# Christian Perspectives
# on Being Human

# Christian Perspectives on Being Human

## A Multidisciplinary Approach to Integration

*Edited by*

## J. P. Moreland
*and*
## David M. Ciocchi

 Baker Books

A Division of Baker Book House Co.
Grand Rapids, Michigan 49516

**Library of Congress Cataloging-in-Publication Data**

Christian perspectives on being human : a multidisciplinary approach to integration / ed-
ited by J.P. Moreland and David M. Ciocchi.
    p.    cm.
Includes bibliographical references and index.
ISBN: 0–8010–6300–0
1. Man (Christian theology) I. Moreland, James Porter, 1948– .
II. Ciocchi, David M.
BT701.2.C474  1993
233—dc20                                                          92–29773

# Contents

# Introduction

## *J. P. Moreland*

As we approach the end of the second millennium in the era of our Lord, the fragmentation and secularization of American culture lies all around us. "Political correctness" pervades many universities, implying that the main heresy is historic, biblical Christianity. Religion has largely become a privatized, personal matter, and our public discourse—the way we frame and discuss issues in the public square—is secular and frequently relativistic. Rhetoric regularly replaces reason in our political process and the makeup man is often more important than the speech writer. Our seemingly unquenchable thirst for entertainment, professional sports, and detailed information about the private lives of celebrities is symptomatic of the fact that many do not have lives of their own and must live vicariously.

In this cultural context, disciples of Jesus of Nazareth have a tremendous responsibility and an unprecedented opportunity to make a difference. We Christians have a passion to be like Jesus Christ. Deep within us is a desire to honor and please him, to enrich his church, and to serve those outside his kingdom in a way that brings honor to him and help to them. Because we have a diversity of spiritual gifts, natural talents, and circumstances of life, as we strive to live lives of excellence, our service will express itself in a variety of ways.

However, all Christians share some basic, fundamental commitments, among which is a dedication to the truth. As Roger Trigg has pointed out, "Any commitment, it seems, depends on two distinct elements. It presupposes certain beliefs [to be true] and also involves a personal dedication to the actions implied by them."[1]

---

1. Roger Trigg, *Reason and Commitment* (Cambridge: Cambridge University Press, 1973), 44.

A commitment to truth implies, in turn, a resolve to cultivate the mind as a part of our discipleship under the lordship of Christ. Among other things, we are to love the Lord our God with all our minds (Matt. 22:37), we are to destroy speculations and every lofty thing raised up against the knowledge of God and take every thought captive to Christ (2 Cor. 10:5), and we are to give everyone a reason for the hope that is within us (1 Pet. 3:15). In short, our desire to serve and honor Christ implies (and presupposes) a desire to know and do the truth, and this implies a need to cultivate our cognitive faculties as part of our service.

In light of all this, the importance of developing a well-reasoned, integrated Christian world view becomes obvious. A world view is a comprehensive conception of the world, a total, structured set of the propositions one believes, especially propositions about reality, knowledge, and values. As we are using the term, a Christian world view is a world view consistent with, guided by, and based on the central propositions that form the core beliefs of "mere" Christianity, that is, the propositions that constitute the essence of historic, orthodox Christian theology. The articulation and defense of a Christian world view is a central component of the task of discipleship and an expression of the Christian conviction that truth exists and is knowable, that all truth is ultimately God's truth, and that truth is universal, objective, and unified.

These convictions about the nature of truth and the importance of a Christian world view form part of the basis of the Christian concern for the task of integration. Let us use the term *theology* to stand for the propositions, theories, and methodologies Christians believe to be rational, true components of historical, biblical Christianity, derived primarily from biblical and systematic theology. In our intellectual life as expressed in the different majors available in a university education, we know that there are other disciplines—psychology or chemistry, for example—that provide propositions, theories, and methodologies thought to be true and rational by proponents of those disciplines. Thus, while there is a unity to truth from a God's-eye perspective, nevertheless, there are different ways of knowing, different sources of knowledge, and different areas of study expressed in the diverse disciplines of the university. The task of integration is the task of relating theology and other disciplines in such a way that one articulates and defends a comprehensive, unified Christian world view in the full light of what it is rational to believe from theology and other disciplines.[2] As Saint Augustine (354–430) once said: "We must show our Scriptures not to be in conflict with whatever [our critics] can demonstrate about the nature of things from reliable sources."[3]

2. For more material on and examples of integration, see Arthur F. Holmes, *Contours of a World View* (Grand Rapids: Eerdmans, 1983); *All Truth Is God's Truth* (Grand Rapids: Eerdmans, 1977); W. David Beck, ed., *Opening the American Mind* (Grand Rapids: Baker, 1991).

3. Augustine *De genesi ad litteram* 1.21. Cited in Ernan McMullin, "How Should Cosmology Relate to Theology?" in *Science and Theology in the Twentieth Century*, ed. Arthur R. Peacocke (Notre Dame, Ind.: University of Notre Dame Press, 1981), 20.

To be engaged in the task of integration is to embark on a journey that is at once exciting and difficult. Integration is no easy task and it is a lifelong project that should occur within an individual believer's life and among the various members of the Christian community working together. Part of the difficulty of this journey is due not only to the massive amount of information and vast array of studies that need to be consulted, but also the fact that there are many different aspects of and attitudes toward integration itself. It is beyond our present scope to attempt to give anything even approximating a typology of these aspects and attitudes.[4] However, it may be helpful to list some examples where the need for integration arises, as well as some of the different ways that theology (as we have defined it) interacts with other disciplines in the process of developing an integrated Christian world view.

Some cases illustrate the need for integration:

1. A biblical exegete becomes aware of how much her own cultural background shapes what she can see in the biblical text, and she begins to wonder whether meanings might not reside in the interpretation of a text and not in the text itself. She also wonders if certain hermeneutical methodologies may be inappropriate given the nature of the Bible as revelation.

2. A psychologist reads literature regarding identical twins who are reared in separate environments. He notes that they usually exhibit similar adult behavior. He then wonders if there is really any such thing as freedom of the will, and if not, he ponders what to make of moral responsibility and punishment.

3. A political science professor reads John Rawls's *Theory of Justice* and grapples with the idea that society's primary goods could be distributed in such a way that those on the bottom get the maximum benefit even if people on the top have to be constrained. He wonders how this compares with a meritocracy wherein individual merit is rewarded regardless of social distribution. Several questions run through his mind: What is the state? How should a Christian view the state and the church? What is justice, and what principles of social ordering ought we to adopt? Should one seek a Christian state or merely a just state?

4. A neurophysiologist establishes specific correlations between certain brain functions and certain feelings of pain, and she puzzles over the question of whether there is a soul or mind distinct from the brain.

5. An anthropologist notes that cultures frequently differ over basic moral principles and wonders whether this proves that there are no objectively true moral values that transcend culture.

6. A businessman notices that the government is not adequately caring for the poor. He discusses with a friend the issue of whether businesses have cor-

4. For a brief typology of different aspects of integration, see William Hasker, "Faith-Learning Integration: An Overview," *Christian Scholar's Review* 21 (March 1992): 234–48.

porate moral responsibilities or whether only individuals have moral responsibility.

7. A mathematician teaches Euclidean geometry and some of its alternatives and goes on to ask the class if mathematics is a field that really conveys true knowledge about a subject matter or if it merely offers internally consistent formal languages expressible in symbols. If the former, then what is it that mathematics describes? If mathematical entities exist and are timeless, in what sense did God create them?

8. An education major is asked to state his philosophy of education. In order to do this, he must state his views of human nature, truth, how people learn, the role of values in education, and so on. He wonders how his Christian convictions inform these issues.

In each case there is a need for the person in question, if he or she is a Christian, to think hard about the issue in light of the need for developing a Christian world view. When one addresses problems like these, there will emerge a number of different ways that theology can interact with an issue in a discipline outside theology. Here are some of the different ways that such interaction can take place:

Propositions, theories, or methodologies in theology and another discipline may involve two distinct, nonoverlapping areas of investigation. For example, debates about angels or the extent of the atonement have little to do with organic chemistry. Similarly, it is of little interest to theology whether a methane molecule has three or four hydrogen atoms in it.

Propositions, theories, or methodologies in theology and another discipline may involve two different, complementary, noninteracting approaches to the same reality. Sociological aspects of church growth and certain psychological aspects of conversion may be sociological or psychological descriptions of certain phenomena that are complementary to a theological description of church growth or conversion.

Propositions, theories, or methodologies in theology and another discipline may directly interact in such a way that either one area of study offers rational support for the other or one area of study raises rational difficulties for the other. For example, certain theological teachings about the existence of the soul raise rational problems for philosophical or scientific claims that deny the existence of the soul. The general theory of evolution raises various difficulties for certain ways of understanding the Book of Genesis. Some have argued that the big bang theory tends to support the theological proposition that the universe had a beginning.

Theology tends to support the presuppositions of another discipline and vice versa. Some have argued that many of the presuppositions of science (e.g., the existence of truth, the rational, orderly nature of reality, the adequacy of our sensory and cognitive faculties as tools suited for knowing the external world) make sense and are easy to justify given Christian theism, but are odd and without ultimate justification in a naturalistic world view. Similarly, some have argued that philosophical critiques of epistemological skepticism and defenses of the existence of a real, theory-independent world and a correspondence theory of truth offer justification for some of the presuppositions of theology.

Theology fills out and adds details to general principles in another discipline and vice versa, and theology helps one practically apply principles in another discipline and vice versa. For example, theology teaches that fathers should not provoke their children to anger and psychology can add important details about what this means by offering information about family systems or the nature and causes of anger. Psychology can devise various tests for assessing whether one is or is not a mature person and theology can offer a normative definition to psychology as to what a mature person is.

These are some of the ways that integration takes place. The present work is an attempt to offer materials for and examples of integration. However, in what follows, the focus will not be on integration in general, but rather on issues specifically involved in clarifying what it is to be a human being. We have chosen this topic for two reasons. First, the present moral and intellectual climate in American culture raises a number of issues about being a human being that call for Christian response. Second, most of the disciplines in the university have something to say about this area of study, and thus issues about being human provide good material for the practice of integration.

In chapter 1, Robert Saucy, a systematic theologian, offers a summary of theological insights about human nature. Among the topics surveyed are the constitutional nature of a human being, the meaning of the image of God, a study of the various theological aspects of being human (e.g., spirit, flesh, heart), theological insights about human functioning, and the nature and effects of the fall of mankind.

Chapters 2 and 3 offer reflections about being human from the field of philosophy. In chapter 2, J. P. Moreland defends a substance dualist view of the

existence and nature of the soul. Moreland summarizes a number of important background issues that help to clarify the different views about the existence of the soul. A number of arguments for dualism in general, and substance dualism in particular are given, and a major objection to substance
dualism is evaluated. In chapter 3, David M. Ciocchi argues that the concept
of freedom plays an important role in our attempt to understand what it is to
be a human being. This concept, he claims, is in effect a family of related ideas,
including both freedom as a condition for moral responsibility ("free will")
and freedom as a characteristic of fully or ideally functioning personhood
("the freedom of personal integrity"). The chapter applies competing definitions of free will to certain theological themes, among them prayer and temptation, and it uses the freedom of personal integrity to help explain the experience described in Romans 7:14–25. The aim of the chapter is to
demonstrate the "integrative" usefulness of philosophy in assisting our development of theological anthropology.

The next section moves into the area of anthropology and psychology. In
chapter 4, Sherwood G. Lingenfelter, an anthropologist, reviews nearly a century of literature by cultural and social anthropologists on the subject of
mind, emotion, culture, and the person. These scholars debate the rationality,
irrationality, and nonrationality of persons, and whether scientific analysis of
mind and persons have universal, developmental, or only relativist validity.
Lingenfelter suggests that all provide valuable insight into what Scripture
terms the "natural man," "alienated mind," and "rebellious heart," and thus
are of value to the biblical scholar when critically examined from biblical and
theological perspectives. Moreover, Lingenfelter compares these secular perspectives on the "natural man" with biblical perspectives on both the "natural" and the "spiritual" man, and shows how each may illuminate the other
toward a more complete understanding of persons.

Nancy Duvall, a psychologist, in chapter 5 discusses the relationship between psychoanalytic perspectives in psychology and Christianity. Duvall
looks at some basic concepts in psychoanalytic theory, unpacks Freud's attitude toward religion, tracks historical developments and revisions in psychoanalytic theory since Freud, and investigates the current interaction between
psychoanalytic thinking and Christianity. Duvall argues that, originally, some
Christian thinkers utilized psychoanalytic theory by distinguishing practical,
clinical helps from Freud's metaphysical assumptions. However, with increasing research, clinical observation, and subsequent revisions in psychoanalytic
theory, the description of humankind embedded in current psychoanalytic
views are much more compatible with a Christian anthropology than was true
of Freud's original view.

In chapter 6, Keith Edwards, also a psychologist, analyzes human nature
and functioning from the perspective of brain studies and neurophysiology.

Edwards describes the functioning of the main parts of the human brain and investigates the implications of brain functioning for human mental life. Edwards stresses that there are mental functions which occur outside of conscious awareness that influence our emotions, thoughts, and behaviors. Research with split-brain patients is used to illustrate out-of-awareness mental activity. Special emphasis is given to the nature of emotions as distinct from language. Finally, Edwards focuses on the relationships among emotions, beliefs, and actions.

The final section of the book approaches questions about being human from New Testament studies, medical ethics, and education. In chapter 7, Walt Russell, a New Testament scholar, argues that the use of passages in Paul's epistles (e.g., Gal. 5–6; Rom. 7–8) to prove that an internal struggle between their "sinful nature" and their "new nature" is a wrong understanding of Paul's argument in those passages. This wrong understanding, claims Russell, is rooted in viewing the flesh and Spirit antithesis in these passages psychologically, rather than in a redemptive-historical manner. Russell shows that Paul, rather than pointing to the internal strife between the parts of a person, uses "flesh" and "Spirit" to refer to the historical identities and behaviors of the total person. Paul's emphasis is not on persons in individual abstraction, but on persons in relation to their corporate identification.

Chapter 8 moves into the field of medical ethics, and Scott Rae asserts that one's view of personhood is critically important in making medical ethics decisions both at the beginning and ending edges of life. Rae shows that attempts to justify various forms of euthanasia are often dependent on a distinction between being a human being and being a person. This chapter examines three areas in which this distinction is made: treating seriously ill newborns, justifying active euthanasia for terminally ill patients, and withdrawing medically provided food and water from patients in a permanent vegetative state. However, claims Rae, the widespread use of this distinction between being a human being and a person is both philosophically problematic and inconsistent with the biblical teaching on the image of God.

Finally, in chapter 9, Klaus Issler, an educator, looks at two discipleship concerns for the maturing believer: educating a sensitive conscience and improving our moral decision-making. As a part of this discussion, Issler offers a review of biblical terms for "conscience" and a three-component model of conscience. Effective growth in Christian character, says Issler, requires that we attend to how our conscience functions.

Before you move to chapter 1, you need to know two things about the book's format that should help you get more out of what follows. First, every chapter except the first (Saucy's) is followed by two brief responses. Saucy's chapter was exempt from this because, in one way or another, chapters 2 through 9 respond to his. These brief responses are offered as examples of how Christian thinkers from one field interact with ideas from a different field in an attempt to move toward an integrated Christian perspective on being human. Second, each chapter closes with a brief bibliography for further study. The works listed are categorized as basic (B), intermediate (I), or advanced (A).

We, the authors, have a long way to go in our attempts to hammer out our considered judgments about a Christian perspective on being human. But we know that the task of integration in this area of study is crucial for the cause of Christ. Thus, we offer the chapters to follow with the prayer that they will be useful to you as you join us on the road to understanding for the glory of God, the good of his kingdom, and the benefit of those who do not know him.

Part 1

# Understanding Human Nature

*The Theological Perspective*

# 1

# Theology of Human Nature

## *Robert L. Saucy*

One of the chief questions facing the modern person is, "Who am I?" Despite facing this issue for probably as long as he has existed, man seems no closer to an agreement on the answer. The perplexity over human nature is understandable when we realize that none of us is self-caused. We are all thrust onto the stage of history by something or Someone beyond us. For the Christian that Someone is God, and the record of his relationship to us as our Creator is provided in Scripture. Although God is the central actor in the biblical record, humanity plays a significant role as the intended covenant partner of God. To bring this relationship to fulfillment, Scripture reveals much not only about God, but also about the nature of humanity. This revelation is not exhaustive in answering all queries of anthropology. Its focus is on that which is central to human life, namely, life before God. But in dealing with this centrality, Scripture speaks to the fundamental questions concerning our nature as human beings. In doing so, it provides the foundation upon which all other anthropological studies must build.

## The Identity of Mankind

"What is man?" A little thought causes one to realize that this most basic question is not easily answered. The human person appears complex and

17

even paradoxical. He is part of nature and yet he cannot be totally explained in terms of the natural world, for he also transcends nature. He yearns for love and good and yet history is largely the record of human nonlove and evil "inhuman" acts. Various nonbiblical explanations have been proffered to the difficult question of human identity, but none provides the comprehensive portrayal of full humanity seen in the biblical revelation and experienced in reality.

### Some Nontheological Explanations of Human Nature

#### The explanations

The various nontheological explanations of human nature have been well summarized around three basic positions.[1] According to the *mythical* understanding the human person is defined as a part of the closed system of nature. Human existence like everything else was the outcome of forces within the universe that operated solely on cause-and-effect principles. Even though the ancient Greeks saw human existence in relation to the gods,[2] that existence was still the fatalistic result of the actions of the "gods" who themselves were part of a nonhistorical realm of being. This view of the ancients is part of the contemporary world as evidenced in the popular devotion to astrology. Views that see human behavior as basically determined may also be seen as related to this position (e.g., classic Freudianism, philosophical behaviourism, and scientific theories that seek to explain human actions in terms of cause and effect).

The *philosophical* anthropology expressed in the Platonic and Aristotelian conceptions of human nature and later in Descartes sees the essence of the human person in a self that is able to objectify and thus transcend the natural world and its own self as a part of that world.[3] This self-transcendence frees the human person from the determinism of nature associated with mythical anthropology. The essence of the person, according to this philosophical understanding, is found in the spirit or mind as distinct from the material nature. This resulted in a dualistic nature of the human being which essentially identified the human person with the spiritual mind and disparaged the body as a temporary shell which was not really part of the person. This in turn often

1. See Ray S. Anderson, *On Being Human: Essays in Theological Anthropology* (Grand Rapids: Eerdmans, 1982), 8–15. Anderson in turn acknowledges his debt to Karl Barth, *The Doctrine of Creation*, ed. G. W. Bromiley and T. F. Torrance, trans. Harold Knight et al., vol. 3, pt. 2 of *Church Dogmatics* (Edinburgh: T. and T. Clark, 1960).

2. The view of the Greeks with their "gods" as well as the philosophical theology that follows is defined as nontheological because human existence is not determined by God and related to him through revelation.

3. This classical philosophical view is largely rejected by secular philosophy today in favor of a physicalism that in essence attempts to extend the scientific understanding of human nature into the realm of philosophy in an identification of all mental events as simply events of the brain.

led to an ethical dualism of spirit as good and body as evil. The impact of this philosophical anthropology has been felt in theologies that tended to draw radical distinctions between the spiritual and material in mankind in opposition to the holistic understanding of human nature in Scripture as a unity of body and spirit.

In the *scientific* understanding of mankind an attempt is made to describe human nature objectively and scientifically from the viewpoint of an outside observer. If this view stays scientific, it does not attempt to answer the final questions of ultimate truth concerning the human person. As such it may be compatible with a biblical anthropology. Often, however, scientific anthropology operates with some degree of philosophical presupposition and thus merges with either the philosophical or mythical anthropologies depending on the worldview assumed. When it does transcend the purely scientific, it generally leads to a materialistic view of human nature.

### The inadequacies of the nontheological anthropologies

When compared to the realities of human existence all forms of nontheological anthropologies reveal serious shortcomings. Three problems may be noted.[4] The first is the transcendent nature of the human person. Whether we conceive of the real human essence as part of nature as in mythical and some scientific anthropologies, or as mind or reason in accordance with the prominent philosophical view, it is obvious that there is always an additional something in the person that makes this explanation. This transcendence over nature is easy to see in the human ability to even make the judgment that man is part of nature. Surely no other part of nature has the ability to explain itself as only part of nature. The explanation of human personhood in terms of the mind also entails a similar inadequacy. As Niebuhr points out, "the very effort to estimate the significance of his rational faculties implies a degree of transcendence over himself which is not fully defined or explained in what is usually connoted by 'reason.'"[5]

A second problem for all of the nontheological views noted above is revealed in the problem of human virtue. Is human nature essentially good or bad? The evils of history are difficult to explain if mankind is fundamentally good. If on the other hand our nature is basically evil, it is difficult to explain how we are able from an evil nature to pronounce this devastating judgment on ourselves. The whole question of human virtue seems to remain ultimately unanswered in a nontheological understanding of mankind.

Finally, the individual personality entailed in human existence is difficult to account for in a nontheological perspective. In naturalism it is lost in the pro-

4. For a good discussion of the problems of non-Christian anthropologies, see Reinhold Niebuhr, *Human Nature,* vol. 1 of *Nature and Destiny of Man: A Christian Interpretation* (New York: Scribner's Sons, 1964), 1–25.

5. Ibid., 1.

cesses of nature. Nature has place for variety, but not true individuality. All is encompassed in natural laws whether conceived physically, psychologically or sociologically. Analogously, the classical philosophical anthropology, which sees the real human essence in the rational capacity, tends to absorb the individual human personality into the ultimate principle of Reason or absolute mind. As we have noted above, the ability of the human being to transcend both nature and reason signifies that the real human essence with individual personality at its core cannot be explained by either.

It should be noted that mankind has frequently, and we might add rightly, recognized that nature and reason are not adequate to fully define the human person. Thus attempt is made to seek the meaning of human life in some sort of divine reality that transcends the natural and rational dimensions of humanity as seen in the contemporary New Age movement. But apart from seeking this meaning in a divine revelation from a personal God, this attempt leads again to the absorption of the human into a sort of divine reality and a monism that finally destroys individuality. New Age physicist and philosopher Fritjof Capra illustrates this when he says that in the ultimate state of conscious "all boundaries and dualisms have been transcended and all individuality dissolves into universal, undifferentiated oneness."[6] The final solution to the true identity of human nature with all of its complexities of being and morality can only be found through a revelation from God. As Neibuhr aptly explains, for man to understand himself means that he must "begin with a faith that he is understood from beyond himself, that he is known and loved of God and must find himself in terms of obedience to the divine will."[7]

### The Biblical View of Human Nature

From the Christian perspective the key to understanding the nature and identity of the human being is found in the first chapter of the Bible. Man is made "in the image of God" (Gen. 1:26, 27). This statement informs us that the identity of man is known only in relation to God. For that which is by nature the "image" of something else can only be fully understood by knowing that which it images.

It is from this perspective that the most important understanding of our being derives and the most significant dilemma of the non-Christian anthropologies is solved. The human being is a personal individual known and loved by God. Each person lives life or "walks" (as Scripture often terms it) responsibly before the God who not only created all things, but continually sustains them. In the apostle's words, "in him we live and move and have our being" (Acts 17:28).

6. Fritjof Capra, *Turning Point: Science, Society and the Rising Culture* (New York: Simon and Schuster, 1982), 371.

7. Ibid., 16.

Not only the question of personality, but the realities of human existence, which we have seen are difficult to encompass in nontheological anthropologies, are solved in Scripture. Declaring that mankind is created from both "the dust of the ground" and "the breath of life" directly from God, Scripture reveals that the human being is both part of nature and transcendent. He shares in the being of the rest of nature, but he also has something that enables him to have a relationship with God which is different than any other part of nature. His ontological structure is thus a duality of material and spirit, with the spirit coming directly from the breath of God and thus having a radically different quality from that of the rest of nature. Monism which denies the reality of both of these dimensions, or any dualistic theory that disparages either aspect as a valuable part of the total human person, is therefore not true to the holism of biblical anthropology.

Finally, the moral ambiguity of human reality evidenced in personal experience and the history of mankind is clearly explained by the picture of mankind in Scripture. As the creature of God who is created "good" (Gen. 1:31) in God's image and who still bears that image, the human person is of great worth. But because of his disobedient turning away from his created relationship to God, man is also sinful. Nowhere are these two fundamental aspects of biblical anthropology revealed more plainly than at the cross of Christ. There the awfulness of human sin is revealed as the deserved judgment of a moral God falls on Christ who stands in the place of all mankind. At the same time the great value of humanity is manifested at the Cross as there in gracious love the Father sent his Son to suffer death for human salvation. It is precisely in coming under the radical judgment and equally radical grace at the Cross that we come to understand the true nature of humanity.[8]

## The Nature of Mankind as the Image of God

The distinguishing attribute of humanity is the truth that among all of creation mentioned in the biblical creation accounts of Genesis mankind alone is made "in the image of God." The meaning of this phrase in relation to the nature of mankind is never expressly elaborated in Scripture. Most theological anthropologies understand it as providing a comprehensive expression of that which distinguishes human nature from the other creation as seen throughout Scripture.[9]

8. Anderson, *On Being Human*, 16.
9. See, for example, Fritz Maas, "אָדָם," in *Theological Dictionary of the Old Testament*, ed. G. Johannes Botterweck and Helmer Ringgren, trans. John T. Willis, 6 vols. (Grand Rapids: Eerdmans, 1974– ), 1:85. Maas expresses this common opinion when he says in relation to the Old Testament that "[the] only certainty here is that the statement ascribes to man an exceptional position." This exceptional position is "derived less certainly from the 'principal passages' . . . than from the overall impression made by the entire OT."

### The Biblical Data

On the sixth day, as the last climactic act of creation, Scripture records, "Then God said, 'Let Us make man in Our image, according to Our likeness'" (Gen. 1:26 NASB). The statement of man's being in the image of God is found explicitly in one form or another six additional times in Scripture. Five of these designate mankind as created in the "image of God" (Gen. 1:27; 9:6; 1 Cor. 11:7) or his "likeness" (Gen. 5:1; James 3:9). The other use refers to the renewal of humanity to the image of God through redemption (Col. 3:10; cf. the similar idea in Eph. 4:24 where the term is not used). Without the specific language, the apostle teaches the same truth in referring to the relation of mankind and God in his address on Mars Hill (Acts 17:28–29).

The Hebrew term *șelem,* translated "image" in the creation account, signifies an "image" in the sense of a plastic copy, a representation of an object by a picture or statue, or a nonphysical picture in the mind or in a dream.[10] The second term *demût,* "likeness," means simply "that which is like something" or similitude.[11] Early patristic interpreters saw a distinction between "image" and "likeness" in which "image" referred to man's natural likeness to God and "likeness" to a spiritual likeness. Although Aquinas followed this understanding (making it central to the traditional Roman Catholic understanding), the Reformers and most modern interpreters rightly see the words more synonymously. The interchangeability of the terms supports this understanding (e.g., Gen. 1:26; 5:3; 9:6). The terms are best understood as complementary in their reference to mankind with the second explaining and supplementing the first. Humanity is created in the *image* of God, namely, an image that is *like* God.

### Various Interpretations of the Meaning of the Image of God

Throughout history the meaning of mankind being created in "the image of God" has received a wide variety of interpretations.[12] Two have been the most prominent. The first, which may be termed substantive or ontological, understands the image as characteristics within the nature of the human being. The second sees the image as relational, that is, it is not defined in terms of some attribute of mankind, but in the relationships of man with God, with

---

10. Seyoon Kim, *The Origin of Paul's Gospel,* 2d ed. (Tubingen: Mohr, 1984), 200.

11. On both terms see also Claus Westermann, *Genesis 1–11: A Commentary,* trans. John J. Scullion (Minneapolis: Augsburg, 1984), 146.

12. Westermann (ibid., 148–54) summarizes the primary opinions throughout history of interpretation into the following six groups: (1) those who make a distinction between the natural and supernatural likeness of God; (2) those who define the image in terms of spiritual qualities or capacities; (3) those who understand the image and likeness as the external form; (4) those who understand the image to consist in the human being as a whole and not in any particular detail of the person; (5) those who see it in the relationship of man to God as God's counterpart; and (6) those who understand the image as signifying mankind as the representative of God on earth.

his fellow man, and even with other creatures. A third view worthy of mention is the functional interpretation, which sees the image not in something that man is or in his relationships, but in the God-given task for mankind to rule over creation (cf. Gen. 1:26, 28).

The most dominant view throughout most of the history of the Church has been the view that sees the image as consisting of characteristics within human nature. Although some, such as modern-day Mormons, have included the human bodily form in the image, it has been more commonly associated with the inner psychological and spiritual qualities of man which are analogous to God's and distinguish man from all other forms of animals. These center in the characteristics of freedom and the capacities for reason and morality.

One variation of this concept is found in Roman Catholic theology. Originally based upon the distinction between the terms *image* and *likeness* found in the creation account, Catholicism has understood *image* to refer to the natural nature of human beings centered in reason and will.[13] *Likeness,* on the other hand, signified the supernatural gift of grace that elevated man into original righteousness and a relationship with God. This gift of grace was an addition to the natural nature of mankind.[14] In the fall man lost the likeness or God-like righteousness, but he retained the image or his human nature fundamentally intact. Thus all people including unbelievers are fully human retaining the ability to reason to truth and will the good. They also in their natural image of God have the ability to receive the grace of God necessary to bring them to the ultimate goal of a saving relationship with God.

The Reformers, viewing *image* and *likeness* as synonymous, applied it to the whole human being. The fall thus affected the entire human being. Since Luther tended to see the image only in relation to the original righteousness of man that related him to God, the image was essentially lost in the fall. The Scriptures that refer to all human beings in the image of God subsequent to the fall (e.g., Gen. 9:6) are therefore understood as pointing to the nobility of the human creature who once bore the image and in whom God wills to recreate it again in Christ.[15] The Calvinistic tradition, viewing the image more broadly, retained the image in fallen mankind but saw all human capacities, including reason and will, as now oriented away from God and incapable in themselves of knowing ultimate truth and choosing the good. Human nature was by creation a nature in relation to God. The entrance of sin,

13. Modern Catholic exegesis no longer makes this distinction in the words of the creation account although the theological distinction is retained in Catholic theology (ibid., 148).

14. For a discussion of the effect of this distinction in the Catholic concepts of nature and grace with regard to the nature of man, see Richard P. McBrien, *Catholicism,* 2 vols. (Minneapolis: Winston, 1981), 1:151–61.

15. Francis Pieper, *Christian Dogmatics,* 4 vols. (St. Louis: Concordia, 1950), 1:519.

therefore, rendered human nature not simply natural, but less than its original nature.

Although the Reformers, in their understanding of the image as the whole person rightly related to God in obedience of will, included a relational dimension, this last aspect has become more prominent in more recent theologies.[16] According to the proponents of this relational position, humanity's creation in the image of God does not relate to the structure of the human being. Rather it focuses on the goal of humanity's creation, namely, to experience a relationship with God. Obviously, this includes man's structure as it is the whole person who is thus related. But the real meaning of *image* is that mankind is created to hear and respond to the Word of God and thus reflect God as in a mirror. In addition to this vertical relationship, the image also includes the horizontal relationship between people. Mankind is truly human not only in relation to God, but also in relation to his fellow human. Thus the image involves the two great commands—love for God and for one's neighbor.

Rejecting the Genesis account of man's original state of righteousness and subsequent historical fall, human creation in the image of God, according to this modern concept, refers to the eschatological goal for mankind, the exemplar of which has already appeared in Christ who is the "image of God." Thus this position is sometimes termed "Christological" or "eschatological," for humanity attains the fullness of this image only in the future through Christ. Unbelieving humanity, although not living in the intended meaning of the image either in relation to God or even man, nevertheless, is said to still stand before God and thus retain the formal aspect of the image. Giving attention to the relational aspects of full humanity are a positive contribution of this interpretation. However, since the image is fundamentally seen only in *redemption,* it does not do justice to the biblical *creation*-image of mankind, nor is it easily applied to the biblical teaching of unbelieving man as seemingly bearing the image in more than form alone.

### The Biblical Meaning of Mankind "in the Image of God"

#### The general meaning

Before looking at the different aspects which comprise the image of God in man, three things may be said about its general meaning. First, it signifies that mankind is God's *representative* in the world. This is suggested in the creation account by the statement about mankind ruling over God's creation. It is also similar to the practice of ancients kings placing statues (images) of themselves throughout their empire to represent their sovereign authorita-

16. E.g., Emil Brunner, *Man in Revolt: A Christian Anthropology,* trans. Olive Wyon (London: Lutterworth, 1939), 102–13; Karl Barth, *The Doctrine of Creation,* ed. G. W. Bromiley and T. F. Torrance, trans. Harold Knight et al., vol. 3, pt. 1 of *Church Dogmatics,* 183–206.

tive presence.[17] Secondly, being in the image of God means not only that we are God's representative, but that we are *representational* of God. Being like God, mankind reflects his nature, that is, when one looks at a human being something of the nature of God shows through which can be seen nowhere else.

Finally, all of what is said about the image, including its representative and representational meanings, may be summarized in saying that the image consists in all that distinguishes mankind from the rest of creation. This distinguishing mark is seen in his God-given crown of "glory and majesty" (Ps. 8:5 NASB). The concept of "glory" carries the idea of that which is *gravitas* or weighty. Applied to man in relation to all other creatures, it means that there is something "weighty" about him, an inner force that is impressive and worthy of respect. As Oehler explains, "Man as a free being is set over nature, and designed to hold communion with God and be his representative on earth."[18] In the following discussion we will see that this exceptional position of mankind in the image of God entails both dimensions of relationship as well as the capacities to fulfill them.

### A being of relationships

Earlier historical discussions of the meaning of the image of God tended to major on the natural capacities or structures of the human being especially those dealing with rationality and morality. The more recent emphasis on the image as relational has rightly called attention to the biblical truth that true humanity cannot be fully described in terms of the essence or ontological structure of the human being, but must also include humanity in actual existence. This is evident when the God whom man images describes himself as "love," which is clearly dynamic and relational.

Having said this, however, it is also clear that the existential dynamic of relationships are not by themselves definitive of the image of God or what it means to be human. Existential relationships are the expression of a prior existing self which possesses the endowments or capacities for active existence. Thus while the full expression of the image of God in humanity includes relationships, these are grounded in and are the expression of the ontological being of the human person. The image thus involves an essential human nature which includes the attributes of existence entailing relationships. These may not be fully developed, but they are nonetheless endowments of the es-

17. For a discussion of the meaning of the image of God including its meaning in the ancient world, see D. J. A. Clines, "The Image of God in Man," *Tyndale Bulletin* 19 (1968): 53–103.

18. A good summary statement is made by the older biblical theologian, Gustav Oehler (*Theology of the Old Testament* [1873; reprint, Grand Rapids: Zondervan, n.d.], 146): "The divine likeness is . . . to be referred to the *whole dignity of man* כָּבוֹד וְהָדָר ['glory and majesty'], comp. Ps. viii. 6[5]), in virtue of which human nature is sharply distinguished from that of the beasts; *man as free being is set over nature, and designed to hold communion with God, and to be his representative on earth.*"

sence of humanity in the image of God even in their potentiality. A person may not be fully expressing the concept of the image while asleep, but he is as such still fully human. So also those who have not yet fully developed their relational capacities, such as infants or the mentally retarded, as well as those who have lost these abilities through accident or old age are still human beings in the image of God. In the final sense, it must be acknowledged that no fallen human fully lives out existentially the meaning of the image.

One human being, however, did live out the existential aspects of the image in its relationships. As that one, Jesus becomes our model of true humanity. His life reveals three basic relationships. He was first and foremost *God-related*, living his life in constant fellowship and dependence on God. This is the most distinguishing aspect of humanity. Man alone is addressed by God and is held responsible for his response. Created in the image of God, the human being is designed to exist in relationship with God as a fish is designed to exist in water.

Humanity as exhibited in the life and teaching of Jesus is also *other-person-related*, that is, the human being was created a social being. This immediately derives from God's triune being, which seems to be hinted at in the creative statement, "Let Us make man in *Our* image" (Gen. 1:26 NASB, italics added). Mankind is created in the image of the scriptural God who as Father, Son and Spirit enjoyed an eternal fellowship of love within his own being. This relational fellowship within the Godhead as well as the identification of God's nature as love are part of the created existence of mankind.

The other-relatedness of humanity is found in the biblical truth that the human being is truly human only in community. Immediately in the case of Adam, it is said that it is not good for a human being to exist alone (Gen. 2:18). Therefore God created woman as the complement of man and the primary example of the necessity of community for the fulfillment of true human life. This should not be interpreted as demanding marriage, otherwise it would deny full humanity to Christ. Rather the man and woman in their gender differences are the clearest evidence of human dependence on the other person for full human existence in its "goodness." Thus, part of living out the image of God involves developing our maleness and femaleness. When the latter are perverted, it is an abuse of the image of God. The other-related dimension of human nature is further exhibited in the frequently found teaching that loneliness is a curse (cf. Ps. 102:5–7), and in the truth concerning goal of redemption, namely, the unity and interdependence of humanity in the body of Christ.

Finally, human existence involves a *relationship with nature*. As the image of God, mankind was given rulership over creation (cf. Gen. 1:26, 28; Ps. 8:4–8). This involved God's call of man into the service of his creation (cf. Gen. 2:5, 15) and the ordering of it for the delight and good of human livelihood. In the knowledge and understanding necessary for this service, humanity acts as God's *prophet* to creation. In the actual rulership he serves as his *king*. And in that his rulership over creation is designed to return it to God and his glory, humanity serves as the divine *priest* for nature.[19] Significantly, in the ancient world only the king or some high ranking official was termed the image of God. Scripture democratizes this exclusivistic concept. All humans are regarded as God's royalty.

### The endowments of personality

True human nature created in the image of God includes not only the relational dimensions, but also the metaphysical endowments necessary to fulfill them. As these are in reality the capacities for human personhood, the central meaning of the image of God in mankind has often been defined fundamentally in terms of the characteristics of personality. Eichrodt expresses this common thought declaring,

> For Man to be created in the likeness of God's image can only mean that on him, too, personhood is bestowed as the definitive characteristic of his nature. . . . This quality of personhood shapes the totality of his psycho-physical existence; it is this which comprises the essentially human, and distinguishes him from all other creatures.[20]

The personhood that mankind shares with God as his image includes the following elements. As will be seen they are inherently interrelated elements, that is, it is impossible to conceive of one without the other. Together they thus constitute the self-ness of a human being.

*Self-conscious rationality.* Human personality, like God's, entails rationality, which, in distinction from what might be called thought in non-human animals, is self-aware. This distinction between human reason and any sort of animal thought is implied in the biblical description of those whose knowledge is only "by instinct [i.e., nature], like unreasoning animals" (Jude 10). The self-conscious thought of mankind in the image of God transcends the stimulus-response instinct of animals, no matter how sophisticated the latter may be. Animals may have desires, but they do not have beliefs about their desires. It is, in fact, such self-conscious rationality that makes personal relationship possible, for genuine relationships require that the persons view themselves as distinct selves in the relationship. For this reason, a newborn baby does not have personal relationships; it is not yet aware of itself. Linguis-

19. See the discussion of the three offices of human relationship to nature in Eric Sauer, *The King of the Earth: The Nobility of Man According to the Bible and Science* (London: Paternoster, 1962), 90–91.

20. Walther Eichrodt, *Theology of the Old Testament*, trans. J. A. Baker, 2 vols. (Philadelphia: Westminster, 1961, 1967), 2:126.

tic ability, which belongs to the human alone among all of the creatures in the Genesis creation account (for no animal learns naturally to talk), rests on this capacity of self-conscious rationality. It has been humorously but rightly said, "Animals don't 'speak' because they have nothing to say."

*Self-determination or freedom.* At the core of the human person, and perhaps the most mysterious element especially in relation to God's sovereignty, is what might be termed the freedom of self-determination. The human being is like God in that he has the ability to create thoughts and actions that have no determinative cause outside of the self. Being a finite being, this human freedom is limited (e.g., it cannot choose to be omniscient or to successfully defy the laws of nature). It is nevertheless real and thus constitutes what might be termed "a little citadel of creativity *ex nihilo*." As this freedom entails choices, which in turn involve rationality, it is obvious that it is related to the previous element of self-conscious thought. It is also foundational for mankind as a moral being.

*A moral nature.* From the initial probation of Adam and Eve in the Garden to the final recompensing of the righteous and unrighteous in eternity, Scripture affirms the moral nature of mankind and holds the human being morally responsible. This may be understood simply as our self-awareness and consequently self-determination in relation to morality. As we will see, sin's entrance into the human race brought bondage with regard to doing good, it did not destroy the capacity of moral distinction. This is seen most clearly in the apostle's teaching that God's law is written in the hearts of all people, and the operation of their conscience is witness to that fact (cf. Rom. 2:14–15).

### Original righteousness

Part of the original dimension of human nature in the image of God was the quality of being sinless or what is termed "original righteousness." Since the meaning of righteousness involves both that which is right and standing in a right relationship with God, it is evident that original righteousness belongs also to the relationship element of the meaning of the image of God. The original righteousness of mankind is seen when all of that which God made is pronounced "very good" (Gen. 1:31; cf. also Eccles. 7:29: "God made man upright"). It is further evident in the apostle's teaching that in salvation mankind is being "renewed according to the image of the One who created him" (Col. 3:10 NASB; cf. Eph. 4:24).

The righteousness of man's original nature needs to be distinguished from a righteousness of character developed through moral action. In creation, therefore, Adam and Eve's righteousness may be said to be that of nature, meaning that they were related to God in sinlessness. But this nature was untested as to character since moral choice was yet to be made through the exercise of the personal endowment of freedom. It should be noted that this distinction in the created endowment of righteousness upon the first human differs from that which is received by the believer in Christ. The righteousness in which the believer stands by virtue of being "in Christ," as well as the righteousness which is worked into the believer's life through the mysterious activity of both the Spirit of God and the working of the person, is the tested and victorious righteousness of Christ which is righteousness both of nature and character.

The image of God in man is thus a broad concept involving man's endowments and actual living existence. It is all that is said in Scripture which describes mankind as a being that has characteristics that are like God's. The ultimate evidence of this is seen in the amazing fact that God in the person of the Son could join himself to humanity *in one Person*. That the characteristics of personality in the divine and human could be joined in such a union clearly indicates a similarity in *being* despite the fact that the divine is infinite and the human finite.

### The Image and the Fall

Scripture clearly views fallen mankind as still in the image of God. The murder of another human being is seen as a heinous crime, for it is striking at a being who even in sin is "in the image of God" (Gen. 9:6). Even the cursing of another human being in anger is an offence to God. James points to the inconsistency of blessing our "Lord and Father" and then cursing men who have been made in his image (James 3:9). The image in sinful mankind is explained in that human beings still have the elements of personality (e.g., self-consciousness, self-determination) which are representational of the nature of God. Moreover, the human person still has the nature that is fulfilled only through relationships with his fellow human and with God. To this might be added the truth that God still determines to maintain a relationship to man as the object of his love.

While Scripture never refers to the image as being "marred" or "disfigured" due to sin, the apostle speaks of the believer in Christ as "being renewed to a true knowledge according to the image of the One who created him" (Col. 3:10 NASB; cf. Eph. 4:24). The language is obviously reminiscent of the Genesis account of man's creation in the image of God and suggests that mankind apart from the renewal of God's salvation is no longer fully "in the image of God." Moreover, since we might say that the image entailed all that is truly human in man, it is necessary to conclude that every aspect of humanity has been affected by sin. That such is the case is clearly manifest in human history and aptly described in Pascal's observation that "[the] greatness of man is so obvious that it can be deduced even from his misery. . . . he has fallen from a better state which in former times was more appropriate to him.

Who does not feel more unhappy at not being a king except a king who has been deposed?"[21]

### The Implications of Mankind in the Image of God

The truth that all people are beings existing "in the image of God" is tremendously significant for human existence. First, if the human being is defined fundamentally as one "in the image of God," then his identity must be sought in relation to God. For it only reasonable that the identity of an "image" is found by knowing the original. Thus the contemporary loss of human self-identity which seems to be experienced especially in Western secular cultures may be explained as due in large part to the loss of a real recognition of and relationship with a personal Creator God.

But the image of God not only means relationship with God but with fellow man as well. A human being is fully human only in community. Thus one's identity is found also in the horizontal relationship of person to person. Nowhere is this illustrated more clearly than in the description of humanity being restored to the image in the church as the body of Christ. Even as members of our physical body can only be seen for what they are in a functioning relationship with the other members of the body, so the individual human finds his or her own real identity in a dynamic relationship with other people.

Secondly, the concept of the image of God reveals the true meaning and purpose of human life in this world, namely, the fulfillment of relationships involved in the image. These reveal that we as human beings exist to live to the love and praise of God, to love our fellow man (which might be interpreted as being a representative of God), and finally, to rule as a beneficent king over God's creation. All through the Scripture these dimensions, especially the first two, are commanded by God for the good of his people. For it is in these avenues that humanity in the image of God finds fulfillment and satisfaction of life. In the final analysis, these are not three tasks but one, one that radiates in our human existence the very nature of God or, as Scripture often states, redounds to the praise of his glory (cf. Eph. 1:12).

The biblical teaching of all mankind being in the image of God finally teaches the value and significance of all human beings. Even more than the biblical writer, modern man with his increased knowledge of the universe is led to ask the question: "What is man. . . ?" (Ps. 8:4). To be sure mankind has made some notable achievements, at least from his perspective. But objectively, in comparison to the vastness of creation, human beings appear as tiny specks. True human significance is difficult to claim unless it is found in the truth of revelation that God has taken thought of man and crowned him with glory and honor (Ps. 8:4–5). As Eichrodt, commenting on Psalm 8, explains: "[It] is

21. Blaise Pascal, "The Greatness of Man's Dignity," in *The Mind on Fire: An Anthology of the Writings of Blaise Pascal,* ed. James H. Houston (Portland, Ore.: Multnomah, 1989), 81.

God's inconceivable marvellous power which alone is the basis of human self-confidence. . . . Ultimately therefore it is a spiritual factor which determines the value Man sets upon himself, namely his consciousness of partnership with God, a privilege of which no other creation is considered worthy."[22] Thus throughout Scripture God sets a high value on mankind (cf. Matt. 10:31; 12:9–12; Mark 2:28). It is this unique value of man as the bearer of the divine image that not only forbids taking human life in murder, but demands the respect and even love for all people. As Calvin says in explaining how we can love even our enemies, "It is that we remember not to consider men's evil intention but to look upon the image of God in them, which cancels and effaces their transgressions, and with its beauty and dignity allures us to love and embrace them."[23]

## The Structure of the Human Being

Scripture uses many different terms in describing the structure or constitution of the human being. Some of these terms (e.g., body, flesh, spirit), as we will see, are clearly used at times for the different substances of material and spirit which make up the dualistic ontological nature of man. But as we have seen, mankind was created to be holistic in function. Thus the biblical writers often use the different terms in an *aspectival* rather than an exclusively *substantival* sense. For example, the term *body* may be used for the whole person emphasizing the aspect of his bodily nature. This holistic perspective of the biblical viewpoint will become evident as we look at some of the key terms used in relation to the nature of man and grasp the fundamental biblical outlook on the constitution of the human being.

### Significant Terms of Human Nature

#### The fundamental structure

The basic structure of human nature is found in the description of man's original creation. Genesis 2:7 (NASB) states, "Then the LORD God formed man of dust from the ground, and breathed into his nostrils the breath of life; and man became a living being [lit. 'soul']." From this passage we learn that the human is a metaphysical composition of that which is material ("dust from the ground") and immaterial ("the breath of life"). The combination of these two elements results in that which is termed a "living soul."[24] These three con-

22. Eichrodt, *Theology*, 2:120–21.
23. John Calvin, *Institutes of the Christian Religions*, ed. John T. McNeill (Philadelphia: Westminster, 1960) 3.7.6.
24. It should be noted that the animals created on the fifth and sixth days of creation are also termed "living souls" (Gen. 1:20, 21, 24). Like human beings they are composed of material that is enlivened with the principle of life. Thus Scripture even refers to the "spirit" of the beasts (Eccles. 3:21). Mankind is unique in that the principle of life in man comes directly from God and is of a different quality than that of animals.

cepts are the basis for three frequently used terms in relation to man's nature, that is, body, spirit, and soul.

The *body* is denoted by various Hebrew terms in the Old Testament, the most prominent being *bāsār,* "flesh." The New Testament writers continued to refer to this aspect of human nature as "flesh" (*sarx*), but more commonly the body was called *sōma.* The body is the physical material side of human nature. It often stands in contrast to the immaterial or spiritual side as is seen in Jesus' warning, "do not be afraid of those who kill the body but cannot kill the soul" (Matt. 10:28). A similar meaning is evident in the statement of James that "the body without the spirit is dead" (2:26; cf. also Isa. 10:18 NASB; Matt. 6:25; 1 Cor. 5:3; 2 Cor. 5:6–8; 12:1–3). *The body* may also in some instances refer to the entire person. Presentation of our "body" to the Lord signifies the presentation of our whole being (Rom. 12:1; cf. 6:13, 16 where "the parts of your body" equals "yourself"). In this holistic usage the emphasis is on the person in his corporeality or his concrete relationship to the material world.

*Body* is also used for the new body to be obtained through the resurrection (cf. 1 Cor. 15:35–49). This body is described as "spiritual." This description does not suggest that it will be immaterial or made of "spirit." Rather it signifies that the new, "spiritual body" will be one perfectly adapted to the redeemed spirit of man. No longer will it be said, "the spirit is willing, but the flesh [i.e., the body] is weak." The body will be a perfect partner for the full life of the human spirit.

The second element in the composition of human nature is *spirit,* represented in Genesis 2:7 by the "breath of life." The root meaning of both the Hebrew (*rûah*) and Greek (*pneuma*) words translated "spirit" is "air in motion, wind, or breath," signifying power or energy. *Spirit* thus has the fundamental meaning of "vitalizing power." It is that which animates. Used in relation to man, it refers to (1) the life or animating principle as opposed to the body or flesh (e.g., Gen. 7:22 NASB; Eccles. 12:7; Matt. 27:50; Luke 8:54–55; John 19:30; Acts 7:59; 1 Cor. 5:5); (2) the seat of various personal activities including thought (e.g., Isa. 29:24; Mark 2:8; 1 Cor. 2:11); emotion (e.g., Gen. 26:35 NASB margin; 41:8 NASB; Ps. 143:4); will (e.g., 1 Chron. 5:26; Ezra 1:5 NASB; Matt. 26:41); and (3) the aspect of man through which he relates to God (e.g., Ps. 51:10; Rom. 8:16; Eph. 4:23 NASB).

In the original creation statement, the union of the material and immaterial or body and spirit constituted the human being as a living *soul* (Gen. 2:7). The Hebrew (*nepeš*) and Greek (*psychē*) words for "soul" come from roots meaning "to breathe."[25] As breathing is the mark of life, so "soul" refers to the creature enlivened by the breath of life or the spirit. The great emphasis in *soul* is thus upon man as a living being. As such it is used in relation to man's

---

25. Some have argued for "throat" (the place of breathing) as the root meaning of *nepeš.*

appetites, yearnings, and desires, whether they be those of the body (e.g., Deut. 23:24 NASB margin; Ps. 107:9 NASB; Prov. 25:25)[26] or those of the inner person (Exod. 15:9 NASB margin; Prov. 21:10 NASB; Jer. 12:7 NASB). It is also linked in this sense with man's longing for God and his word (e.g., Pss. 42:1, 2; 63:1; 119:20). As evidenced in these references to human passions and longings, *soul* has the characteristics of all of the aspects of human personality, that is, thought, emotion, and volition.

*Soul* is also used for the life of an individual (e.g., Gen. 35:18 NASB; Exod. 21:23 NASB; Rom. 11:3 [GK.]). In such uses it refers not to life in the abstract, but the living self in all of its dynamic. Since this life is manifest most clearly in the personal characteristics of the inner person, *soul* sometimes is used along with *body* ("flesh") to represent the whole person (e.g., Isa. 10:18 NASB; Ps. 63:1). At times the soul is distinguished from the body as that which cannot be ultimately affected by physical death (e.g., Matt. 10:28; John 12:25). Thus, the soul and body are different entities that, taken together in unity, form the whole person. It should be noted, however, that while soul and body are different entities in these instances, the emphasis is not on a division of the person into material and immaterial essences. Rather the emphasis is on the truth that the life of the soul is given by God and lived before him. As such it is life that cannot be limited by the death of this present body. Closely related to this concept are the many instances when *soul* is best understood simply as the "person" or "self."

In sum, then, *soul* in its most comprehensive sense stands for the entire person—the human being is a "living soul." As the uses above indicate, *soul* may be used for various aspects of the person, even the person who survives the death of this body. But even in these uses, there is the underlying thought that these actions or characteristics of the soul are those of the whole person.

The concept of soul is thus broader than that of spirit. As seen in Genesis 2:7 the soul is the total person enlivened by spirit. The spirit is thus a metaphysical entity, namely, the principle of life which empowers, while the soul is the individual subject or bearer of that life. The spirit is thus immaterial in essence, whereas the soul encompasses the total person, material and immaterial. Because it is used for the entire person, it is possible in certain contexts to distinguish the soul from the body (e.g., Matt. 10:28). But this is because the real person inheres in the immaterial aspect in separation and not because it becomes identical to "spirit." Thus the same disembodied person may be termed a "spirit" (e.g., Heb. 12:23) when viewed from the perspective of ontological nature, and a "soul" from the perspective of a "person" (e.g., Rev. 6:9).

26. In many of the references using *soul* cited above, the versions simply use the personal pronoun for the Hebrew wording, e.g., Deut. 23:24: "until you are satisfied" is literally "according to your satisfaction of your soul." The NASB often helpfully has the literal translation in the margin.

In certain Pauline texts soul is distinguished from spirit (cf. 1 Cor. 2:14–15, the natural or "soulish" person and the "spiritual" person). This has led some to see the soul and spirit as two distinct elements in human nature. The distinction, however, is not between two different essences. With the coming of the Holy Spirit under the new covenant, the apostle found it useful to distinguish between the believer, who is endowed with the Holy Spirit, and the unsaved, natural person. Thus the former, under the influence of the Spirit, is termed "spiritual," whereas the unsaved person living a natural, earthly life is called "soulish." The distinction, therefore, does not refer to different elements in the human person, but to different states of the entire person.

*Other important terms*

In addition to the three fundamental terms related to the human structure, there are several other significant anthropological terms used in Scripture that describe aspects of human nature. *Flesh* points to mankind as clothed in material substance. As noted above, the Old Testament does not have a separate word for "body," but most often uses *flesh*. It may refer to the soft flesh as opposed to bones or blood (e.g., Gen. 2:21; Prov. 5:11; 1 Cor. 15:50) or to the whole external body as opposed to the inner person (e.g., Ps. 16:9 NASB; 84:2; Gal. 2:20 NASB; Phil. 1:22–24 NASB). Finally, it describes the whole man along with the other creatures who live in corporeity (Gen. 6:17 NASB; 1 Pet. 1:24, 25 NASB). The significant meaning of *flesh* is clearly seen in this last sense when it is contrasted to *spirit*. Warning against reliance on Egypt, Isaiah writes, "Now the Egyptians are men and not God; their horses are flesh and not spirit" (31:3). In contrast to spirit, flesh is weak, transitory, and mortal. Thus the psalmist declares his trust in God and lack of fear for man stating, "What can mere man [lit. "flesh"] do to me?" (56:4 NASB; cf. also Gen. 6:3 NASB; 2 Chron. 32:8; Isa. 40:6 NASB; Jer. 17:5).

This primary description of mankind as flesh, and therefore weak and powerless, becomes the basis for the significant use of *flesh* in the New Testament for the principle of sinfulness. Apart from God weak, fleshy mankind is morally weak and comes under the domination of sin's power. In this ethical sense, then, *flesh* denotes the human person living as mere man apart from the power of God and thus under sin. In this sense, all the unsaved live in the realm of "the flesh" (cf. Rom. 8:5–13), and believers also still struggle with the remnants of the old "fleshly" principle that tempts them to live independently of God (cf. Gal. 5:17). Man as flesh is weak, but God provides hope in the sending of his Spirit for "all flesh" (cf. Joel 2:28 NASB).

One of the most significant terms in relation to human functioning is also the most frequently used, namely, *heart*. While it is used for the bodily organ, the term *heart* is overwhelmingly found in a metaphorical sense for the center of the human person. If the soul stands for the totality of the person, the heart is the inner operating center of the soul (cf. Prov. 4:23). As the center of the person, the heart refers to the inner person in general and to the attributes of human personality. According to Scripture, the functions of thought, emotion, and will all take place in the heart. Prominent among these is the teaching that man reasons and knows with his heart (e.g., Deut. 29:2–4 NASB; Ps. 90:12; Prov. 15:14). This is especially true in the Old Testament where there is no separate term for "mind." The function of what we know as the mind is performed in the heart. As evidence of this truth, the term *heart* is found by far most frequently in the portions of Scripture known as Wisdom Literature, such as Proverbs and Ecclesiates, and in the strongly didactic book of Deuteronomy. These portions are given that we might discern and come to "know" God's way of wisdom. Even in the New Testament, the heart continues this Old Testament function despite the addition of the Greek term *nous* for mind (e.g., Luke 2:19; 5:22; 9:47 NASB; Heb. 4:12).

The heart is also the seat of human volition, the place of motives, desires, and decisions (e.g., Exod. 35:5 NASB; Deut. 8:2; Ps. 21:1–2; Acts 8:22; Rom. 2:5). Finally, the heart is the seat of human feelings or moods (e.g., Prov. 14:30; 23:17) with the whole spectrum of emotions being attributed to it (e.g., sadness, 1 Sam. 1:8 NASB; joy, Prov. 15:30; fear, Deut. 28:65; uncertainty, John 14:1). All of these functions of personality (reason, emotion, will) are united inseparably in the heart. The thought of a person acting out of either reason or emotion as separate entities is contrary to biblical thought.

As the center of the inner person, the heart also denotes that which is innermost or hidden (e.g., "the heart of the sea," Ps. 46:2). Thus Scripture portrays the heart of man as hidden and finally inaccessible. Only God searches and knows the heart ( Ps. 139:23–24; Prov. 24:12; Jer. 17:9–10; 1 Cor. 4:5). What is commonly referred to as the realm of the unconscious, which so often affects the conscious life, lies in the depth of the heart where thought, emotion, and will are joined into one center of the human person.

In sum, the heart is the center or focus of man's personal life, the spring of all his motives, longings, moral choices and actions. It is the reflection of the real person (Prov. 27:19). Thus it is the heart of man that God considers in his evaluation of man and not the outward appearance (1 Sam. 16:7), a principle we would do well to follow to the extent that we can perceive another's heart. Finally, and most importantly, it is to the heart that God addresses his word and expects a response.

As indicated, the concept of that which we know as *mind* is connected in the Old Testament almost entirely with the word *heart*.[27] When translated "mind" the focus is on the heart as the seat of recollection (e.g. Isa. 65:17, "The former things will not be remembered, nor will they come to mind [lit. 'heart']"), reason (e.g., 1 Kings 3:12, "a wise and discerning heart"), and in-

---

27. In some English versions the Old Testament words *nepeš* ("soul") and *rûah* ("spirit") are also occasionally translated "mind" (e.g., Gen. 23:8 KJV).

tention or direction (Prov. 16:9, "In his heart a man plans his course"). Mind in the Old Testament is never separated from the entire person and is therefore holisticly related to the emotion and will. Thinking is not abstract or disinterested thought. Rather it represents the rational grasping of an object by the whole person via the faculties of investigation and analysis in such a way that the emotion and will respond in an appropriate manner. In Old Testament thought, the thinking function of the mind is never aimed at theoretical contemplative thought, but rather the right conduct of life.

This Hebrew concept of mind continues on in the New Testament where it is also frequently associated with the heart (cf. Luke 1:51; 2:19; 9:47 NASB; Heb. 4:12). But under the influence of the Greek world where the mind or reason played a central role, the New Testament writers also used other terms the most prominent of which is *nous* and its cognates. In general these terms signify the cognitive, reasoning, and purposive faculty of the human person. Although the terms are derived from the Greek culture, their New Testament meaning retains more of the Old Testament concept where rational thought is closely associated with the entire person, especially the will.

The New Testament "mind" is thus not simply a neutral faculty of human reason; by virtue of its understanding in relation to God or lack thereof, it represents a disposition or attitude of the person. Thus the mind can be described as depraved (Rom. 1:28), unspiritual (Col. 2:18), or futile (Eph. 4:17 NASB). On the other hand, the mind can be renewed by the Spirit (cf. Rom. 12:2; Eph. 4:23) and described as the "mind of Christ" (1 Cor. 2:16).

It may be said in general that in the holistic understanding of Scripture, the "mind" in Scripture represents the thinking aspect of the heart. This relationship is explained by Ridderbos when he says, "one can perhaps say that the heart is still more inclusive than the *nous,* in that the *nous* speaks of the human ego from the viewpoint of thinking—though this . . . is not in the least conceived of only as an intellectual faculty—whereas the affections, aspirations, passions, desires dwell in the heart and spring forth from it."[28] It is significant that faith, which obviously entails thought, is nevertheless always associated even in the New Testament with the heart indicating that true believing is more than an intellectual activity.

Another important aspect of the makeup of the human being is termed *conscience.* Derived from the Greek term *suneidēsis,* which is literally "a knowing with," the conscience is the human faculty of moral self-awareness. Again in relation to scriptural understanding of man as a holistic being, the conscience is not conceived of as a faculty detached from the person. It is rather man himself who is aware of his willing and acting. Thus the one with a "weak

28. Herman Ridderbos, *Paul: An Outline of His Theology,* trans. J. R. DeWitt (Grand Rapids: Eerdmans, 1975), 119.

conscience" (i.e., lack of clear moral convictions due to lack of instruction) may also be described as a "weak" person (1 Cor. 8:7, 11-12).[29] Further evidence of this can be seen in the absence of a separate term for conscience in the Old Testament. Like the mind, its function belongs primarily to the heart, the center of the person. It is clearly the conscience that is meant when David's heart is said to strike him (1 Sam. 24:5 NASB margin; 2 Sam. 24:10 NASB margin), or his heart stumbles (1 Sam. 25:31 NASB margin; cf. also Job 27:6 NASB). The action of conscience is also evident in the misery of unconfessed sin in Psalm 32:3–4.

The function of the conscience is seen clearly in Romans 2:14-16 where it acts as a witness and judge of human actions, either accusing or defending those who do them. Its activity is primarily retrospective judging of past actions, but it also evaluates future actions urging compliance with the moral standard (e.g., Rom. 13:5; 1 Cor. 10:27; 1 Pet. 2:19 NASB). This standard against which one's conscience judges his actions includes the moral law of God written in every human heart (Rom. 2:15) and moral concepts derived from cultural tradition (cf. 1 Cor. 8:7, 12).

Since sin not only disrupts the ability to perceive God's law clearly, but has also corrupted the human traditions incorporated into a person's moral standard, the activity of the conscience cannot be trusted for infallible moral judgment. It needs to be instructed by God's revelation concerning the true moral standard (cf. Rom. 10:2; 1 Cor. 8:7–11). However, Scripture warns against ever trampling on the conscience even before it is fully instructed (1 Cor. 8:7–11; 10:28; Rom. 14:23). Such action not only yields a defiled (bad or pained) conscience (1 Cor. 8:7; Heb. 10:22), but also brings a dangerous desensitizing of this moral faculty, that is, a searing of the conscience (1 Tim. 4:2; cf. Eph. 4:19). A "good" or "clear" conscience is an important aspect of true human life (cf. 1 Tim. 1:5, 19; 3:9; 2 Tim. 1:3; 1 Pet. 3:16), for it signifies an inward healing of the divided person. Such a healing of the conscience comes ultimately through the cleansing of Christ's saving work (Heb. 10:22; cf. 1 Pet. 3:21).

Scripture uses many other terms in relation to the human person. For example, the bowels, liver, and kidneys are frequently associated with spiritual and emotional states (e.g., Ps. 73:21 NASB margin, where "kidneys" is parallel with "heart"). Likewise, the outward members of the body represent human capacities and activities. For example, the hand frequently is used for man's power (e.g., 1 Sam. 25:26). The terms discussed above, however, are primary in providing an understanding of the biblical perspective of the structure of human beings.

29. Christian Maurer, "συνοιδα κτλ" *Theological Dictionary of the New Testament,* in vol. 7, ed. Gerhard Friedrich (Grand Rapids: Eerdmans, 1971), 914–15.

## The Basic Nature of the Human Being

Something of the general perspective of human nature has been seen in the discussion of the various terminology. But it will be helpful, especially in the light of much current thought, to draw this together in a brief summary of the biblical picture of the basic nature of the human being. According to Scripture the nature of the human person is a basic duality which is intended to function holistically.[30]

### A basic duality

Much of modern thought (including biblical scholarship) has come to view the human being in such a holistic fashion that human existence is limited to existence in the body. One major source of this thinking has been a massive interdisciplinary study of the human brain. Psychologists, neurophysiologists, brain surgeons, evolutionary biologists, and even computer scientists have joined forces in an attempt to understand the complexity of the operation of the brain and the resultant human behavior. Because electrical and chemical stimulation of the brain can elicit a variety of behaviors, many have concluded that there is no separate entity in man such as a spirit or mind distinct from the physical brain. Man, it is claimed, is ultimately monistic in essence and that essence is material. The mind is reducible to the physical operation of the brain.

Many biblical scholars, while not willing to reduce man to material monism, nevertheless, view him as so holistic that while mind and brain are not identified, neither are they separable. This is allegedly derived from the Hebraic view of Scripture which is said to have been subsequently corrupted in later theology by Greek dualism. Although expressed some time ago, the explanation of H. Wheeler Robinson represents many today: "For the Hebrew man is a unity and that . . . unity is the body as a complex of parts, drawing their life and activity from a breath-soul, which has no existence apart from the body."[31] More recently Christian psychologist David Myers affirms a union of mind and body to the extent that our minds "are manifestations of our bodies."[32]

---

30. For a recent defense of "holistic dualism" involving biblical, scientific, and philosophical data, see John W. Cooper, *Body, Soul, and Life Everlasting: Biblical Anthropology and the Monism-Dualism Debate* (Grand Rapids: Eerdmans, 1989).

31. H. Wheeler Robinson, "Hebrew Psychology," in *The People and the Book,* ed. Arthur S. Peake (Oxford: Clarendon, 1925), 366.

32. David G. Myers, *The Human Puzzle: Psychological Research and Christian Belief* (New York: Harper and Row, 1978), 268. A similar understanding is seen in the explanation of the evangelical scientist, Richard Bube, "Other Options?" *Journal of the American Scientific Affiliation* 24 [March 1972]: 14–15 : "The soul is . . . a reality which is produced as an emergent property of the living system of a human being. As life is produced as an emergent property of a non-living system by the appropriate patterned interaction of non-living subsystems, so soul is produced as an emergent property of non-soul subsystems when they interact according to the appropriate pattern."

A third factor behind much of the modern unitary thought regarding human nature comes from the idea of evolution. According to Rahner, "the contemporary world-picture is characterised by a pre-decision for unity and development; it sees matter, life and spirit as held together in one single history of evolution."[33]

While the overall picture of human life in Scripture is holistic, it is nevertheless the holism of a basic duality.[34] In the central Scripture establishing the nature of man at creation, God used the matter of the earth and his own breath (i.e., spirit) to create Adam. This combination of material and spirit resulted in a holistic "living soul." There is no indication in the creation account that this combination was ever intended to be separated. However, Scripture indicates that the being of man can be and is separated. This separation is seen particularly at the point of physical death which entered human existence as a result of sin (cf. Rom. 5:12). The separation of the person at death into the two original elements is clearly explained by the writer of Ecclesiastes when he says, "then the dust will return to the earth as it was, and the spirit will return to God who gave it" (12:7 NASB). The separability of spirit and body is further seen in passages that indicate that the body is somehow the dwelling of the inner person (e.g., Job. 4:19; 2 Pet. 1:13). Moreover, the inner person continues to exist following the separation (e.g., 2 Cor. 5:5–8; Phil. 1:20–25; Heb. 12:23). Interestingly, it is even possible for Paul to conceive of the possibility of an out-of-body experience apart from death (2 Cor. 12:2–4).

These passages demonstrate not only the basic duality of the nature of the human person, but also that the primacy of the person resides in the immaterial or spiritual aspect. At the separation, the "self" continues to exist in a conscious state in the spirit aspect of human nature apart from a material body. Such a human condition, however, is always viewed in Scripture as incomplete. Thus the Bible affirms the resurrection of the body for all people that the human person may again become whole as intended in creation.

### A functional holism

Although the human person by constitution is a basic duality, these two aspects of his nature are joined together in a functional holism of life. The body is not the whole person (materialism), nor is it the prison house of the soul (Platonic philosophical dualism). Instead, the body or "the outer man" is designed as a partner of the spirit or "the inner man" (cf. 2 Cor. 4:16 NASB). The body is the only avenue of expression for the inner person in the world of time and sense. It is really only in bodily form that we can present ourselves a living sacrifice to God in this world (Rom. 12:1).

33. Karl Rahner, *Concerning Vatican Council II,* trans. Karl-H. and Boniface Kruger, vol. 6 of *Theological Investigations* (London: Darton, Longman and Todd, 1969), 148.

34. For an exposition of the biblical duality of the human constitution, see Robert H. Gundry, *Sōma in Biblical Theology* (Grand Rapids: Zondervan, 1987), 83–156.

Thus Scripture teaches that the human person functions in psychosomatic wholeness. The most obvious expression of this is seen in the way personal psychological qualities are attributed to a great variety of physical parts of the body. This includes the peripheral parts of the body such as the face, mouth, eyes, nostrils, arms, hands, feet and neck. Even more forcefully in connection with the inner body, emotional states are attributed to the bowels, kidneys, and above all the heart. Even the bones are given psychological significance.[35]

This holism of the human person is seen further in the teaching of the interaction of the body with the spiritual nature. According to the writer of Proverbs, bringing the words of God into one's heart results in "health" to the "whole body" (Prov. 4:22 NASB; cf. 3:7-8; 17:22). The primary flow is from the inner person to the body, indicating the primacy of the spiritual side of human nature. But the effect can also be from the body to the spirit. Thus the psalmist can write that wine "makes man's heart glad" (104:15 NASB; cf. Prov. 31:6).

*Some implications of the nature of the human person*

The nature of the human person as the totality of material and spiritual aspects leads to the conclusion that the person acts as a totality. It is not the body or the mind, but the unified psychosomatic person who is involved in life's relationships and activities. While it is no doubt possible to see different circumstances as related more to one aspect of life than the others, it is finally impossible to radically isolate human experiences into physical, emotional, or spiritual compartments. This would be especially true of the relationship of the emotional and spiritual since both relate primarily to the inner person. Wholeness in the spiritual or emotional realms can only be achieved when the total self is involved. Moreover, since the human person is defined primarily as the image of God, wholeness in any realm cannot be finally achieved apart from a relation to God.

The holistic character of human nature also demands that human life be seen as a whole. Human relationship to God, others, self, and creation leads to a complex of spiritual, social, economic, political and physical interests in the world. As the different aspects within the unified person cannot be separated, so his relations to his outside environment in these various dimensions of life cannot be separated. Man relates to them as a unitary organism. Thus all interests are interrelated and finally all are related to God.

These implications from the nature of a human being have clear implications for the ministry of the church which is involved in God's saving purpose to restore true human personhood upon his people. People must be viewed holistically and ministry directed to the needs of the whole person, physical,

35. For a good discussion of the Old Testament conception of the human person as a psycho-physical organism, see Aubrey R. Johnson, *The Vitality of the Individual in the Thought of Ancient Israel* (Cardiff: University of Wales, 1964), 37–87.

emotion, and spiritual. Moreover, ministry must somehow be relevant to the various relationships that the unified human being has to the world about him.

## The Functioning of the Human Person

Having seen that the nature of the human being is a complex whole, it follows that the actual functioning of this holistic being would also involve complexity. Without attempting a full-orbed biblical study of human behavior,[36] certain basic principles of how the various aspects of human nature function together in human behavior are clearly taught in Scripture.

### Human Life Is Lived from the Heart

According to Scripture, the heart is the fountainhead of behavior. It is not only the center which reflects the real person (Prov. 27:19), but the organ of personality or that through which the human person or soul functions.[37] The human life is lived from the heart. The writer of Proverbs declares, "Above all else guard your heart, for it is the wellspring of life" (4:23). The Hebrew term translated "wellspring" is literally "issues," signifying not only the place from which something goes forth, but the course it takes. The heart is not only the source of activity in human life, but is also that which determines the direction and course of that life (e.g., Eccles. 10:2; Deut. 30:17). It is "an organ of self-expression,"[38] "the meeting-place of all man's powers of mind and the starting-point of all his activities,"[39] the "totality of the soul as a character and operating power."[40] An important fact in this regard is the predominantly religious use of the heart in Scripture. As mankind was created to walk before God, so that walk is always determined by the heart.[41]

It must be recognized that the heart as the director of life has different levels. Some things that come to the heart may be said to lie only on its surface and have little effect on behavior. Other things lie at quite a different depth

---

36. Traditionally, theological anthropology has focused primarily on the structural or onto-logical nature of man with studies on human function being much more limited. One work that includes considerable material on the nature of human functioning is the somewhat dated, but still useful classic, Franz Delitzsch, *A System of Biblical Psychology* (1867; reprint, Grand Rapids: Baker, 1966).

37. M. Scott Fletcher, *The Psychology of the New Testament* (London: Hodder and Stough-ton, 37. 1912), 77.

38. Johnson, *The Vitality of the Individual*, 81.

39. Fletcher, *The Psychology of the New Testament*, 76.

40. Johannes Pedersen, *Israel: Its Life and Culture,* rev. edition, 2 vols. (London: Oxford University Press, 1926), 1:104.

41. See F. H. Von Meyenfeldt, "The Old Testament Meaning of Heart and Soul," in *Toward a Biblical View of Man: Some Readings,* ed. Arnold H. De Graaff and James H. Olthuis (Toronto: The Association for the Advancement of Christian Scholarship, 1978), 71–73.

and form the real nucleus of the heart. As Pedersen says, "there may be a difference between the momentary and the stable points of gravity in the soul [i.e., the heart as acting center of the soul]." At any moment, therefore, the actions of the person may actually be from different levels of the heart so that the deepest-lying contents do not always make themselves felt.[42]

Because we as humans act out of the contents of our hearts, Scripture makes the care of one's heart the supreme task of man. The heart may be director of human behavior, but the person has the responsibility of directing the director, that is, controlling what goes into and stays in the heart. Thus the writer of Proverbs exhorts us to guard our hearts, valuing it above all other treasures. This responsibility is finally performed only through the enablement of God (cf. Ps. 86:11; Jer. 32:39).

### The Unified Nature of the Heart in Behavior

In attempting to understand human behavior, it is important to grasp the biblical truth that in the heart, the operating center from which all behavior flows, thought, feeling, and will all come together in a unified whole. This unification of the elements of personality in human action is seen in the fact that "[w]illing, thinking, experiencing, are never distinguished in Scripture with terminologic sharpness."[43] A good example of this is the biblical word *know* which indicates not merely propositional knowledge, but also experience (e.g., "Adam knew his wife Eve," Gen. 4:1 NASB margin). As Dentan says, "[G]enuine knowledge involved the whole of a man's personality—his mind, his feelings, and his deeds."[44] Similarly, the Hebrew word often translated "intent" combines both thought and will. And the verb *to hear* in Scripture clearly includes the thought of obedience.

Human behavior is, therefore, always the manifestation of all of the elements of the total human person in unity.[45] Attempts to act out of reason apart from the emotion, or vice versa, are not only alien to biblical thought but are finally impossible. This is not to say that there are often conscious conflicts between reason and emotion even as there are conflicting thoughts in the mind or conflicting emotions. In the actual behavior, however, the person, unless deranged, acts unitedly in these realms. In this connection, it must be remembered that the realm of the heart includes the unconscious. Thus the thought of the heart involved in any action may not be consciously recognized. But whether recognized or not, biblically, human behavior involves the total person acting holistically.

42. *Ibid.*, 166.
43. Delitzsch, *A System of Biblical Psychology*, 207.
44. Robert C. Dentan, *The Knowledge of God in Ancient Israel* (New York: Seabury, 1968), 40.
45. On the biblical unity of the person involving mind, emotion, and will in human behavior, see Pedersen, *Israel* #1:125–28.

### The Functioning of the Heart

Regarding the union of thought, emotion, and will in human actions, Scripture reveals a certain priority of the thinking element. We are exhorted to personal transformation "by the renewing of your mind" (Rom. 12:2 NASB). Newness is accomplished through being "renewed in the spirit of your mind" (Eph. 4:23 NASB). Obedience stems from commitment to teaching (Rom. 6:17). Spiritual warfare involves "taking every thought captive to the obedience of Christ" (2 Cor. 10:5 NASB). The centrality of the mind in right behavior is evident in the biblical truth that the direction of human life is ultimately a conflict between the truth and the lie even as it was in the Garden of Eden. Thus Jesus says that it is the truth that sets the person free to live or behave according to his true created nature (John 8:32). While this truth is embodied in the person of Jesus (cf. 8:36), the knowledge of Jesus is finally attained through his word. Thus the heart is above all the place where God addresses his word to man and from which man responds to that word.

From the beginning point of thought, the flow of the heart's operation moves to emotion and finally to action. The significance of emotions or feelings in human life has probably not received the attention it deserves in theological anthropology. Nevertheless, Scripture is replete not only with displays of human feelings, but their centrality to true life.[46] The picture of emotions is that they stem from the way the heart views or thinks about experience.[47] As Pannenberg, following Augustine, explains, "The question . . . is not so much *whether* the devout mind can feel anger, but rather *why* it feels anger; not *whether* it grows sad, but *at what* it feels sadness; not *whether* but *why* it is afraid."[48] Thus Jesus weeps over the reality perceived by his mind in the death of Lazarus. Similarly, the recognition of the believer's eschatological future produces an inexpressible joy which gives encouragement and strength during suffering (cf. 1 Pet. 1:6–8).

The importance of emotions in human life is seen in that they ultimately drive the behavior. Augustine recognized this truth, describing the affects as the feet of the soul. They either lead us closer to God or carry us farther from him; but without them we will go nowhere.[49] This truth is behind the biblical concept of not simply *reading* Scripture, but *meditating* on it. The repetition and other aspects involved in meditation is designed to let the truth touch the emotions and thus effect a change of life. Biblically speaking, one has not hid-

46. Jonathan Edwards, *Religious Affections,* ed. John E. Smith, vol. 2 of *The Works of Jonathan Edwards,* ed. John E. Smith et al. (New Haven: Yale University Press, 1959).

47. On emotions as the result of the construals of the mind, see Robert C. Roberts, *Spirituality and Human Emotion* (Grand Rapids: Eerdmans, 1982), 12–24.

48. Wolfhart Pannenberg, *Anthropology in Theological Perspective* (Philadelphia: Westminster, 1985), 259. See pp. 244–65 for further discussion of the place of emotions.

49. Ibid.

den Scripture in the "heart" until it affects not only the thinking, but the feeling and behavior.

While recognizing the general flow among the elements of the heart from thought to emotion and then behavior, the inseparable conjunction of these three elements in the heart leads to the further truth that they function interrelatedly. That is, each function in turn affects the others. Emotions, therefore, not only affect actions, but also thought. Similarly, actions affect both thoughts and emotions. This total combination of mind, emotions and actions is seen, for example, in Paul's exhortation to the Philippian believers. They were to let their "mind dwell" (i.e., ponder to the point of emotional involvement leading to behavior)[50] on those things which are positive (4:8–9). These things, which had been demonstrated in the life of the apostle, were then to be practiced. As a consequence, the Philippians would experience the presence of the God of peace. A more pointed example of the effect of actions on thought is seen in James' teaching that although faith clearly produces works, works also "perfect" faith (cf. 2:22 NASB). The idea is that the actions produced by faith (which includes thought) in turn have the effect of strengthening and maturing that faith.

The union of thought, emotion, and volition in the heart and their interrelatedness of function indicate that all three are involved in human behavior. Any attempt to facilitate a change of heart necessary for human change and growth must consider the place of all of these dimensions of the person as they function in the heart.

## The Fall of Man

Whether we examine our own individual experiences or consider the whole course of human history, realism compels us to conclude that something is wrong with human nature. High ideals of love and goodness are continually present, but frequently not experienced and never in their perfection. Scripture accounts for this reality of human experience in its doctrine of sin or human alienation from God, the source of all true love and goodness.

### The Original Probation of Man in Eden

At the creation God provided for every need of original mankind. Placed in a park-like garden, Adam and Eve were richly supplied with provisions for physical life with trees described as "pleasing to the sight and good for food" (Gen. 2:9 NASB). They were also given a command in the form of a prohibition not to eat of "the tree of the knowledge of good and evil" (2:17). This command as the word of God was to open up the possibility of a personal rela-

---

50. H. W. Heidland, "λογίζομαι," *Theological Dictionary of the New Testament*, ed. Gerhard Kittel and Geoffrey W. Bromiley, trans. Geoffrey W. Bromiley, 10 vols. (Grand Rapids: Eerdmans, 1967), 4:289.

tionship with the one who spoke it. As Westermann explains, "a personal relationship to God is part of human existence as a whole and it only becomes possible through a commandment of God; Deut 8:2."[51] The prohibition thus acknowledges the freedom of the human being above any animal and places a limit on it. The limit is finally for the protection of man, for to have life man the creature must remain in a relationship with God the source of life. The command also provided an opportunity for man to develop moral character. The prohibition which the tempter turns into a temptation is used by God as a test so that man's moral nature may develop character through the exercise of moral choice.

### The Fall and the Essence of Sin

The nature of the temptation and the first sin of man reveals the essential nature of sin and the crucial problem of mankind. The "knowledge of good and evil" associated with the prohibited tree in the Garden signifies the knowledge that determines what is good and evil—in other words, moral autonomy. The true knowledge of good and evil, or the prerogative to determine morality, belongs to God alone as sovereign creator. Perhaps more than anything else in a moral universe this characteristic identifies God as God. Man's morality is thus intended to be dependent upon God's "knowledge of good and evil." In taking to themselves this determining moral knowledge, mankind in reality assumed the place of God. Thus there was truth to the tempter's words, "you will be like God, knowing good and evil" (Gen. 2:5; cf. also the similar words of God in 3:22).

The first sin of mankind thus reveals the essential nature of sin, which in turn is seen in its various manifestations throughout Scripture. Sin involves assuming the position of godhood over one's life and living independently from the true God. Sin is not in the first instance a specific act or thought, but self-godhood. Thus theologians following Scripture have seen the essence of sin in terms of pride[52] (cf. Ps. 10:4; Prov. 6:17; 8:13; 16:5; Isa. 14:12–14) or unbelief, which may be explained as the result of pride (cf. Rom. 14:23; John 8:8–9). Sinful behavior simply flows from this basic stance of life which refuses to hold in faith the truth expressed by the apostle that God is the one in whom man lives and moves and has his being (Acts 17:28; cf. Rom. 14:23, "everything that does not come from faith is sin"). In assuming the place of God, man must attempt to live above his fellow man, a purpose prompting thoughts and actions of self-centered lovelessness in relation to others.

The reason why mankind chose to turn away from God receives no explanation in Scripture. There is never any suggestion as has sometimes been of-

---

51. Westermann, *Genesis 1–11*, 223.

52. For an interesting discussion of the pride of sin in its various forms and effects, see Niebuhr, *Human Nature*, 178–240.

fered by interpreters that the cause of sin lay in human finitude, for example, in ignorance or spiritual impotence. To explain sin in terms of the good created nature of man in any cause-and-effect relationship would finally be explaining evil in terms of good. This in turn would finally deny morality since the boundary of evil and good would disappear. In sum, Scripture consistently sees the origin of sin, whether in the angelic or human realm, in terms of the unexplained use of created freedom to turn against its source in exceeding the limits which the Creator has established for the benefit of the creature (cf. Ezek. 28:15).

## The Effects of the Fall

The choice of original man to disobey God's command and choose his own autonomy resulted in a serious disruption of the original human situation. The effects were not only immediate upon Adam and Eve; they extended to the entire human race affecting every aspect of life—personal, social, economical and environmental.

### The Immediate Effects of the Fall

#### The fundamental effect—death

The command of God carried the penalty of death for disobedience (Gen. 2:17). Scripturally, death is simply the absence of life. It relates to both the spiritual realm of the human being or the inner person, as well as the body. Death occurs when something is separated from that which is its life. Since the living God is the "fountain of life" (Ps. 36:9), the action of man in turning from him can only result in death. Thus death is not only the divine judgment, but is also the natural result of sin.

On the day that man sinned, he experienced personal separation from God resulting in the death of spirit or the inner person. This was immediately evident in his hiding from God in fear (Gen. 3:8, 10). Spiritual death not only signified alienation from God, but also resulted in alienation from his fellow human being (Gen. 3:12). Moreover, it brought disorder to man's inner being. For the first time he experienced the inner chaos of shame and guilt. Shame is the awareness that something is now lacking or is not right in oneself. Thus man, aware of his lack, sought to hide himself from the gaze and exposure of others (Gen. 3:8). As shame relates to another, guilt relates to oneself, indicating an internal split between one's moral standard and actions. The attempts by both the man and the woman to attribute the sinful act to someone else were only attempts to resolve this inner tension by self-acquittal (cf. 3:12–13).

The true nature of spiritual death is seen in these effects of sin on the inner person. Spiritual death is not annihilation of the person or even the person's spirit. It is rather the disruption and chaos of the created structure of the human person, the opposite of that condition of total well-being which Scripture so often describes by the term *šālôm*, peace.

Along with spiritual death, the process of physical death also came into effect on the day that Adam and Eve disobeyed God. They would still continue to live for many years, in the case of Adam over eight hundred years. But that which leads to physical death was now at work in them. That this process began when spiritual death occurred is suggested by the holistic nature of the human being discussed earlier. While the Scripture does not explain the relationship, it clearly suggests that disruption in the realm of the spiritual nature inevitably has an effect on the body. Thus Adam's physical nature, which prior to the entrance of sin was not dying, was from this time forward affected with the death principle.

### The judgment on woman, man, and nature

Sin not only affected man's relation to God necessitating death, it also brought the judgment of God upon the fundamental areas of human life on earth.[53] In the case of woman, the judgment touched the two traditionally central areas of her life. With her husband she was intended to enjoy the blessing of children (Gen. 1:28) in the union of a harmonious marriage (2:18, 22–25). It was exactly these two areas of the marriage relationship and motherhood in which the biblical woman found great fulfillment in life, that God touched with judgment (3:16). She would continue to bear children, but from now on it would be with pain.[54] Her marriage of loving union would now be fraught with struggle and the once loving leadership of her husband would now be a rulership. As Wenham remarks, "Though created to be man's companion, she is told that her desire for independence will conflict with his demand for submission. Under the curse, those who were created to be one flesh will find themselves tearing each other apart."[55]

The judgment of God similarly touched the fundamental area of the man's life, namely that of providing for the family. Instead of the abundance of easily obtained food provided in the Garden, the ground was cursed so that Adam would now have to "toil" for the fruit of it in order to live. The word translated "toil" (3:17 NASB) or "painful toil" (NIV) is the same Hebrew word as used for the "pain" of the woman in childbearing. It signifies almost any suf-

53. Gerhand Von Rad, *Genesis: A Commentary,* rev. ed. (Philadelphia: Westminster, 1972), 93–94: "The woman's punishment struck at the deepest root of her being as wife and mother, the man's strikes at the innermost nerve of his life: his work, his activity, and provision for sustenance."

54. The Hebrew wording, "your pain and your childbearing" (3:16) is commonly understood as a hendiadys: "your pain in childbearing." Cassuto and some others have also understood the words as meaning, "your *suffering* in general, and more particularly that of *your childbearing*" (U. Cassuto, *A Commentary on the Book of Genesis,* 2 vols. [Jerusalem: Magnes, 1961], 1:165.

55. Gordon J. Wenham, *Genesis 1–15,* Word Biblical Commentary (Waco, TX: Word, 1987), 89.

fering, emotional and physical, related to that which is toilsome or hard to bear. There is thus a parallel between the judgment on the woman and that on the man. The fundamental areas of their lives are touched by the judgment of God to remind them of the presence of sin. Such a disturbing of the basic areas of human life on earth can also be seen as an action of God's grace designed to induce man to long for that which was lost through sin and return to God, the source of a life of *šālôm*.

The judgment on man involved the cursing of the land. From the scriptural statements that God's blessing on a land meant an abundance of water and fertility (cf. Gen. 2:8–14; Deut. 33:13–16), the cursing may be seen to signify the lack of these, causing the difficulty to produce provisions for human life. But it also signifies other major changes of nature. The New Testament teaching that creation was subjected to "futility" (i.e., inability to attain its purpose) and enslaved to "corruption" (i.e., decay and death) is linked by most interpreters to human sin and the cursing of the ground in Genesis 3 (cf. Rom. 8:20–21).[56] The cursing of the ground was thus a radical negative transformation of creation from its original "good" condition. According to the apostle's teaching this curse will be lifted only with the final perfection of those in Christ who will be revealed in glory as his children (cf. Rom. 8:19, 21).

The cursing of the ground at creation, therefore, not only provides for the judgment of God, but also relates to the original design that creation needs the rulership of man to fulfill its purpose. In the words of Cranfield, "We may think of the whole magnificent theatre of the universe together with all its splendid properties and all the chorus of sub-human life, created to glorify God but unable to do so fully, so long as man the chief actor in the drama of God's praise fails to contribute his rational part."[57]

### The Racial Effects of the Fall

That the judgments of that first sin continued to effect the human race both in a disturbed life on earth and death is evident in history. But Scripture also connects the truth of the universal presence of evil in the human heart with the sin of Adam. This connection is clearly seen in the apostle's teaching that "through one man sin entered into the world, and death through sin, and

---

56. Of the "subjection" of creation, C. E. B. Cranfield, *A Critical and Exegetical Commentary on the Epistle to the Romans,* The International and Critical Commentary, 2 vols. (Edinburgh: T. and T. Clark, 1975), 1:413 says, "There is little doubt that Paul had in mind the judgment related in Gen. 3:17–19, which includes (v. 17) the words 'cursed is the ground for thy sake.'" For the Jewish background of this New Testament understanding, see Ernest Käsemann, *Commentary on Romans,* trans. and ed. Geoffrey W. Bromiley (Grand Rapids: Eerdmans, 1980), 233.

57. Cranfield, *Romans,* 414.

so death spread to all men, because all sinned" (Rom. 5:12 NASB; cf. 1 Cor. 15:21–22).

The explanations of the connection of subsequent generations of humanity with Adam's act has been variously interpreted. Some have denied a real connection and treated Adam as only a bad example who had a pernicious effect on his progeny. Others acknowledge the inheritance of a corrupt sinful nature from Adam, but attach no guilt to the inherited depravity of nature until the individual actually affirms this nature in a personal act of sin himself. The biblical teaching, however, seems to demand more than these views. All of humanity, which constitutes a single race, is somehow seen as directly related to the sin of the first human being and sharing in its consequences.

In the apostle's teaching in Romans 5:12–19 the connection of mankind to Adam and his sin is viewed as parallel to that of the believer and the righteous action of Christ. Thus even as Christ's "act of righteousness" is accounted to all who are related to him, so also the "one transgression" of Adam is accounted to all mankind related to him (v. 18). In both cases the result is that the individuals related to both Adam and Christ are viewed as participating in the actions of these two individuals.

Various explanations of this connection of all men to Adam have been proposed with none receiving general acceptance. Perhaps the best solution is found in the biblical teaching of the unity or corporateness of humanity in which the individual and the group to which he belongs are closely identified. Also termed "corporate personality," the union of the individual and the community were such that the entire group could be conceived of as acting in the individual (e.g., the sin of Achan in Josh. 7:10–12). While this has something of a representative idea, it also has a certain reality of relationship which may be seen most clearly in the concept of "being in Christ." The union of all human beings with Adam by natural birth is thus analogous to the union of the new humanity with Christ even as the apostle portrays the parallel between the two individuals in Romans 5. As all who are "in Christ," by virtue of their corporate union with him, participate in his "act of righteousness," so all who are in Adam, by virtue of their natural corporate union with him, participate in his "one transgression" (Rom. 5:18; cf. 1 Cor. 15:21–22). In this concept of corporateness a real unity of mankind is affirmed without attempting to explain its exact nature.[58]

While the scriptural teaching of the connection of all human beings to the sin of Adam is difficult to understand, it nevertheless presents the best explanation of the reality that there is in fact a union of all people in the problem of sin. Moreover, the plan of salvation whereby the many are brought to glory

---

58. For a discussion of the concept of corporateness in relation to Adam's sin, see G. C. Berkouwer, *Sin,* trans. Philip C. Holtrop, vol. 11 of *Studies in Dogmatics* (Grand Rapids: Eerdmans, 1971), 508–17.

through participation in the actions of one Savior rests on this same corporate concept.

The scriptural truth that all humanity participates in the sin of Adam leads to the result that all people come into this world burdened with sin. Not only does every person sin at some time (cf. 1 Kings 8:46; Ps. 143:2; Prov. 20:9; Rom. 3:9–11, 23; Gal. 3:22), they sin because they are born into the world in a sinful state. Such "original sin," as it is often termed, is clearly taught in Scripture. Sin is present from birth (cf. Ps. 51:5; 58:3; Prov. 22:15; Job 14:1–4); it pollutes mankind from the beginning so that they are all described as being "objects of wrath *by nature*" (Eph. 2:3 NASB, italics added). Finally, it is difficult to account for the universality of the practice of sin apart from something that is native to fallen human nature.

To say that all are born in a sinful state means first that in relation to the holiness of God, every aspect of their nature has been corrupted by sin. Thus the human mind, conscience, heart and will are all said to be permeated by sin (cf. Gen. 6:5; Jer. 17:9; Rom. 8:7; 1 Tim. 4:2). This should not be interpreted as meaning that all are equally depraved. Scripture recognizes not only that some commit worse sin than others (e.g., Gen. 15:16; 2 Tim. 3:13), but also that the natural fallen human being can perform certain "good" actions on the natural level (cf. Matt. 5:46–47; 7:11). But even these good actions are finally conditioned by sin. That is, they are done independently of God and thus in reality under the principle of the first sin (i.e., acting as one's own god). True "goodness," which is goodness produced through a relation to God and designed to display his glory, is therefore impossible for the natural human person (cf. Rom. 3:12). This truth is evident from human history where, in spite of the universal teaching of love, the world seems as far, if not farther, from peace and harmony today than ever before.

In addition to corruption in relation to God's holiness, original sin entails guilt in relation to his justice. The universe is finally a moral universe, and mankind in the image of God is a moral being. Thus man's life entails the principle of justice, meaning that obedience and disobedience must be treated differently. Scripture, therefore, teaches not only that God hates evil, but that his judgment must fall on evil in distinction to his favor upon righteousness. Mankind by nature, under the state of sin, is alienated from God. Living as his own god, he is violating the law of God and consequently stands guilty under the judgment of the wrath of God (cf. John 3:36; Eph. 2:3).

The teaching of Scripture that all of humanity shares in the sin of Adam, with the result that every individual is by nature burdened with sin and under the judgment of God, reveals the sad plight of the human condition apart from God. Rather than negating the stature of the human being, however, it attests to the significance with which God treats the human being. Human actions, even in opposition to God, are important and have great significance.

As noted earlier, the full seriousness of human sin is revealed clearly when the wrath of God is poured out against his Son who took our place on the cross. But in this very act, God asserts not only that human beings are sinful, but that they are of such significance in his eyes that he gave his beloved Son to restore them to wholeness.

## Suggested Readings

Anderson, Ray S. *On Being Human: Essays in Theological Anthropology.* Grand Rapids: Eerdmans, 1982. [A]

Baker, William H. *In the Image of God.* Chicago: Moody, 1991. [B]

Barth, Karl. *Church Dogmatics.* Vol. 3, pts. 1–2, *The Doctrine of Creation.* Edited by G. W. Bromiley and T. F. Torrance. Translated by Harold Knight et al. Edinburgh: T. and T. Clark, 1956–60. [A]

Berkhof, Hendrikus. *Man in Transit.* Wheaton, Ill.: Key Publishers, 1971. [B]

Berkouwer, G. C. *Studies in Dogmatics.* Vol. 8, *Man: The Image of God.* Translated by Dirk W. Jellema. Grand Rapids: Eerdmans, 1962. [A]

Brunner, Emil. *Man in Revolt: A Christian Anthropology.* Translated by Olive Wyon. Philadelphia: Westminster, 1947. [A]

Carey, George. *I Believe in Man.* Grand Rapids: Eerdmans, 1977. [I]

De Graaff, Arnold H., and James H. Olthuis, eds. *Toward a Biblical View of Man: Some Readings.* Toronto: Association for the Advancement of Christian Scholarship, 1978. [A]

Delitzsch, Franz. *A System of Biblical Psychology.* 2d ed. Translated by Robert E. Wallis. Edinburgh: T. and T. Clark, 1879. [A]

Hoekema, Anthony. *Created in God's Image.* Grand Rapids: Eerdmans, 1986. [I]

Kümmel, Werner G. *Man in the New Testament.* Revised and enlarged edition. London: Epworth, 1963. [A]

Laidlaw, Robert. *The Bible Doctrine of Man.* Edinburgh: T. and T. Clark, 1895. [A]

Lee, F. H. *The Origin and Destiny of Man.* Nutley, N. J.: Presbyterian and Reformed, 1974. [B]

McDonald, H. D. *The Christian View of Man.* Westchester, Ill.: Crossway, 1981. [I]

Niebuhr, Reinhold. *The Nature and Destiny of Man.* Vol 1, *Human Nature.* New York: Charles Scribner's Sons, 1964. [A]

Pannenberg, Wolfhart. *Anthropology in Theological Perspective.* Translated by Matthew J. O'Connell. Philadelphia: Westminster, 1985. [A]

Robinson, H. Wheeler. *The Christian Doctrine of Man*. Edinburgh: T. and T. Clark, 1926. [A]

Sauer, Eric. *The King of the Earth: The Nobility of Man According to the Bible and Science*. London: Paternoster, 1962. [I]

Stacey, W. D. *The Pauline View of Man*. New York: St. Martin's, 1956. [A]

Torrance, T. F. *Calvin's Doctrine of Man*. Grand Rapids: Eerdmans, 1957. [A]

Verduin, Leonard. *Somewhat Less than God: The Biblical View of Man*. Grand Rapids: Eerdmans, 1970. [I]

Wolff, Walter. *Anthropology of the Old Testament*. Philadelphia: Fortress, 1974. [A]

Part 2

# Basic Questions about Human Nature

*Christian Perspectives from Philosophy*

# 2

# A Defense of
# a Substance Dualist View
# of the Soul

## J. P. Moreland

In chapter 1, Professor Saucy reminded us of the biblical model of being human: A human being is a unity of two distinct entities—body and soul. The soul, while not by nature immortal, is nevertheless capable of entering an intermediate disembodied state upon death and, eventually, being reunited with a resurrected body. The name for this view is substance dualism. St. Thomas Aquinas (1225–1274) is a classic representative of the position.

In the modern world, substance dualism has fallen on hard times, even among believers. Christian psychologist David Myers boldly asserts that "[in] contrast to the [unbiblical] dualistic body-soul image which has shaped Western thought, the Old and New Testaments consistently convey a unity of mind and body. No sharp distinction is made between the two."[1]

Why is dualism in disfavor today even among many Christian thinkers? No doubt, a full answer to that question would involve many factors. But I think

1. David G. Myers, *The Human Puzzle* (New York: Harper and Row, 1978), 268. Myers fails to recognize the fact that unities can contain multiplicities within them and that two entities can be inseparable even though non-identical.

55

the chief reason is the rise of *scientism,* roughly, the notion that a claim about the nature of reality is true and reasonable if and only if it is a scientific claim.[2] More specifically, there are three aspects of scientism that have made dualism implausible to many modern people:

> *Crude empiricism:* Something is true or reasonable if and only if it is testable with the five senses. Seeing is believing, and since the soul is embarrassingly invisible, it either does not exist or if it does, no one could verify its existence.
>
> *Scientific naturalism:* Science has been successful in treating all objects, including living organisms (e.g., human beings), as merely physical systems. Immaterial entities like souls are not included in science and since science (especially physics and chemistry) is the best (perhaps only) way to know what is real, we ought to abandon belief in the soul.
>
> *Evolution:* Darwin was and his modern followers are committed to a materialist view of living things.[3] The reason is obvious. If living things are merely the result of a physical process (the mechanism(s) of evolution) operating on physical materials (a mixture of inorganic chemicals on the early earth in some prebiotic soup), then the product of this process will itself be physical. As Darwin pointed out, if entities like souls exist, the best explanation for them is that God was their creator. And if God is allowed to intervene at this point, he could have done so at other points in the development of life. This would tend to cast doubt on the adequacy of evolution as a complete explanation of the origin and development of life.

The issue of substance dualism, then, is not an isolated question of merely intellectual interest. A broad, world view clash between scientific naturalism and Christian theism is lurking behind the scene.[4] Thus, substance dualism is of interest to the believer because it seems to be the most natural way to understand biblical anthropology and, further, if substance dualism is true, it weakens the adequacy of scientific naturalism as a total, self-contained account of the origin, development, and nature of life, especially human life.

Moreover, substance dualism makes belief in life after death more reason-

---

2. Cf. J. P. Moreland, *Christianity and the Nature of Science* (Grand Rapids: Baker, 1989), chap. 3.

3. Cf. Howard E. Gruber, *Darwin on Man: A Psychological Study of Scientific Discovery* (Chicago: University of Chicago Press, 1974), 211; Paul Churchland, *Matter and Consciousness* (Cambridge, Mass.: MIT Press, 1984), 20–21.

4. See Richard Swinburne, *The Existence of God* (Oxford: Clarendon, 1979), 152–79; J. L. Mackie, *The Miracle of Theism* (Oxford: Clarendon, 1982), 119–32.

able. It should be clear why. If we are simply material beings, then when our bodies die, we die because we *are* our bodies, nothing more, nothing less. However, if we have souls, then while the soul may become extinct at death, it could be that I can survive the death of my body because my soul could continue to exist.[5]

In this chapter, I will not respond directly to the tenets of scientism listed above, even though I think each of them is implausible. Instead, I want to give a brief, simply-stated case for substance dualism. The case will proceed in four stages: first, some preliminary background issues will be discussed, including definitions of physicalism and substance and property dualism; second, arguments will be given that, if successful, count equally in favor of property and substance dualism (defined below) compared to physicalism; third, arguments will be given that, if successful, count in favor of substance dualism compared to both property dualism and physicalism; fourth, I shall respond to the objection most frequently raised against dualism.

## Preliminary Background Issues

### The Mind/Body Problem

In some contexts, it is important to make a distinction among the mind, the soul, the spirit, or the self. But for our purposes, we will use these interchangeably. Our main concern here is to focus on the mind/body problem and defend the claim that, in addition to a body, brain, and central nervous system, a human being has an immaterial component as well. The main issue in the mind/body problem is this: is a human made of only one component, say, matter, or two components, matter and mind?

Currently, there are two main positions taken on the mind/body problem: *physicalism* and *dualism*. The former claims that a human being is completely physical, the latter that a human being is both physical and immaterial. There are different versions of physicalism but we will not explore them here.[6] Dualism, in turn, comes is two major varieties: *substance dualism* and *property/ event dualism*. In order to clarify these different views, we must first look at the nature of substances, properties, and events.

5. Many Christian thinkers who deny substance dualism maintain belief in the afterlife by claiming that at death, one becomes extinct, while at the general resurrection, God recreates us *ex nihilo*. However, this view seems exegetically strained to say the least, and it suffers from problems with personal identity. On this last point, see Stephen Davis, "The Resurrection of the Dead," in *Death and Afterlife*, ed. by Stephen Davis (N. Y.: St. Martin's, 1989), 119–44.

6. For a brief overview of the options, see Joseph Owens, "Mind-Body," in *Handbook of Metaphysics and Ontology*, ed. by Hans Burkhardt and Barry Smith (Munich: Philosophia Verlag, 1991), 1:557–60.

### Substance, Property, Event

A *substance* is an entity like an acorn, a leaf, a dog, or an angel. Substances have a number of important characteristics. First, substances are particular, individual things. A particular acorn cannot be in more than one place at the same time. Second, a substance is a continuant, that is, it can change by gaining new properties and losing old ones, yet it remains the same thing throughout the change. A leaf can go from green to red, yet the leaf itself is the same entity before, during, and after the change. Third, substances are basic, fundamental existents. They are not *in* or *had by* other things. My dog Fido is not in or had by something more basic than he. Rather, properties (and parts) are in substances that have them. For example, Fido has the property of brownness. Fourth, substances are unities of parts, properties, and capacities (dispositions, tendencies, potentialities). Fido has a number of properties (brownness, weighing twenty-five pounds) and a number of parts (four legs, some teeth). Further, he has some capacities that are not always actual (the capacity to bark even when he is being silent). As a substance, Fido is a unity of all the properties, parts, and capacities had by him. Finally, a substance has causal powers. It can act as a causal agent in the world. A dog can bark, a leaf can hit the ground. Substances can cause things to happen.

In addition to substances, there are also entities called *properties*. A property is an existent reality, examples of which are brownness, wisdom, painfulness. As with substances, properties have a number of important features. First, a property is a universal that can be in more than one thing at the same time. Redness can be in a flag and an apple at once. Second, a property is immutable and unchanging. When a leaf goes from green to red, the *leaf* changes by loosing an old property and gaining a new one. But the property of redness does not change and become the property of greenness. Properties can come and go, but they do not change in their internal constitution or nature. Third, properties can, or perhaps must, be had by other things more basic than they. They are in the things that have them. For example, redness is in the apple. The apple has the redness. One does not find redness existing alone all by itself. Generalizing, substances have properties; properties are had by substances. Finally, there are entities in the world called *events*. Examples of events are a flash of lightning, the dropping of a ball, the having of a thought. Events are temporal states or changes of states of substances. An event is the coming, continued possession, or going of a property by a substance at or through a particular time. This shirt being green now, that acorn changing shape then are examples of events.

### Options Regarding the Mind/Body Problem

We are now in a position to understand the different mind/body views mentioned above. According to physicalism, a human being is merely a physical entity. The only things that exist are physical substances, properties, and events. When it comes to humans, the physical substance is the body or brain and central nervous system. The physical substance called the brain has physical properties, such as a certain weight, volume, size, electrical activity, chemical composition, and so forth.

There are also physical events that occur in the brain. According to physicalism, when someone has an occasion of pain or an occurrence of a thought, these are merely physical events, namely, events where such and such C-fibers are firing or certain electrical and chemical events are happening in the brain and central nervous system.

So far, we have been using the terms *physical* and *matter* without defining them. Unfortunately, there is no clear definition of matter, and actually we know precious little about what matter is. But examples of matter are not hard to come by. Material objects are things like computers, carbon atoms, and billiard balls. Material properties are the properties that one finds listed in chemistry or physics books, for example, hardness, occupying and moving through space, having a certain shape, possessing certain chemical, electrical, magnetic, and gravitational properties, having density and weight, and being breakable, malleable, and elastic. A physical event would be the possession, coming, or going of one or more of these properties by a physical substance (or among physical substances) at a time.

There is one very crucial observation to make about material substances, properties, and events. *No material thing presupposes or has reference to consciousness for it to exist or be characterized.*[7] You will search in vain through a physics or chemistry textbook to find consciousness included in any description of matter. A completely physical description of the world would not include any terms that make reference to or characterize the existence and nature of consciousness.

Dualists disagree with physicalists. According to the former, mental entities are real. As with matter, it is hard to give a definition of mental entities. But examples of mental entities are easy to supply. First, there are various kinds of sensations: experiences of colors, sounds, smells, tastes, textures, pains, itches. Sensations are individual things that occur at particular times. I can have a sensation of red after looking in a certain direction or by closing my eyes and daydreaming. An experience of pain will arise at a certain time, say, after I am stuck with a pin.

Further, sensations are natural kinds of things that have, as their very essence, the felt quality or sensory property that makes them what they are. The

7. Frank Jackson attempts to give a "topic neutral" definition of a mental entity (e.g., a pain, sensation, desire) as an entity which is such that it would not exist if there were no sentient creatures. See his *Perception* (Cambridge: Cambridge University Press, 1977), 1–2. As Jackson points out, in the sense mentioned above, no material entity fits this definition (unless, of course, a phenomenalist account of material objects is given where a material object just is a bundle of actual or possible ideas).

nature of a sensation is revealed to us through introspective awareness. Part of the very essence of a pain is the felt quality it has; part of the very essence of a red sensation is the presentation of a particular shade of color to my consciousness.

Sensations are not identical to things outside a person's body. For instance, a feeling of pain is not the same thing as being stuck with a pin and shouting, "Ouch!" Sensations are essentially characterized by a certain conscious feel, and thus they presuppose consciousness for their existence and description. In short, they are modes of consciousness. If there were no conscious beings, there would be no sensations.

Second, there are things called propositional attitudes: having a certain mental attitude that expresses a proposition which is part of a that-clause. For example, one can hope, desire, fear, dread, wish, think, believe that P, where P may be the proposition "The Royals are a great baseball team." Propositional attitudes include at least two components. First, there is the attitude itself. Hopes, fears, dreads, wishes, thoughts, and the like are all different states of consciousness, and they are all different from each other based on their conscious feel. A hope is a different form of consciousness than an episode of fear.

Second, they all have a content or a meaning embedded in the propositional attitude, namely, the propositional content of my consciousness while I am having the propositional attitude. My hope that P differs from my hope that Q, because P and Q are different propositions or meanings in my consciousness. Arguably, if there were no conscious selves, there would be no propositional attitudes.

Third, for many dualists there are acts of will or purposings. What is a purposing? An example may help. If, unknown to me, my arm is tied down and I still try to raise it, then the purposing is the "trying to bring about" the raising of my arm. Intentional actions are episodes of volition by conscious selves wherein and whereby they do various actions. They are acts of will. Such acts are episodes that are done by conscious selves. In sum, all of the above are cited by dualists as examples of mental entities.

In addition to the differences between physicalists and dualists, there is also an intramural debate between *property dualists* and *substance dualists*. According to property dualists, there are some physical substances that have only physical properties. A billiard ball is hard and round. In addition, there are no mental substances. But there is one material substance that has both physical *and* mental properties—the brain. When I experience a pain, there is a certain physical property possessed by the brain (a C-fiber stimulation with chemical and electrical properties) and there is a certain mental property possessed by the brain (the pain itself with its felt quality). The brain is the possessor of all mental properties. I am not a mental self that *has* my thoughts and experiences. Rather, I am a brain and a series or bundle of successive experiences themselves. Finally, just as wetness is a real property that supervenes over a water molecule, so mental properties supervene upon brain states. This view has an implication for life after death. When a water molecule is destroyed, the property of wetness *had* by that molecule ceases to exist. Similarly, when the brain is destroyed, the conscious properties and events *had* by the brain cease to exist.

Substance dualism holds that the brain is a physical substance that has physical properties and the soul is a mental substance that has mental properties. When I am in pain, the brain has certain physical (e.g., electrical, chemical) properties, and the soul has certain mental properties (the conscious awareness of the pain). The soul is the possessor of its experiences. It stands behind, over, and above them and remains the same throughout my life. The soul and the brain can interact with each other, but they are different entities with different properties.

Keep in mind that substance dualists need not, and probably should not, believe that the soul is simple. An entity is simple in that it has no internal differentiation within it. A simple entity is fundamental and basic. It is not composed of more basic properties or parts. It does not contain further divisions within it. In my view, the soul is a substance. However, it is not simple but complex. To be sure, the soul's complexity is not like that of a material object, say, a table. A table is a complex unity which is extended in space and whose parts (the left leg, the right leg) occupy different spatial locations. Moreover, one can destroy the table by breaking it up and its parts can still survive. They are independent parts, capable of existing on their own independently of the whole table itself or of the other parts of the table. For example, if the table is destroyed, each leg will still exist and can be put by itself in different places in the garage.

The soul has a different type of complexity. The soul is a deep unity of parts, properties, and capacities. The soul is diffused throughout the body and can enter into complex cause-effect interactions with that body. Our vast array of intellectual, emotional, and volitional capacities differ from each other and the soul is a deep unity of this complex array of internal differentiations. Of course, the soul is not a mere heap of parts. One's sensory abilities cannot survive the soul's destruction nor can they be separated from one's intellectual abilities and put in different places in the garage. Thus, the soul's parts are inseparable parts and the soul, as a whole, is prior to its parts. So while the soul's unity is different and, in fact, deeper than that of a table, the soul is still a *complex* unity and not a simple entity.

Why is this important? As Keith Edwards points out in chapter 6, the soul can fragment when multiple personalities develop or when the brain is split. In order for the soul to function as a unity (at least in an embodied state), psychological maturity must be present and an intact, functioning brain must be operating. Substance dualists distinguish between what the soul *is* and how the soul *functions*. The soul is a substance, a unity, a single unified, enduring I. But the soul's different capacities may function together in harmony or disharmony.

For the substance dualist, multiple personalities and split brain phenomena do not prove that the soul is not a unified, enduring substance in its *being*. They merely provide evidence that the soul will *function* in a fragmented way if certain psychological problems or neurophysiological conditions obtain.

### The Nature of Identity

It is time to turn to a topic that will explain our strategy for defending dualism: the nature of identity. Bishop Joseph Butler (1692–1752) once remarked that everything is itself and not something else. This simple truth has profound implications. Suppose you want to know whether J. P. Moreland is Eileen Spiek's youngest son. If J. P. Moreland is identical to Eileen Spiek's youngest son, then in reality, there is only one thing we are talking about: J. P. Moreland who *is* Eileen Spiek's youngest son. Furthermore, J. P. Moreland is identical to himself; he is not different from himself. Now if J. P. Moreland is *not* identical to Eileen Spiek's youngest son, then in reality we are talking about two things, not one.

This illustration suggests a truth about the nature of identity known as Leibniz' Law of the Indiscernibility of Identicals: For any entities x and y, if x and y are identical (they are really the same thing; there is only one thing you are talking about, not two), then any truth that applies to x will apply to y, and vice versa. This suggests a test for identity: if you could find one thing true of x not true of y, or vice versa, then x cannot be identical to (be the same thing as) y.

Further, if you could find one thing that could *possibly* be true of x and not y (or vice versa), even if it isn't actually true, then x cannot be identical to y. For example, if J. P. Moreland is five feet eight inches tall, but Eileen Spiek's youngest son is six feet tall, then they are not the same thing. Additionally, if J. P. Moreland is five feet eight and Eileen Spiek's youngest son happens to be five feet eight as well, but it would have been possible for J. P. to be five feet nine while Eileen's youngest son is five feet eight (suppose J. P. had eaten more Wheaties as a child than he, in fact, did eat), then they are not the same thing either. Even though the two do not in fact differ regarding their height, if it were merely possible for them to have differed in this way, then that is all we need to establish the fact that they are not identical.

What does this have to do with the mind/body problem? Simply this: Physicalists are committed to the claim that alleged mental entities are really identical to physical entities (e.g., brain states), properties of the brain, overt bodily behavior or dispositions to behave (e.g., pain is just the tendency to shout "Ouch!" when stuck by a pin instead of pain being a certain mental feeling). If physicalism is true, then everything true of the brain (and its properties, states, and dispositions) is true of the mind (and its properties, states, and dispositions) and vice versa. If we can find one thing true, or even possibly true of the mind and not the brain, or vice versa, then dualism is established. The mind is not the brain.

Keep in mind that the relation of identity is different from any other relation, for example, causation or constant connection. It may be that brain events cause mental events or vice versa (e.g., having certain electrical activity in the brain may cause me to experience a pain, having an intention to raise my arm may cause bodily events), it may be that for every mental activity a neurophysiologist can find a physical activity in the brain with which it is correlated. But just because A causes B (or vice versa), or just because A and B are constantly correlated with each other, that does not mean that A *is identical to* B. Something is trilateral if and only if it is triangular. But trilaterality (the property of having three sides) is not identical to triangularity (the property of having three angles), even though they are constantly conjoined.

It is not enough to establish physicalism that mental states and brain states are causally related or constantly conjoined with each other in an embodied person. *Physicalism needs identity to make its case, and if something is true, or possibly true of a mental substance, property, or event that is not true, or possibly true of a physical substance, property, or event, physicalism is false.*

The considerations to follow will all be variations and elaborations of two basic arguments. Argument one has already been mentioned: If we can find one thing true or possibly true of mental entities (substances, properties, events) not true or possibly true of physical entities, then physicalism is false and dualism is true (taking it to be the only other live option).[8] Argument two goes like this: There are certain abilities human beings have (e.g., free will and moral responsibility, rationality, and they remain the same through the loss and gain of body parts or mental events). These abilities could not be present if physicalism or property dualism were true and, thus, the presence of these abilities supports substance dualism.

Can a case for dualism be made? Most definitely. In what follows, I will first list some arguments that give equal support to both property and substance dualism, then offer some arguments that show the superiority of substance dualism over both physicalism and property dualism.

8. This argument can be stated so as to involve the truth of two different premises. Premise 1 is called the Cartesian intuition: something is true or possibly true of a particular mental entity (substance, property, event) or type of mental entity that is not true or possibly true of a particular physical entity or type of entity (e.g., matter is not painful, mental states have no electrical charge, it is possible for persons to exist in a disembodied state). Premise 2 focus on the *nature of identity:* $(x)(y)[(x=y)\rightarrow\Box(x=y)]$. For all x and y, if x is identical to y, then, necessarily, x is identical to y. In other words, it is a necessary feature of a thing that it be identical to itself. For more on the nature of identity and identity statements, see Saul Kripke, *Naming and Necessity* (Cambridge, Mass.: Harvard University Press, 1972).

## Arguments Supporting Property and Substance Dualism

### *The Distinctiveness of Mental and Physical Properties and States*

Mental events are episodes of thoughts, feelings of pain, and episodes of having a sensory experience. Physical events are happenings in the brain and central nervous system that can be described exhaustively using terms from chemistry and physics. However, physical events and properties do not have the same features that hold for mental events and properties. My thoughts, feelings of pain, or sensory experiences do not have any weight, are not located anywhere in space (my thought of lunch cannot be closer to my right ear than my left one), are not composed of chemicals, do not have electrical properties. However, the brain events associated with, for example, my thoughts—indeed, material things in general—*do* have these features.

Try this experiment. Try to picture a pink elephant in your mind, or if you do not have a vivid imagination, look at a colored object, close your eyes, and you will continue to see an after-image of that object. Now, if you imagine a pink elephant or have an after-image of blue, there will be a pink or blue property (a sense datum or a sensory way of experiencing) or an awareness of a pink or blue property in your mind ofb which you can be aware. There will be no pink elephant outside you, but there will be a pink mental image or an awareness of pink in your mind.

Now at that time there will be no pink or blue entity nor any awareness of such an entity in your brain, no neurophysiologist could open your brain and see a pink or blue entity or an awareness of a pink or blue entity while you are having the sensory experience. But, then, the sensory event has a property—pink or blue (or being an awareness of pink or blue)—that no brain event has. Therefore, they cannot be identical. The sense image is a mental entity.

Regarding the distinctiveness of mental and physical properties and states, Roderick Chisholm has made the following point:

> Let us consider some particular psychophysical identity statement—the statement, say, that thinking about unicorns is the same thing as to have Q fibres that vibrate in manner N. One cannot *understand* such a statement, of course, unless one can grasp or conceive the property or properties that are referred to. . . . To the extent that we can understand the statement in question, we can *see* that the two properties referred to are not the same property—just as we can see that the property of believing that all men are mortal is different from that of wondering whether there is life in outer space. It has been held, not implausibly, that to deny the validity of such rational insights is to undermine the possibility of every type of reasoning.[9]

9. Roderich Chisholm, "Mind," in *Handbook of Metaphysics and Ontology,* ed. by Hans Burkhardt and Barry Smith (Munich: Philosophia Verlag, 1991), 2:556.

### Self-Presenting Properties

Consider the following argument:
(1) No physical properties are self-presenting.
(2) All mental properties are self-presenting.
(3) Therefore, no mental properties are physical properties.

Mental properties, like feeling sad, experiencing red, having a thought that three is an odd number, are self-presenting. They present themselves directly to the subject, they are psychological attributes, they are directly present to a subject because that subject simply has them immediately in his field of consciousness. There are two pieces of evidence for the claim that mental properties are, while physical properties are not self-presenting: *private access* and *incorrigibility.*

First, *private access.* I have private access to my own mental life. I am in a privileged position to know about what I am thinking and sensing compared to anyone else. Whatever ways you have for finding out if I am presently sensing a red after-image (e.g., by analyzing my brain states), those ways are available to me. But there is a way of knowing I am having a red after-image not available to anyone else—my own immediate awareness of my own mental life. I am in a position to know my own mental life in a way not available to anyone else. But that is not the case for any physical entity, including my brain and its various states. Physical objects, including my brain, are public objects and no one is in a privileged position regarding them. A neurophysiologist can know more about my brain than I do, but he cannot know more about my mental life. I have private, privileged access to my mental life because it contains self-presenting properties. But physical properties are not self-presenting.

Not only do I have private access to my mental states, but also I can sometimes know them *incorrigibly.* If something is incorrigible to a knowing subject, then that subject is incapable of being mistaken about that thing. For example, I can be wrong if I think that a chair is in the next room. But I cannot be wrong about the fact that I at least *think* that the chair is there, that is, that a certain, specific thought is occurring to me. The former claim is about a physical object (the chair); the latter is about a mental state within me—a thought that I am currently having. In general, claims about physical states, including claims about my brain and its properties/states, can be mistaken. But if I am being attentive, I can incorrigibly know my episodes of thought (that I am having such and such thought right now) and, perhaps, my sensory experiences (that I am experiencing green now).

In sum, physical states/properties are not self-presenting, but mental states/properties are, as evidenced by the twin phenomena of private access and incorrigibility. Thus, physical states/properties are not identical to mental states/properties.

### The Subjective Nature of Experience

The subjective character of experience is hard to capture in physicalist terms. The simple fact of consciousness, constituted by the subjective feel or texture of experience itself, is a serious difficulty for physicalists. To see this, consider the following example. Suppose a deaf scientist became the world's leading expert on the neurology of hearing. It would be possible for her to know and describe everything there is to the physical aspects of hearing. In our example, nothing physical is left out of the description. However, something would *still* be left out of such a description—the experience of what it is like to be a human who hears. As Howard Robinson puts it, "The notion of *having something as an object of experience* is not, *prima facie,* a physical notion; it does not figure in any physical science. *Having something as an object of experience* is the same as the subjective feel or the *what it is like* of experience."[10]

Subjective states of experience are real—I experience sounds, tastes, colors, thoughts, pains, and so forth—and they are essentially characterized by their subjective nature. Speaking of the character of subjective awareness, Thomas Nagel has this to say:

> If physicalism is to be defended, the phenomenological features [the felt quality or experiential texture of experiences that make them the kinds of things they are, e.g., the painfulness of pain, the sounds, colors, odors of sensory experiences] must themselves be given a physical account. But when we examine their subjective character it seems that such a result is impossible. The reason is that every subjective phenomenon is essentially connected with a single point of view, and it seems inevitable that an objective, physical theory will abandon that point of view.[11]

### The Existence of Secondary Qualities

Secondary qualities are qualities such as colors, tastes, sounds, smells, and textures. Primary qualities are qualities that are thought to be among the properties that characterize matter—weight, shape, size, solidity, motion. Physicalism seems to imply that secondary qualities do not exist in the external world. For example, we are led to believe that color is really nothing but a wavelength of light. So, in general, physicalism reduces secondary qualities to being nothing but primary qualities. We are left with a picture of matter bereft of secondary qualities.

But the world of our common sense experience is replete with secondary qualities. Thus, such qualities must exist. But, some argue, if they do not exist

---

10. Howard Robinson, *Matter and Sense* (Cambridge: Cambridge University Press, 1982), 7.

11. Thomas Nagel, "What is it like to be a bat?" in *Mortal Questions* (Cambridge: Cambridge University Press, 1979), 167. Nagel seems to present two different arguments here: the argument from the subjective, phenomenal quality of an experience, and the argument about the irreducibility of a first-person point of view to a third-person perspective.

in the external world as properties of matter, they must exist as mental entities in the conscious minds of experiencers themselves. As Frank Jackson says:

> It is a commonplace that there is an apparent clash between the picture Science gives of the world around us and the picture our senses give us. We *sense* the world as made up of coloured, materially continuous, macroscopic, stable objects; Science and, in particular, Physics, tells us that the material world is constituted of clouds of minute, colourless, highly-mobile particles. . . . Science forces us to acknowledge that physical or material things are not coloured. . . . This will enable us to conclude that sense-data are all mental, for they are coloured.[12]

In other words, some argue that science does away with secondary qualities, but since we know they do exist—we see them—they must exist in our minds as mental entities because they are not aspects of matter.

### Intentionality

Some have argued that the mark of the mental is something called intentionality. Intentionality is the mind's "of-ness" or "about-ness." Mental states point beyond themselves to other things. Every mental state I have is of or about something—a hope that Smith will come, a sensation of the apple, a thought that the painting is beautiful. Mental states can even be about things that do not exist, for example, a fear of a goblin or a love for Zeus.

Now intentionality is not a property or relation of anything physical. Physical objects can stand in various physical relations with other physical objects. One physical thing can be to the left of, larger than, or the thing causing the motion of another physical object. But one physical object is not *of* or *about* another one.

When I am near a podium, I can relate to it in many ways: I can be two feet from it, taller than it, and my body can bump into it. These are all examples of physical relations I sustain to the podium. But in addition to these, I can be a conscious subject that has the podium as an object of various states of consciousness I direct toward it; for instance, I can have a thought about it, a desire for it (perhaps I want one like it), I can experience a sensation of it, and so forth. These are all mental states and they have intentionality (of-ness, about-ness) in common. In sum, mental states possess intentionality, physical states do not. Mental states are not physical states.

## Arguments Supporting Substance Dualism

The arguments listed above favor dualism over physicalism. But it can be argued that they count equally in favor of substance and property dualism. I

12. Frank Jackson, *Perception* (Cambridge: Cambridge University Press, 1977), 121.

will not dispute that claim, but instead offer a series of arguments that, if successful, lend support to substance dualism and count against both physicalism and property dualism. The following are designed to show that substance dualism is superior to both physicalism and property dualism.

### Our Basic Awareness of the Self

When we pay attention to our own consciousness, we can become aware of a very basic fact presented to us: we are aware of our own self (ego, I, center of consciousness) as being distinct from our bodies and from any particular mental experience we have. We simply have a basic, direct awareness of the fact that I am not identical to my body or my mental events; rather, I am the self that *has* a body and a conscious mental life.

An experiment may help convince you of this. Right now I am looking at a chair in my office. As I walk toward the chair, I experience a series of what are called phenomenological objects or chair representations. That is, I have several different chair experiences that replace one another in rapid succession. As I approach the chair, my chair sensations change shape and grow bigger. Further, because of the lighting of the study, my chair experiences change color slightly. Now, the chair doesn't change in size, shape, or color; but my chair experiences do.

I am, of course, aware of all the different experiences of the chair during the fifteen seconds it takes me to walk across my study. But if I pay attention, I am also aware of two more things. First, I do not simply experience a series of sense-images of a chair. Rather, through self-awareness, I also experience the fact that it is I myself who has each chair experience. Each chair sensation produced at each angle of perspective has a perceiver who is I. An "I" accompanies each sense experience to produce a series of awarenesses—"I am experiencing a chair sense image now."

There is a second thing of which I am aware. I am aware of the basic fact that the same self that is currently having a fairly large chair experience (as my eyes come to within 12 inches of the chair) is the very same self as the one who had all of the other chair experiences preceding this current one. In other words, through self-awareness, I am aware of the fact that I am an enduring I who was and is present as the owner of all the experiences in the series.

These two facts—I am the owner of my experiences and I am an enduring self who possesses all of my experiences through time—show that I am not identical to my experiences (or my body in whole or in part), but I am the thing that has them. In short, I am a mental substance. Only a single, enduring self can relate and unify experiences.

### First Person Not Reducible to Third Person

A complete physicalist description of the world would be one in which everything would be exhaustively described from a third person point of view in terms of objects, properties, processes, and their spatiotemporal locations. For example, a description of an apple in a room would go something like this: there exists an object three feet from the south wall and two feet from the east wall and that object has the properties of being red, round, and sweet, among others.

The first person point of view is the vantage point that I use to describe the world from my own perspective. Expressions of a first person point of view utilize what are called indexicals—words like *I, here, now, there, then*. Here and now are where and when I am; there and then are where and when I am not. Indexicals refer to me myself. The word *I* is the most basic indexical and it refers to my self which I know by acquaintance with my own consciousness in acts of self awareness. That is, I am immediately aware of my own self and I know who *I* refers to when I use it—it refers to me as the owner of my body and mental states.

According to physicalism, there are no irreducible, privileged first person perspectives. Everything can be exhaustively described in an object language from a third person perspective. A physicalist description of me would say that there exists at a certain location a body that is five feet eight inches tall and weighs 160 pounds. The property dualist would add a description of the properties possessed by that body, for example, the body is feeling pain, thinking about lunch, and can remember being in Grandview, Missouri, in 1965.

But no amount of third person descriptions captures my own subjective, first person acquaintance of my own self in acts of self awareness. In fact, for any third person description of me, it would always be an open question as to whether the person described in third person terms was the same person as I am. I do not know my self because I know some third person description of a set of mental and physical properties and I also know that a certain person satisfies that description. I know myself as a self immediately, through being acquainted with my own self in an act of self awareness. I can express that self awareness by using the term *I*.

*I* refers to my own substantial soul; it does not refer to any mental property or bundle of mental properties I am having nor does it refer to any body described from a third person perspective. *I* is a term that refers to something that exists and *I* does not refer to any object or set of properties described from a third person point of view. Rather, *I* refers to my own self with which I am directly acquainted and which, through acts of self awareness, I know to be the substantial possessor of my mental states and my body.

### Personal Identity Through Change

Imagine a wooden table that had all its parts removed one by one and replaced with metal parts. Now suppose someone took the original wooden parts and made a new table. Which one would be the original table—the metal one or the wooden one? The answer seems to be clear. The original table would be the wooden one. Why? Because if something is made out of matured stuff called parts, then it cannot remain identical to itself if it gains new parts and loses old ones. If a table here now is going to be the very same table as one that was here, say an hour ago, this table must be made out of the same stuff as the one an hour ago. If not, then they are different tables. In general, physical objects cannot remain literally the same if they gain new parts and lose old ones.

But now a question arises regarding persons. Am I literally the same self that I was a moment ago? An hour ago? Seven years ago? I am constantly losing parts. Each moment I lose hundreds of thousands of skin, hair, and other microscopic parts. In fact, every seven years my cells are almost entirely replaced. Do I maintain literal, absolute sameness through change? The same difficulty arises for property dualism. I can also gain and lose mental properties, for example, pains, thoughts, and sensations come and go, or my ability to have memories can be lost through amnesia. Can I gain and lose mental properties and be literally the same person?

Substance dualists argue that persons do maintain absolute identity through change, because they have, in addition to their bodies and current mental experiences or mental capacities (say, the capacity to remember a childhood event), a soul that remains constant through change, and personal identity is constituted by sameness of soul, not sameness of body or mental abilities like memory.

Physicalists and property dualists have no alternative but to hold that personal identity through change is not absolute. Usually they argue that persons are really ancestral chains of successive, momentary "selves" (called person-stages) connected with one another in some way. At each moment a new self exists (since the organism is constantly in flux, gaining new parts and mental experiences and losing old parts and mental experiences) and this self resembles the self prior to and after it.

The relation of resemblance between selves plus the fact that later selves have the same memories as earlier selves and the body of each self traces a continuous path through space and time when the whole chain of selves is put together, constitute a relative sense of identity. At this moment I merely resemble a self that existed a moment ago (my body resembles that body, my memories resemble the memories of that earlier self, my body was reached by the body of the earlier self through a continuous spatial path).

So substance dualists hold to a literal, absolute sense of personal identity and physicalists and property dualists hold to a loose, relative sense of personal identity that amounts to a stream of successive selves held together by resemblance between each self in the stream, similarity of memory or brain, similarity of character traits, and/or spatial continuity.

But now certain problems arise for physicalism and property dualism. 1) The fact that I can have a memory that an earlier self had presupposes that I am the same person as that earlier self. Memory presupposes personal identity, it does not constitute it. The same can be said for the other traits listed in the preceding paragraph. 2) In self awareness, I seem to be aware that I am literally the same self who continues to exist throughout my life and that unites my stream of consciousness into one stream that is mine. How can a physicalist or property dualist explain this basic awareness? 3) Why should "I" ever fear the future, say, going to the dentist next week? When it gets here, "I" will not be present; rather, another self who looks like me (or has my memories) will be there, but "I" will have ceased to exist. 4) Why should anyone be punished? The self who did the crime in the past is not literally the same self who is present at the time of punishment. Physicalism and property dualism seem to require a radical readjustment of these basic, common-sense notions because these notions presuppose a literal, absolute sense of sameness through change, and this makes sense only if the soul is a substance that is a continuant. If the intuitions expressed in points one through four above are reasonable, then this provides evidence for substance dualism.

### Free Will, Morality, Responsibility, and Punishment

When we use the term *free will* we mean what is called libertarian freedom: given choices A and B, I can literally choose to do either one, no circumstances exist that are sufficient to determine my choice, my choice is up to me, and if I do one of them, I could have attempted to have done otherwise. I act as an agent who is the ultimate originator of at least some of my own actions.[13]

If physicalism is true, then determinism is true as well. If I am just a physical system, there is nothing in me that has the capacity to freely choose to do something. Material systems, at least large scale ones, change over time in deterministic fashion according to the initial conditions of the system and the laws of chemistry and physics. A pot of water will reach a certain temperature at a given time in a way determined by the amount of water, the input of heat and the laws of heat transfer.

Now, when it comes to morality, it is hard for a physicalist to make sense of moral obligation and responsibility. They seem to presuppose freedom of the will. If I "ought" to do something, it seems to be necessary to suppose that I *can* do it. No one would say that I ought to jump to the top of a fifty-floor building and save a baby, or that I ought to stop the civil war in 1993, because I do not have the ability to do either. If physicalism is true, I do not

13. My arguments in this and the next section claim that libertarian freedom is the correct account of much of human action and that this account is needed to make sense of our moral and rational activity. Not all substance dualists agree with me here. See chapter 3 by David M. Ciocchi for an alternative account of human action.

have any genuine ability to choose my actions. It is safe to say that physicalism requires a radical revision of our common-sense notions of freedom, moral obligation, responsibility, and punishment. On the other hand, if these common-sense notions are true and the libertarian account of them is corrrect, then physicalism is false.

The same problem besets property dualism. There are two ways for property dualists to handle human actions. First, some property dualists are *epiphenomenalists*. According to epiphenomenalism, when matter reaches a certain organizational complexity and structure, as is the case with the human brain, then matter produces mental states like fire produces smoke, or the structure of hydrogen and oxygen in water produces wetness. The mind is to the body as smoke is to fire. Smoke is different from fire (to keep the analogy going, the physicalist would identify the smoke with the fire or the functioning of the fire), but fire causes smoke, not vice versa. The mind is a byproduct of the brain and the mind causes nothing. It merely "rides" on top of the events in the brain. It should be obvious that epiphenomenalism denies free will, since it denies that mental states cause anything.

A second way that property dualists handle human action is through a notion called state-state causation (also called "event-event" or merely "event causation"). To understand state-state causation, consider a brick that breaks a glass. The cause in this case is not the brick itself (which is a substance), but the brick's being in a certain state, namely, a state of motion. The effect is the glass being in a certain state, namely the breaking of the glass. Thus, one temporal state or event (an event is another name for a temporal state)—the moving of a brick—causes another state to occur—the breaking of the glass. When one billiard ball causes another one to move, it is the moving of the first ball that causes the moving of the second ball. In general, then, state-state causation involves a state of one thing existing as an efficient cause that is prior to an effect, which is the production of a state in another thing.

Agent causation is what is required for libertarian freedom of the will and it is the view of causation embraced by many substance dualists. An example of agent causation is a typical case of a human action—my raising of my arm. When I raise my arm, I, as a substance, simply act by spontaneously exercising my causal powers. *I* raise my arm; I freely and spontaneously exercise the powers within my substantial soul and simply act. No set of conditions exists within me that are sufficient to determine that I raise my arm.

William Rowe offers the following definition for something X, say, Jones, being the agent-cause of some event e, say, the raising of his arm:[14]

14. See William Rowe, "Responsibility, Agent-Causation, and Freedom: An Eighteenth-Century View," *Ethics* 101 (January 1991): 237–57. I have changed some of Rowe's wording on page 238 of the article to capture some of his later qualifications of the formula cited on that page.

1. X is a substance that had the power to bring about e.
2. X exerted its power to bring about e.
3. X had the ability to refrain from exerting its power to bring about e.

In agent causation, substances simply act; in state-state causation, a state within a substance is the cause of an effect. According to state-state causation, when I raise my arm, there is some state within me that causally necessitates that my arm go up (e.g., a state of desiring that my arm go up or a state of willing that my arm go up).

Unfortunately for property dualists, state-state causation is deterministic. Why? For one thing, there is no room for an agent, an "I" to intervene and contribute to my actions. I do not produce the action of raising my arm; rather, a state of desiring to raise an arm is sufficient to produce the effect. There is no room for my own self, as opposed to the mental states within me, to act.

For another thing, all the mental states within me (my states of desiring, willing, hoping) are states deterministically caused by prior mental and physical states. "I" become a stream of states/events in a causal chain. Each member of the chain determines that the next member occur.

In sum, property dualism denies libertarian freedom, because it adopts either epiphenomenalism or state-state causation. Thus, property dualism, no less than physicalism, is false, given the truth of free will, moral ability, moral responsibility, and punishment.

### Physicalism and Property Dualism Are Self-Refuting

A number of philosophers have argued that physicalism and property dualism must be false because they imply determinism and determinism is self-refuting. H. P. Owen states, "determinism is self-stultifying. If my mental processes are totally determined, I am totally determined either to accept or to reject determinism. But if the sole reason for my believing or not believing X is that I am causally determined to believe it I have no ground for holding that my judgment is true or false."[15]

Others have pointed out that property dualism suffers at the hands of this argument no less than does strict physicalism. Speaking of epiphenomenalism, A. C. Ewing maintains, "if epiphenomenalism is true, it follows that nobody can be justified in believing it. On the epiphenomenalist view what causes a belief is always a change in the brain and never the apprehension of any reason for holding it. So if epiphenomenalism is true, neither it nor anything else can ever be believed for any good reasons whatever."[16] In order to understand these statements, let us first examine the nature of self-refutation and then see why physicalism and property dualism are self-refuting.

15. H. P. Owen, *Christian Theism* (Edinburgh: T. and T. Clark, 1984), 118.
16. A. C. Ewing, *Value and Reality* (London: George Allen and Unwin, 1973), 77.

First, what is self-refutation? A statement is about a subject matter. "All electrons have negative charge" is about the subject matter called electrons. Some statements refer to themselves, that is, they include themselves in their own field of reference. "All English sentences are short" refers to all English sentences whatsoever, including that very sentence itself. Now sometimes a statement refers to itself and it fails to satisfy its own criteria of rational acceptability or truthfulness. "I do not exist" and "There are no truths" are self-refuting. They refer to themselves and they falsify themselves. Self-refuting statements are necessarily false, that is, they cannot possibly be true.

Why are physicalism and property dualism self-refuting? The simple answer is that they undercut the necessary preconditions for rationality itself to be possible. In other words, they make rationality itself impossible. If someone claims to know that physicalism or property dualism are true, or to embrace them for good reasons, if one claims that they choose to believe in them because of good reasons, then these claims are self-refuting. At least three factors must be assumed if there are to be genuine rational agents who exhibit rationality. All three are ruled out by physicalism; only the last two are inconsistent with property dualism.

First, humans must have genuine *intentionality*; they must be capable of having thoughts and sensory awarenesses *of* or *about* the things they claim to know. For example, one must be able to see or have rational insight into the flow of an argument if one is going to claim that a conclusion follows from a set of premises. We can simply see that if you have (1) If P, then Q, and (2) P, therefore, you also have (3) Q. This requires an *awareness of* the logical structure of the syllogism itself.

As we saw earlier, intentionality is a property of mental states, not physical ones. Thus, this first feature of rationality is incompatible with physicalism, though it is compatible with property dualism. Intentionality is not a physical property, but it could be claimed that it is a mental property of the brain.

Second, in order rationally to think through a chain of reasoning such that one sees the inferential connections in the chain, one would have to be the same self present at the beginning of the thought process as the one present at the end. As Immanuel Kant argued long ago, the process of thought requires a genuine enduring "I."

In the syllogism above, if there are three different "selves," each of whom reflect on a different premise, then there is literally no enduring self who thinks *through* the argument and *draws* the conclusion. As H. D. Lewis noted, "one thing seems certain, namely that there must be someone or something at the centre of such experience to hold the terms and relations together in one stream of consciousness."[17] But we have already seen that physicalism and property dualism deny a literal, enduring I, and substitute for it a series of selves. Thus, they are at odds with this necessary condition for rationality.

17. H. D. Lewis, *The Self and Immortality* (New York: Seabury, Crossroad Books, 1973), 34.

Finally, rationality seems to presuppose an agent view of the self and genuine libertarian freedom of the will. There are rational "oughts." That is, given certain evidence, I "ought" to believe certain things. I am intellectually responsible for drawing certain conclusions, given certain pieces of evidence. If I do not choose that conclusion, I am irrational. But ought implies can. If I ought to believe something, then I must have the ability to choose to believe it or not believe it (or at least I must be free to do something that will put me in a position to have or not to have the belief). If one is to be rational, one must be free to choose his beliefs in order to be reasonable. Often, I deliberate about what I am going to believe or I deliberate about the evidence for something. But such deliberations make sense only if I assume that what I am going to do or believe is "up to me," that is, that I am free to choose and, thus, I am responsible for irrationality if I choose inappropriately.

But we have already seen that physicalism and property dualism rule out libertarian freedom. In sum, physicalism and property dualism rule out the possibility of rationality. It is self-refuting to *argue* that one *ought* to *choose* physicalism or property dualism on the *basis* of the fact that one *should see* that the *evidence* is *good* for physicalism or property dualism. Substance dualism, it would seem, is the best view of the self consistent with the preconditions of rationality.[18]

## A Major Objection to Dualism

We do not have space to look at all the objections that have been raised against dualism. In my view, most of them are expressions of scientism mentioned in the introduction (e.g, naturalistic evolution is the correct picture of how we got here and it implies physicalism). However, one problem comes up most frequently and it may be the most important one to consider. Physicalists claim that on a dualist construal of a human being, mind and body are so different that it seems impossible to explain how and where the two different entities interact. How could a soul, totally lacking in any physical properties, cause things to happen to the body or vice versa? How can the soul move the arm? How can a pin-stick in the finger cause pain in the soul? Opponents of dualism claim that because most current forms of dualism imply this problematic interaction between mind and body, then such forms of dualism ought to be abandoned.

This objection assumes that if we do not know *how* A causes B, then it is not reasonable to believe *that* A causes B, especially if A and B are different.

18. William Hasker offers a form of dualism (he calls it "emergentism") that could be taken as property dualism, but in my view, it is actually a form of substance dualism (a possibility for which he explicitly allows). See "Brains, Persons, and Eternal Life," *Christian Scholar's Review* 12 (1983): 294–309.

But this assumption is not a good one. We often know that one thing causes another without having any idea of how causation takes place, even when the two items are different. As C. D. Broad argued long ago:

> One would like to know just how unlike two events may be before it becomes impossible to admit the existence of a causal relation between them. No one hesitates to hold that draughts and colds in the head are causally connected, although the two are extremely unlike each other. If the unlikeness of draughts and colds in the head does not prevent one from admitting a causal connection between the two, why should the unlikeness of volitions and voluntary [bodily] movements prevent one from holding that they are causally connected?[19]

There are several cases where we know that one thing causes another even though we do not know how causation works and even though the causes are different from the effects.[20] Even if one is not a theist, it is not inconceivable to believe it possible for God, if he exists, to create the world or to act in that world, even though God and the material universe are very different. A magnetic field can move a tack, gravity can act on a planet millions of miles away, protons exert a repulsive force on each other, and so forth. In these examples, we know *that* one thing can causally interact with another thing, and we can even describe the interaction, even though we have no idea *how* such interaction takes place. Some interactions are simply taken as basic and ultimate. Further, in each case the causes would seem to have a different nature from the effects—forces and fields vs. solid, spatially located, particle-like entities.[21]

In the case of mind and body, we are constantly aware of causation between them. Episodes in the body or brain (being stuck with a pin, having a head injury) can cause things in the soul (a feeling of pain, loss of memory), and the soul can cause things to happen in the body (worry can cause ulcers, I can

19. C. D. Broad, *The Mind and Its Place in Nature* (London: Routledge and Kegan Paul, 1925), 98. Cf. C. J. Ducasse, *Nature, Mind, and Death* (La Salle, Ill.: Open Court, 1961), 424–43.

20. See Mark Bedau, "Cartesian Interactionism," in *Midwest Studies in Philosophy X: Studies in the Philosophy of Mind*, ed. by Peter A. French, Theodore E. Uehling, Jr., and Howard K. Wettstein (Minnesota: University of Minnesota Press, 1986), 483–502; see also John Foster, "In Defense of Dualism," in *The Case for Dualism*, ed. by John R. Smythies and John Beloff (Charlottesville: University Press of Virginia, 1989), 1–25.

21. If there is any place where a request for a mechanistic explanation of how a causal process takes place should be fruitful, it would be in science. But as these examples show, even in science it is often the case that a picture of how causation takes place is lacking and yet belief that causation is present is still justified. In metaphysics, the request for a mechanism of causation is even more dubious if that request is taken as a necessary condition for justifying belief that causation is real. For example, we know that if we burn a green leaf, we "cause" the color green to no longer be instanced by the leaf. But how a physical event of burning can cause a universal—a nonspatial, non-temporal entity—to no longer enter into an instancing relation with a particular (the leaf) is not clear.

freely and intentionally raise my arm). We have such overwhelming evidence *that* causal interation takes place, that there is no sufficient reason to doubt it.

Furthermore, it may even be that a "how" question regarding the interaction between mind and body cannot even arise. A question about how A causally interacts with B is a request for an intervening mechanism between A and B that can be described. You can ask how turning on the key starts your car because there is an intermediate electrical system between your key and your car's running engine that is the means by which turning on your key accomplishes the event, namely, the starting of your car. Your "how" question is a request to describe that intermediate mechanism. But the interaction between mind and body may be, and most likely is, direct and immediate. There *is* no intervening mechanism and, thus, a "how" question describing that mechanism does not even arise.

Like many other problems raised against dualism, the objection we are currently examining is often just an expression of physicalist bias.[22] I conclude, therefore, that this objection does not carry sufficient weight to abandon a dualist construal of mind and body.[23]

22. As an example of this, Peter Smith and O. R. Jones "argue" against dualist interactionism by claiming that such interaction "goes clean against a fundamental principle of the physical sciences, namely that the causes of physical changes are other entirely physical events." See *Philosophy of Mind* (Cambridge: Cambridge University Press, 1986), 58. But they seem to reverse the order between philosophy and science, and this reversal results in the question-begging claim just mentioned. If dualism is true, then the physical sciences are not the only thing needed to account for human nature and action. Thus, the philosophical case for and against dualism is epistemologically prior to scientific considerations, not vice versa. For defenses of the priority of philosophy in general, and philosophy of mind in particular to science, see George Bealer, "The Philosophical Limits to Scientific Essentialism," in *Philosophical Perspectives, I: Metaphysics, 1987,* ed. by James E. Tomberlin (Atascadero, Calif.: Ridgeview, 1987), 289–365; "The Logical Status of Mind," in *Midwest Studies in Philosophy X: Studies in the Philosophy of Mind,* ed. by Peter A. French, Theodore E. Uehling, Jr., and Howard K. Wettstein (Minneapolis: University of Minnesota Press, 1986), 231–74. Further, their view entails determinism, and we have already seen reasons for rejecting determinism. Finally, if one tries to offer a physicalist account of how human action and cognitive abilities are possible, then this strategy backfires in the face of something called the frame problem. See Daniel Dennett, "Cognitive Wheels: The Frame Problem of AI," in *Minds, Machines, & Evolution,* ed. by Christopher Hookway (Cambridge: Cambridge University Press, 1984), 129–51. An intelligent creature is able to learn from past experience, anticipate future senarios to alternative actions available to the creature, and to think things out before it acts. Dennett acknowledges (pejoratively) that dualism can explain this ability to "look before one leaps" by the simple notion that the soul can learn from experience. But the physicalist is hard pressed to explain this ability, and the frame problem may be fairly presented as a counterargument to those who demand an explanation of how a causal process takes place before we are justified in believing that it takes place, especially when the explanation must operate within physicalist constraints. For a helpful discussion of dualist interaction and the conservation of energy, see Robert Larmer, "Mind-Body Interaction and the Conservation of Energy," *International Philosophical Quarterly* 26 (September 1986): 277–85.

23. For a caricature of the substance dualist understanding of interaction, see Paul Churchland, *Matter and Consciousness,* 18–20.

## Summary

In the 1600s, the great Reformed pastor, Richard Baxter, was faced with lukewarmness in the church and unbelief outside the church. To counteract these trends, Baxter wrote a book in 1667 that gave solid, intellectual arguments for the existence of the soul and the reality of the future life. This chapter has been written in the spirit of Baxter's pastoral model. I have tried to offer a case for substance dualism in a way understandable to the non-philosopher. A more detailed case can be found in the sources listed in conjunction with this chapter.[24] Currently, there is a revisionist trend among some Christians. This trend denies that substance dualism is the biblical view. However well intentioned, this trend is not an accurate representation of biblical teaching and, in my view, is not demanded by the requirements of intellectual integrity.

## Suggested Readings

### Christianity and Dualism

Cooper, John W. *Body, Soul, & Life Everlasting*. Grand Rapids: Eerdmans, 1989. [B]

Taliaferro, Charles. "Philosophy of Mind and the Christian." In *Christian Theism and the Problems of Philosophy*. Edited by Michael D. Beaty, 230–53. Notre Dame: University of Notre Dame Press, 1990. [I]

### Dualism and Life After Death

Davis, Stephen T., ed. *Death and Afterlife*. (N. Y.: St. Martin's, 1989). [I]

Habermas, Gary, and J. P. Moreland. *Immortality: The Other Side of Death*. Nashville: Thomas Nelson, 1992. [B]

### Dualism and the Metaphysics of Substance

Connell, Richard J. *Substance and Modern Science*. Notre Dame: University of Notre Dame Press, 1988. [A]

### Personal Identity

Madell, Geoffrey. *The Identity of the Self*. Edinburgh: Edinburgh University Press, 1981. [A]

Perry, John. *A Dialogue on Personal Identity and Immortality*. Indianapolis: Hackett, 1978. [B]

### Defenses of Dualism

Foster, John. *The Immaterial Self*. London: Routledge, 1991. [A]

---

24. For more on the soul and life after death, see Gary Habermas and J. P. Moreland, *Immortality: The Other Side of Death* (Nashville: Thomas Nelson, 1992).

Habermas, Gary, and J. P. Moreland. *Immortality: The Other Side of Death*. Nashville: Thomas Nelson, 1992, chap. 2–3. [B]

Robinson, Howard. *Matter and Sense*. Cambridge: Cambridge University Press, 1982. [A]

Swinburne, Richard. *The Evolution of the Soul*. Oxford: Oxford University Press, 1986. [I or A]

Smythies, John R., and John Beloff, eds. *The Case for Dualism*. Charlottesville: University Press of Virginia, 1989. [A]

# A Response to J. P. Moreland

## Nancy S. Duvall

My response to Moreland's argument for substance dualism involves some background issues, attention to the argument itself, and consideration of the implications especially as it relates to the field of psychology.

In relation to background issues, I would like to highlight Moreland's comments about scientism, the view that only science can describe the nature of reality. The world view of scientism was a very pervasive cultural assumption and very much part of my early psychological training. I remember what a mind-expanding concept it was when I encountered Alfred North Whitehead's *Science and the Modern World* and his contention that science was only one way of deriving a view of the world and reality. That gave me the mental space and freedom to actively think about science and the limits of science. Though I was not a Christian at the time, that kind of freedom of inquiry ultimately helped me recognize the limits of science and created space for the truth of revelation, which represents a different perspective from man's view which is what science represents.

As an example of the reign of scientism, I had gradually and unconsciously accepted science's definition of substance, that is, material substance, which is one of Webster's definitions. I, and I believe many persons, had forgotten the historic meaning of substance, which Webster's dictionary lists as the first definition, "a real unchanging essence or nature of a thing." Moreland's chapter puts us back into the more historical and less narrow definition, and thus gives us mental space to investigate the arguments of physicalism versus dualism.

Finally, as a background issue, I would like to highlight Moreland's approach which is that of a philosopher, and whose primary approach is reason.

God gave us not only the five senses to take in data (the basis of empiricism and science); he also gave us intellect and reasoning within us to integrate the data and I believe it honors God when we are able to articulate the faith, or in this instance an anthropological view.

As to the defense of substance dualism, I think that Moreland's argument is well presented and logical. I cannot argue with his presentation, nor do I wish to do so. What I would say is that he has articulated what I had as a graduate student concluded, though his reasoning is more carefully specified. I remember the time in graduate school when I had the rather awkward question of whether I had chosen the right profession of clinical psychology. I had this lurking question that possibly psychiatry had the "real" answers for hurting people and possibly clinical psychology was second best. After all, psychiatry was medically and biologically based. Psychiatrists could give medicine (matter) and that could help people. I knew that medication could be helpful, but, I also knew that careful listening to someone and helping them understand their anxiety was also very helpful and furthermore that the psychotherapy approach involving listening and talking might have more lasting results, whereas medication might need to be continued. Medication could be truly helpful, but might not give the enduring results. I therefore decided that there was a place for psychotherapy, and not just medication. Implicitly, and not nearly as articulately as J. P. Moreland's presentation, I was deciding that there was a legitimate realm of the mind that was not just reducible to the brain.

This leads to the implications of Moreland's argument for substance dualism. If substance dualism is not true, there really is no room for psychology or psychotherapy, but everything psychological should be reduced to biology, chemistry, and physics. In fact, some of the early attempts at psychology, such as Freud's psychoanalysis and B. F. Skinner's behaviorism, were ultimately attempts to reduce psychology to instincts à la Freud, or to reduce all psychology to overt behaviors (without acknowledging anything but visible external behavior) à la Skinner. Freud's metapsychology has shifted radically to a more personal and relational view of humankind, and B. F. Skinner's behaviorism has failed as a viable anthropology, though many of his learning principles apply within certain limited realms. In general the history of psychology went through a period of trying to emulate the physical sciences since physicalism was the prevailing view. Words like "soul" were totally absent from psychology books. But now psychology is becoming a study of "the psyche" again. There is a recognition that one needs to understand not only the brain, but the mind. Moreland's view of substance dualism gives the underlying basis for a true psychology.

# A Response to J. P. Moreland

## Keith J. Edwards

One of the benefits of participating in writing for this volume has been the opportunity to interact with scholars from other disciplines on what it means to be human. In reading Moreland's chapter I have developed a deeper appreciation for the power of logical arguments and tightly reasoned dialog. I have been trained as a scientist in the empirical tradition of logical positivism. While I understand the limitations of this paradigm, I am still more comfortable with testing the validity of a statement in the laboratory of observation than I am with logical argumentation. In the security of one's laboratory, it is possible to become complacent about the language we use and the assumptions we make in reporting our observations and trying to communicate what we think they mean. Reading Moreland's chapter has given me a deeper appreciation (obviously a soul experience) for logic and rational discourse.

### Concurrence Versus Identity

Among the various ideas he has presented, one that is particularly salient for me is the definition of identity. In the area of neurophysiology, consciousness is always associated with electrical activity in the brain. If there is no electrical brain activity, then we say the person is dead. Since brain activity is so essential for consciousness, it is easy to fall into the logical fallacy of equating the two. But there is a more serious consequence of such thinking than the violation of rules of logic. The serious consequence is the depersonalization of human life. Making the electrochemical activity of the brain identical to consciousness leads to a reduction of the person to a mass of impersonal, chemical and electrical components that, but for the complexity of the organization of the constituent elements and a morality based on social consensus, is no more significant than the computer on which I am typing this chapter or the weeds my son is pulling out of the ground. This brings me to what I see as the most significant contribution of Moreland's chapter: the reclaiming of the significance of the person.

As he notes in his introduction, dualism has fallen on hard times. We could also say that the value of human life has also fallen on hard times. He clearly exposes reductionistic implications of the physicalist's and property dualist's paradigms and establishes a sound basis for the dignity of the person.

## Do Animals Have Souls Too?

One question Moreland's chapter raises for me is, "Do animals have souls?" My reading of his chapter tells me that Moreland must believe that animals have souls. If this is the case, then I would want to know more about the similarity and differences he sees between humans and animals. First, let me tell you why I come to this conclusion about Moreland's view on the matter. The mental events of consciousness, which he describes as evidence of a non-material substance called the soul, are not uniquely characteristic of humans. As I have noted in my chapter, perceptions are mental events that represent interpretations of sensations in light of prior experience. Both animals and humans experience these mental events. Since such mental events are evidence for the soul and are also characteristic of animals and humans, animals must have souls, according to Moreland's argument.

Similarly, Moreland makes several references to self-awareness as being a form of mental activity that is evidence for the existence of the soul. With humans, we can observe self-awareness because people can talk about their internal states. With animals, we are limited to inferring self-awareness from behavior. One type of behavior that is evidence of self-awareness is observational learning. A number of researchers have shown that naive animals can learn complex discriminating behaviors simply by observing the performance of trained animals.[25] Since the observing animals do not directly experience the reinforcing stimuli, their learning must be a result of vicarious experience (observational learning) based on some degree of symbolic representation and hence self-awareness. Again, if, as Moreland has argued, such mental events are evidence for the existence of the soul, then I am led to conclude that animals have souls.

If we accept the proposition that animals have souls, then what is it that is distinct about human nature? My understanding of the Bible in regard to hu-

25. E. Roy John, "A model of consciousness," in *Consciousness and Self-Regulation: Advances in Research,* ed. Gary E. Schwartz and David Shapiro (New York: Plenum, 1976), 2.

man nature is that we are distinct from the rest of creation in that we possess a unique, created spiritual essence; what I have assumed was the human soul. In Genesis 2:7 we read that God breathed on man and he became a living being. We are the only member of creation that is said to receive this infusion of life from the breath of God. We were placed in a position of authority over all the rest of creation. Since Scripture teaches that God is a Spirit and we must worship him in spirit and in truth, I assume that our spiritual nature, our spirits, our souls, are all terms referring to the image of God in us. Assuming that animals do have souls, then what is the basis for a morality that places a unique value on human souls, a value so high that God sent his Son to redeem us? What is unique about human nature? The commandment, "You shalt not murder," is clearly meant to apply to men and women and not animals. If animals have souls, what is the difference between animals and humans that is the basis of our moral principles on the sanctity of human life? Certainly, a key quality of human souls is their future eternal existence. Jesus came and died to redeem the souls of humans. If animals have souls, are they eternal? I would like to have had Moreland address this issue to some extent in his chapter since it is so directly relevant to what it means to be human.

## Self Knowledge

One of the main points made in my chapter is that our conscious mental life is influenced by various brain events over which we have only some direct volitional control. This state of affairs is due, in part, to a brain which mediates the processing of sensations at many levels that are outside of our conscious awareness. We also learn strategies for protecting our self from psychological pain by using psychological defenses that keep us from becoming aware of perceptions that would lead to unacceptable feelings or thoughts. In the human mind, there is much that goes on outside of conscious awareness. The unconscious is both a psychological and a neurological reality. On the other hand, Moreland emphasizes the unique qualities of the conscious self as the possessor of one's experience and that one has "privileged access to [one's] mental life." There is nothing said about the status of out-of-awareness mental activity. How do we square these two views?

I would suggest that the views come together in the notion of the fragmented soul, as Moreland describes it. Because of fear and denial we fragment our selves as a way of coping with the fearful and painful realities that seem overwhelming and threaten our survival. We are in need of restoration to wholeness. There are two verses in the Psalms that support this view of the fractured self and the need for restoration. Both of them were penned by David, whose own system of denial was broken with Nathan's confrontation. In Psalm 51:6, he writes, "Surely you desire truth in the inner parts; you teach me wisdom in the inmost place." In a similar vein, he says in Psalm 139:23–24,

"Search me, O God, and know my heart; test me and know my anxious thoughts. See if there is any offensive way in me, and lead me in the way everlasting." This Scripture teaches that there are aspects of our mental life of which we may not be aware but which God can reveal to us. This is consistent with Moreland's claim that we can become aware of our sensations and perceptions through introspective awareness. The psychology of defenses tells us that we don't always want to know the "truth" such introspection might reveal. The psalmist reveals that God desires us to see the depth of our own souls, to be healed, and to know wisdom. The apostle Paul tells us in Romans 7–8 that truth without the saving grace of God we receive through faith in Christ would be devastating. The main goal of ministries like teaching, preaching, and counseling is to guide seekers to know truth in the context of grace as the path to love, joy, and peace.

# 3

# Human Freedom

*David M. Ciocchi*

Anyone who wants a genuinely biblical understanding of what it is to be a human being will discover that the concept of *freedom* is essential to that understanding. This discovery is likely to lead to another insight—that understanding freedom requires some help from the discipline of philosophy. In this chapter I will draw on philosophy for assistance in exploring the nature and significance of the concept of freedom. Although I will restrict my attention to theological anthropology, much of what I will say is applicable to a wide range of other subjects, including ethics, sociology, psychology, political science, and cultural anthropology. This wide applicability should come as no surprise, for if having freedom really is essential to being human, then any study about human beings will at some point address the concept of freedom.

It can be misleading, though, to talk about *the* concept of freedom. There is in fact a whole family of freedom concepts, and I believe the best place to begin this chapter is with a look at the members of this family. One way of classifying them is by putting them in three general categories. The first of these is what I call the *freedom of permission,* a category that covers all those senses of human freedom involving authority, rights, and privileges. Each one of these freedoms amounts to the permission to do as we please in some particular context, usually within defined limits. A prominent biblical example is Paul's discussion of freedom in Christ in his first letter to the Corinthians.[1]

1. For an excellent discussion of this concept of freedom, see Gordon D. Fee, *The First Epistle to the Corinthians,* New International Commentary on the New Testament (Grand Rapids: Eerdmans, 1987). Note especially his treatment of 6:12, 8:9, and 9:1.

This first category suggests the second, for if we have rights and privileges, it must be because we can exercise them responsibly. The freedom of permission implies the *freedom of moral responsibility,* or, as it is more commonly called, *free will.* Free will is the sense of freedom that serves as the foundation for moral responsibility. This category is made up of competing definitions of *free will,* all of which aim to explain why it makes good sense to use the traditional vocabulary of the moral life, such as *good* and *evil* or *praise* and *blame,* not to mention a considerable range of theological terms, such as *righteousness, sin,* and *divine judgment.* To be free in this sense is to be a responsible agent, to be worthy of praise or blame and deserving of punishment or reward. The Bible clearly teaches that all human beings have this freedom of moral responsibility, but the same thing cannot be said about the third category of freedom, the *freedom of personal integrity.* This category consists of various accounts of what it is to be the kind of person one wants to be. If I am able to live a life of consistently translating my values into action, then I have the freedom of personal integrity. If I find myself torn between my values and certain desires which conflict with those values, with the result that I frequently violate my conscience, then I lack the freedom of personal integrity. Unless I am an extremely pathological case, I still have free will, and so am responsible for my moral failures, but I am without the peace of mind and consistency of action associated with personal integrity.[2] The classic biblical text relevant to this sense of freedom is Romans 7:14–25, a passage I will return to later in this chapter.

I will limit my discussion to the freedom of moral responsibility (free will) and the freedom of personal integrity, devoting a major section of this chapter to each of these senses of freedom. In the first section I will discuss free will, describing its leading definitions and applying them to a series of issues in theological anthropology. I will present each definition as fully and fairly as I can, leaving it to the reader to determine which one he thinks is correct. In the second section I will describe two accounts of the freedom of personal integrity. I will then apply them to the exposition of Romans 7:14–25, showing how the accounts can assist us in our understanding of the text and, by extension, in our understanding of ourselves.

## The Freedom of Moral Responsibility

### *Preliminary Issues*

Any theological anthropology faithful to the biblical text will affirm that human beings are morally responsible for their actions. It is not possible to take the Bible seriously and at the same time deny the concept of responsi-

---

2. I will say more about the relationship between these two senses of freedom in my section on the freedom of personal integrity (see pp. 101–6).

bility a place in what we might call "minimal orthodoxy," that is, those beliefs that must be beyond theological dispute. There is plenty of room for dispute, though, about which definition of free will provides the correct or most adequate account of moral responsibility, and there is a long history of such disputation in the literature of theology and philosophy. Before I present the competing definitions of free will I must discuss a few preliminary issues.

First, free will is a *necessary*, but not a *sufficient*, condition for moral responsibility. To say that A is a necessary condition for B is to say that without A, B would not take place or exist; to say that A is a sufficient condition for B is to say that given A, B must take place or exist. Free will is not a sufficient condition for responsibility because it is possible for a person to freely choose to do something yet not be morally responsible for the outcome of that act. This is the case when someone is unavoidably ignorant of a key piece of information about the situation in which he is acting. For instance, if I choose to drink a glass of punch without knowing that it has been poisoned, then my ignorance exempts me from any responsibility for my subsequent illness or death. A full account of moral responsibility requires an analysis of the sort of knowledge a person must have to be properly held accountable for an act.

Second, a believer in free will need not suppose that *all* human behavior is freely chosen. It is clear enough that at least some behavior may be due to factors independent of a person's free choosing, such as reflex actions, actions done under the influence of powerful drugs, or behavior determined by severe mental or physical illnesses.

The third and last of these preliminary matters is closely related to the second one. Even though some human behavior is not freely chosen, and even though there are special cases in which it is difficult if not impossible to ascribe moral responsibility to a person, a believer in free will affirms that *much* or *most* of the behavior of human beings is either freely chosen or the result of earlier free choices (e.g., the drunk driver who chose to drink and drive). The upshot of this is that the believer in free will regards freedom and moral responsibility as the typical or *paradigmatic* human condition. This fits the biblical teaching that God is the judge of us all: *all* human beings, not just most of us, will be held to account for the lives we have lived.

### The Conditions for Free Will

Free will, then, is a necessary condition for moral responsibility, and much or most human behavior is either freely chosen or the result of earlier free choices, so that the paradigmatic human condition is one of freedom and moral responsibility. The question now is: what *is* free will, or what *makes* a choice a genuinely free choice? We are looking for a *definition* of free will, and any candidate that deserves serious consideration will meet the following three conditions: the *ability condition,* the *control condition,* and the *rationality condition.*[3]

The first two conditions may really be two ways of saying the same thing. The *ability condition* requires that the agent—the person making a choice—be able to choose and act differently from the way he actually does. This is usually called "the ability to choose (or do) otherwise," and it has long been standard fare in philosophical discussions of free will. Now if the agent has the ability to choose otherwise, then it seems fair to say that he was in control of his choosing, so that to meet the first condition is also to meet the second one. The *control condition* requires that it is the agent himself who determines what the actual choice shall be. If I choose freely, then what I choose is "up to me," I am in control of it.

The *rationality condition* presupposes a belief-desire psychology in which the agent evaluates options on the basis of their likelihood of bringing about the things he desires. A free choice, then, is a choice that the agent himself believes is likely to bring about a state of affairs that he finds desirable (or to avoid a state of affairs that he finds undesirable). Another way of saying this is that the rationality condition requires the agent to have a *personal reason* for the choice he makes, that is, to have some reason for making the choice that appeals to him even if (perhaps) it does not appeal to anyone else. If you and I are invited to play tennis, and you want to improve your skill at the game, then you have a personal reason for choosing to accept the invitation. I, however, may have no interest in tennis, no desire ever to play the game again. Barring some other *personal* reason for accepting the invitation, I would not be free to choose to accept it.[4]

### The Competing Definitions of Free Will

I will now present three definitions of free will. They are *anarchic free will, libertarian free will (incompatibilism),* and *soft determinist free will (compatibilism).* Each of these definitions is actually a genus that exists in a variety of species or forms, so that it is possible to say something about free will that, for instance, one libertarian philosopher would accept and another would reject. My aim is as far as possible to present only the conceptual core of a definition, so that what I say will be acceptable to anyone who accepts that definition.

The first definition, *anarchic free will,* is not an intellectually serious account of freedom, and as far as I know there is no one who actually advocates it today. I am including it in this chapter because a knowledge of it will help

3. For a fuller account of the conditions for free will, see Richard Double, *The Non-Reality of Free Will* (Oxford: Oxford University Press, 1991), 218–21.

4. That is, I would not have *free will* with respect to the choice, but I would have the *freedom of permission* with respect to it. I would have the right, or perhaps "privilege" is more appropriate here, to accept the invitation; but without a personal reason for doing so, I would not have the free will to exercise my privilege.

us in understanding the other two definitions, both of which are live options for students of theological anthropology. Anarchic free will traces its lineage to the Greek philosopher Epicurus (341–270 B.C.), who had adopted the metaphysics of the Greek atomists. The atomists said that reality consists only of atoms moving in space, and that all atomic motions are purely mechanical, rather like a universe of colliding billiard balls. Epicurus was principally interested in ethics, and he was apparently disturbed by the thought that this mechanical universe precluded free will and moral responsibility. With that in mind he modified atomic theory by postulating occasional random "swerves" of individual atoms. These "swerves" are causeless and thus unpredictable, and yet they are somehow supposed to account for free will.[5]

As the Epicurean view explains it, free will is something that is finally beyond explanation of any sort, since its expressions are uncaused. A free act is something that just happens, something that is in no way connected to the belief-desire psychology of the person who "chose" to perform it. As an example of this anarchic free will, suppose that I have a gentle friend named Benny, a man who wouldn't hurt a fly, much less me. One day I see Benny carrying a baseball bat (something he's never done before), and I stop to ask him about it. Before I can get a word out, he clobbers me over the head with the bat. When he visits me in the hospital (without the bat), he tells me tearfully that he regrets what happened: it was after all, free will, just something that happened. He didn't want it to happen, had no personal reason for it; quite the contrary, he just found himself carrying that bat, and found (to his horror) that he was using it to strike his friend.

The anarchic free will definition fails to meet any of the three conditions for serious accounts of free will. The agent could not have "done otherwise" because it is not clear that he *did* anything at all—his atoms swerved, he found his limbs moving in certain ways. The anarchic "free choice" is something that happens *to* the agent rather than something the agent *does,* so it is clear enough that he has no control over it. He is instead its victim. Further, the agent in anarchic freedom need have no personal reasons for his allegedly free choices. Benny, for instance, had no desire to hit me over the head; there was nothing about his "free choice" that appealed to him in any way.

The failure of anarchic free will is more than made up for by its attractive competitors, one of which is *libertarian* or *incompatibilist free will.*[6] The libertarian definition is perhaps most easily understood by examining the way it

---

5. Since the extant writings of Epicurus do not mention the swerve, we are indebted to Epicurus's disciple Lucretius for our knowledge of it. See Lucretius, *On the Nature of Things,* 2:251–93.

6. *Libertarian* is from *liberty,* a synonym for *freedom.* This definition is also called "incompatibilist free will" because those who advocate it claim that free will is *incompatible* with *determinism,* the philosophical thesis which says that for everything that ever happens there are conditions such that, given them, nothing else could happen.

handles the ability condition for free will. According to libertarian philosophers, the free agent has the *categorical ability* to choose (and do) otherwise than he actually does. That the agent's ability is *categorical* implies that an agent who made a particular choice might actually have refrained from doing so; that is, being just what he was and feeling just what he felt, and being in just those circumstances, he might still have chosen differently. In other words, there was nothing in his character and circumstances that determined that he make that particular choice rather than some other choice. It was not necessary that anything *be* different to bring it about that this agent *choose* differently. He might have refrained from making the choice he made; that he did not refrain must finally be attributed to his (libertarian) free will rather than to anything else.

To understand the libertarian definition better, it would help to apply it to a particular instance of an agent's making a free choice. Suppose that there is a concert pianist named Mary who has a free hour this evening before she must leave for her scheduled performance at the local music center. Suppose further that there are just three options for the use of this hour that appeal to her, that is, just three options that are live options for her because she has personal reasons for them. Each option is such that it would take all, or most, of the hour, so she can only choose one of them. First, she might watch the evening news. Her personal reason for this option is that the news is covering a story about a major earthquake in a city where her brother lives, and she is concerned about him. Second, she might take a long walk to comply with her doctor's orders that she exercise so as to help prevent the occurrence of another heart attack (she had one a couple of months ago). Her personal reason for this is the concern she feels about her health, a concern that leads her to want to do all she can to take proper care of herself. Finally, she might use the hour to practice for her upcoming concert. This is her last chance to practice, and her personal reason for doing so is her worry about one of the pieces she is to play—she doesn't feel that she's got it "right" just yet. Let's say that Mary uses her free will to choose to devote the hour to taking a walk.

The libertarian philosopher would argue that his definition of free will can account for Mary's choice in a way that meets all three of the conditions for free will. Mary chose to take a walk, but she had the categorical *ability* to choose otherwise. There was nothing in her character and circumstances that determined that she make this particular choice. She might actually have refrained from taking the walk, and instead have chosen one of her other options. That she chose the walk rather than any other of her options is to be attributed entirely to her (libertarian) free will. Clearly, then, Mary was in *control* of her choosing. It was "up to her" whether she took the walk or chose one of her other options: she didn't suddenly find her legs taking her out walking as if she were a victim of anarchic freedom. Her free choice was truly hers, an expression of her own belief-desire psychology, and so it meets the *rationality* condition. Mary's concern for her health gave her a personal reason for choosing to take the walk.

The *soft determinist* or *compatibilist* definition of free will presents a sharp contrast to libertarianism.[7] According to soft determinist philosophers, the free agent has the *hypothetical ability* to choose (and do) otherwise than he actually does. This means, roughly, that the agent *would* have done otherwise *if* he had wanted to. I may have freely chosen to play tennis this afternoon rather than to go swimming; that I wanted (preferred) to play tennis does not imply that I lacked the ability to swim this afternoon. I *could* have gone swimming, and the proof of this is that had I preferred to swim, I *would* have gone swimming. What the soft determinist is doing here is to equate free will with the agent's acting on his preference. In other words, a free choice is to be understood as the agent's choosing to do whatever matters most to him at the time of choice.

This soft determinist definition of free will presupposes that the agent himself, the person as the locus of free will, is virtually if not precisely identical to his *character*. It is hard to define "character," but in this context it means roughly a more-or-less structured set of beliefs and desires. Given the agent's character and the particular circumstances in which he finds himself, he cannot fail to have a preference (so the soft determinist claims), a particular option that matters more to him at this time than any other option. His personal reason or reasons for choosing to act on this option will prevail over any reasons he may have for other options, if any. To put it another way, whatever matters most to the agent will *determine* which choice he makes. This will be his choice, under his control, "up to him," for his character determines his choice, and he *is* his character.

By contrast, the libertarian refuses to equate the agent with his character. The agent, as a locus of free will, is something more than his own character—his character has a say, but not the final say, in a libertarian free choice. What the libertarian affirms with the soft determinist is that the agent's character and circumstances will *determine the range of options from which he will make his free choice.* That is, the agent's character and circumstances limit the options for which he has personal reasons (rationality condition). As Mary faces her free hour, she has personal reasons for some possible actions but not for others. For instance, she has a personal reason for practicing a troublesome piece she will be playing later at the concert, but she has no personal reasons for polishing her piano, eating laundry detergent, or singing the National An-

7. This definition is at times called "soft determinism" to differentiate it from "hard determinism" which denies free will and moral responsibility. It is more frequently called "compatibilism" to indicate that it regards free will and determinism as *compatible*, that is, as *logically consistent*, with each other.

them. The libertarian free agent's character determines the range from which he will make his free choice, but it does not determine *which* option from that range he will choose. *That* choice is what free will is all about (according to the libertarian), and it is finally mysterious, beyond full explanation, for full explanations presuppose the very determinism the libertarian rejects. In this respect libertarianism is akin to anarchic free will, for both these definitions refuse to subject free choices to the deterministic explanations favored by the soft determinist.

The soft determinist insists that his account of free will is consistent with our ordinary ways of thinking about freedom, and that it does a good job of meeting the three conditions for free will. Consider once again Mary's freely choosing to take a walk. The soft determinist meets the *ability* condition by claiming that Mary had the hypothetical ability to choose (and do) otherwise, for *if* she had preferred to do otherwise she would have. She had the ability to act on the other options in her range, but Mary, being Mary, and having had a heart attack recently, preferred to take care of her physical health. The choice was "up to her" *(control* condition) because it was an expression of her character and she *is* her character. Finally, the *rationality* condition is met because Mary had a personal reason for her choice, her overriding concern for her health.

There is one more matter to discuss before I make some theological applications of these definitions of free will. If we suppose that Mary's concern for her health was truly "overriding," that it genuinely mattered more to her than any of her personal reasons for those other options, then the soft determinist's account of the choice seems to make better sense than the libertarian's. In fact, we often make choices in which the option we've selected is clearly the one we prefer, the one that has no serious rivals. In such cases it seems odd to claim that we have the *categorical* ability to choose otherwise, as presumably the libertarian would want to claim. The fact is, though, that the libertarian would *not* want to claim this. No definition of free will requires that all human behavior be freely chosen, and the libertarian philosopher typically regards much or even most behavior as fully determined by the agent's character and circumstances. The libertarian restricts the operation of free will to those cases in which the agent has the categorical ability to choose (and do) otherwise, even though that means that many choices some of us might regard as free must not be free after all, at least not in the sense of being expressions of libertarian free will. It may be that Mary really does care more about her health than about anything else at her time of choice, and if this is so then the soft determinist will, and the libertarian will not, regard her choice as free. Libertarians generally consider free will to cover a smaller part of human behavior than do soft determinists.

## Theological Applications of Free Will

At the beginning of this chapter I claimed that the concept of freedom is essential to a genuinely biblical understanding of what it is to be a human being. In what follows I will defend this claim with a series of theological applications of the freedom of moral responsibility (free will), each one selected to show how the competing definitions of free will can affect our thinking in theology, particularly in theological anthropology. The applications will address *paradox, temptation, prayer,* and *evil.* I will make each application in a suggestive and open-ended way, revealing something but not everything about the strengths and weaknesses of both libertarianism and soft determinism.

The first application will address the concept of *paradox* in theology, and in order to get started on it I need to say a few words about *logical consistency* and *inconsistency.* Two statements are logically consistent if it is possible for them both to be true (e.g., "My car is a Honda" and "My car is a 1988 model"); two statements are logically inconsistent if it is not possible for them both to be true. One type of logical inconsistency is *contrariety,* which exists when we have two statements that cannot both be true but might both be false (e.g., "My car is a Honda" and "My car is a Ford"). Another and perhaps more familiar type is *contradiction,* that involves two statements which are related in such a way that one must be true and one must be false (e.g., "My car is a Honda" and "My car is not a Honda" when in each statement "my car" refers to the same object).

A *paradox* is a set of two or more statements that are *apparently inconsistent* with each other but (so someone believes) are not really inconsistent. We talk about paradox whenever it appears that some of what we believe fails to fit together logically, when we are believers in *A* and believers in *B,* but are unable to show that it is possible for them both to be true. In such a case we must appeal to the concept of paradox because if *A* and *B* are *really* inconsistent, then at least one of them must be false.

This issue is a particularly important one for Christian theology. It is commonplace to find this or that thinker accusing the Christian faith of harboring logical inconsistencies in its theological formulations. If there really were logical inconsistencies in our theology, then at least some of our theology would be false. There are two things that need to be said here. First, human beings are finite creatures who simply cannot have the exhaustive knowledge God possesses. There will always be things we do not understand, things that puzzle us, and this is true for everyone, for the atheist and the Hindu as well as for the Christian. A triumphalist approach to theology in which we talk as though we could iron out *all* difficulties and answer *all* questions in final, definitive ways is foolish at best. Second, as we face our finitude we must make policy decisions about how to respond to those parts of our theology that don't seem to fit together logically. One possible decision is to make the appeal to paradox, maintaining that although *we* cannot explain how for instance Jesus can be both God and man, *God* can, so that the alleged inconsistencies among our theological beliefs are only apparent, not real. There may be cases in which the appeal to paradox is unavoidable, but there is another policy decision we might reasonably make when confronted with an apparent inconsistency in our theology. We might decide to use the intellectual tools we have to construct arguments showing that what we believe really is logically consistent and therefore *can* be true (showing that our beliefs *are* true, if and to the extent that this can be done, is another matter altogether).

One of the most common appeals to paradox in theology has to do with the relation between divine sovereignty and human responsibility. A typical instance of this can be found in Anthony Hoekema who claims that it does not seem possible "for us to harmonize these two apparently contradictory thoughts: that God is totally sovereign over our lives, directing them in accordance with his will, but that nevertheless we are required to make our own decisions and are held totally responsible for them."[8] What needs to be noticed here is that this appeal to paradox presupposes both a certain understanding of the sovereignty of God (Hoekema says "totally sovereign") and a certain definition of the free will that grounds human responsibility—specifically, it presupposes *libertarian* free will. What Hoekema is talking about really does appear to involve a logical inconsistency; in fact, I am prepared to say that in this case appearance is reality, and the appeal to paradox fails. Let me explain.

If we take a strongly deterministic view of the sovereignty of God ("God is *totally* sovereign"), then we are implying that God has ultimate control over all events, including all human choices. This is a theological determinism in which through the will of God there are antecedent conditions for each human choice such that, given those conditions, no other choice could (actually) have been made. And this in its turn is logically at odds with libertarian free will, a definition that insists that freedom involves the *categorical* ability to do otherwise, so that the free agent could (actually) have refrained from making the choices he made. A deterministic account of the sovereignty of God and a libertarian account of free will are really, and not just apparently, inconsistent, so there is no paradox here after all. These two positions cannot both be true: one of them must be false.

If I am a theologian who believes in libertarian free will, then I have an intellectual choice to make. I may affirm both a deterministic divine sovereignty and libertarianism, making that appeal to paradox which I have just argued is not legitimate in this case; *or* I may attempt to formulate divine sovereignty in some way that is neither apparently nor actually inconsistent with libertar-

8. Anthony A. Hoekema, *Saved By Grace* (Grand Rapids: Eerdmans, 1989), 5.

ian free will.[9] This latter choice seems to me to be the more reasonable of the two, for it is an expression of the policy decision to use our intellectual tools to resolve where possible apparent inconsistencies are among our theological beliefs. There is nothing in this choice that precludes an eventual return to the appeal to paradox should the appeal to reason fail.

If I am a theologian who believes in soft determinist free will, then I will have no need of either reformulating my positions to eliminate apparent inconsistencies or of appealing to paradox should my reformulations fail to be convincing. This is because soft determinism and theological determinism are logically consistent. It is possible to affirm both that God has ultimate control over all events, including all human choices, and that we human beings necessarily act on our preferences, that is, that we have free will in a sense that is compatible with determinism.

Even if I am right in all that I have said about paradox, it does not follow that soft determinism is true and that libertarianism is false, but only that the soft determinist escapes the libertarian's logical problem about the relation between divine sovereignty and human responsibility. This does not mean that the soft determinist theologian has no intellectual problems of his own, including ones generated by his anti-paradox joint affirmation of theological determinism and soft determinist free will. He does have problems, and the most significant of them is one I will discuss later in the section on evil and free will.

The second application will address the concept of *temptation*. I will center my attention on what is probably the best known biblical text about temptation, which reads as follows: "No temptation has overtaken you but such as is common to man; and God is faithful, who will not allow you to be tempted beyond what you are able, but with the temptation will provide the way of escape also, that you may be able to endure it" (1 Cor 10:13 NASB).[10] Notice the dual reference to *ability*. In this context it is clear that the believer's responsibility to endure temptation presupposes his ability to do so, and this is just what we would expect, given that (1) ability is a condition for free will, and (2) free will is a condition for responsibility.

The libertarian definition of free will requires that the free agent has the *categorical ability* to choose (and do) otherwise, and it is not difficult to apply this sense of ability to 1 Corinthians 10:13. To say, as the apostle does, that God will not permit us to be tempted beyond our (categorical) ability to endure means that in any given case of temptation, it is actually possible for the

9. For examples of this position, see Jack W. Cottrell, "The Nature of the Divine Sovereignty," in *The Grace of God, the Will of Man*, ed. Clark H. Pinnock (Grand Rapids: Zondervan, 1989), 97–119, and William Lane Craig, *The Only Wise God* (Grand Rapids: Baker, 1987).

10. For a more extensive treatment of the relation between temptation and free will, see my "Understanding Our Ability to Endure Temptation: A Theological Watershed," *Journal of the Evangelical Theological Society* 35 (1992): 463–79.

believer to endure and actually possible for him to fail to endure. If the believer endures, then he (actually) could have done otherwise; if he fails to endure, then again, he (actually) could have done otherwise. In other words, the believer as a free agent has a two-way ability to respond to temptation. God promises that no temptation will be so great that it overwhelms him, so endurance will always be (actually) possible. If the believer fails to endure, it will not be God's fault, but rather the believer's, who is guilty of using his two-way ability the wrong way.

The soft determinist definition of free will requires that the free agent has the *hypothetical ability* to choose (and do) otherwise. This sense of ability can be applied to 1 Corinthians 10:13 as well, but doing so produces a result that some will regard as counterintuitive. To say that God will not permit us to be tempted beyond our (hypothetical) ability to endure means that in any given case of temptation the believer will endure *if* he wishes to endure. God has promised that there shall be no temptations sufficient to overwhelm the believer, and this means that the believer is left to act on his own preference. This preference, though, is the *necessary* expression of his character as mediated by the present set of circumstances. This in turn implies that whether the believer in a given case of temptation chooses to endure or not to endure, he could not (actually) have done otherwise. According to the soft determinist, the believer facing a temptation cannot fail to act on the option that means the most to him at that time—his ability to respond to temptation is a one-way ability.

The soft determinist understanding of 1 Corinthians 10:13, and of temptation in general, is open to the objection that it permits the believer who gives in to temptation to excuse himself by saying "I couldn't (actually) do otherwise, so you must not hold me responsible." Of course the soft determinist will reply that this person didn't *want* to do otherwise, that he acted on *his* preference. But this will not be enough to silence the objector. It will not be enough because the soft determinist and the objector have differing moral intuitions. To the soft determinist, the one-way ability to respond to temptation by acting on one's preference is sufficient to ground the believer's moral responsibility. But to the objector (a libertarian), this will not do. He will say that moral responsibility requires the two-way ability which allows the believer the possibility of rising above the limitations of the present state of his character, so that he can (actually) choose to endure temptation any time he is faced with one.

Whether it is the soft determinist's or the libertarian's moral intuitions that are correct is a question that probably cannot be answered through argumentation, at least not directly. I think it can be argued, though, that the libertarian's understanding of the believer's response to temptation has logical implications that are inconsistent with both the Bible and experience. The Bible affirms a connection between what a person is and what he does (e.g., John

8:42; 1 John 2:18, 19; 3:9), and it considers this to be a necessary connection, for "a good tree cannot produce bad fruit, nor can a bad tree produce good fruit" (Matt. 7:18 NASB). It also speaks of spiritual growth (e.g., in 2 Peter 3:18), a theme that implies a connection between the believer's stage of growth and his actual behavior, including his response to temptation. Even as 1 Corinthians 10:13 presupposes the *ability* condition for free will, so these passages and others like them presuppose the *rationality* condition for free will, which insists that genuinely free choices express the belief-desire psychology of the agents making them. It seems to me that the libertarian is open to the charge that his categorical ability violates the rationality condition—and with it both biblical teaching and our life experience—by severing the connection between the believer's spiritual condition and his response to temptation.

This is the problem: if the categorical ability view is correct, then from the moment he comes to faith, the believer might actually (a) invariably choose to endure temptation, thus living from the outset like a perfected saint, or (b) invariably choose to give in to temptation, thus living from the outset like an apostate. There is nothing in the libertarian account of free will to preclude these extreme possibilities. The libertarian cannot find a way out by appealing to the believer's character, for by definition a libertarian free choice—which we are supposing the believer's response to temptation to be—is never determined by the character of the free agent. Nor can the libertarian find a way out by appealing to the intervention of God, since that would put God in the position overriding the very libertarian free will he has supposedly given to the believer as a necessary condition for the believer's moral responsibility. The upshot of this apparently unavoidable implication of libertarian categorical ability is that it severs the connection between the believer's spiritual condition and his response to temptation by permitting him to live like a perfected saint or like an apostate *without ever having had to develop into one.* This is contrary not only to biblical teaching but also to our experience of our own and others' responses to temptation.

The third application will address the biblical concept of *prayer.* I will center my attention on a single biblical text which contains one of the Bible's strongest prayer promises: "And this is the confidence which we have before Him, that if we ask anything according to His will, He hears us. And if we know that He hears us in whatever we ask, we know that we have the requests which we have asked from Him" (1 John 5:14, 15 NASB). At first glance there seems to be nothing in this passage, and perhaps nothing in the concept of prayer itself, that would lead us to consider competing defintions of free will. A closer look will give us a very different picture of things.

The language of this passage makes it clear enough that the "will of God" must have reference to the *revealed* will of God, because it speaks of a confidence based on the knowledge that the requests we have made actually are according to God's will. This, of course, tells us nothing about requests of the "if it be your will" type. We are concerned here only with those requests that God promises to grant because they are in keeping with what he has declared that he wants for us and from us. Now one of those things that he wants from us is that we forgive one another (e.g., Eph. 4:32).

Consider this case: I have two Christian sisters, Mary and Martha, who have had a quarrel and will not speak with each other. Their feud is so bitter that it has divided our family and made everyone unhappy. Now I *know* that it is the will of God that my sisters forgive each other, so I decide to ask God to bring this about. If I take 1 John 5:14, 15 at something like face value, then if my prayer is made in faith and meets all other biblical requirements, I can be confident that God will grant me my request, that is, that he will bring it about that Mary and Martha forgive each other.

At this point a consideration of free will is appropriate, even necessary. My understanding of this passage presupposes that we have soft determinist free will, for only on that supposition can God grant me my request without violating the free will of my sisters. They must choose to forgive, and if free will is necessarily acting on one's preference (the soft determinist view), then God can by his power work "in their hearts" to bring it about that they will prefer forgiving each other to continuing to fight. If God does this, then Mary and Martha will freely choose (in the soft determinist sense) to forgive each other. By contrast, in the conceptual world of libertarianism talk about God's bringing it about that my sisters "freely choose" to forgive each other makes no sense. He could *determine* that they "forgive" each other, but he could not bring it about that they do this *freely*, because libertarian free will requires the categorical ability to choose (and do) otherwise than one actually does. A libertarian freely chosen action can have no causally sufficient antecedent conditions; that is, it cannot be determined by anything or anyone but the free choosing of its agent. What a libertarian God could guarantee me with respect to my petition would be an attempt on his part to influence Mary and Martha in the direction of mutual forgiveness. In other words, he would "give it his best shot," but the final outcome would depend on Mary's and Martha's exercise of their libertarian free will. They can "bring it about" that they freely choose to forgive each other; God cannot bring this about.

The libertarian's general point here is that whether in answer to prayer or for any other reason, God does not determine the particular free choices of human beings. One implication of this is that whatever else 1 John 5:14, 15 and other strong prayer promises may mean, they do not mean that God can or will guarantee to bring it about that particular human beings will make particular choices in response to our prayers. Since so many of our petitions involve matters bearing on the free choices of ourselves and others, this consequence of libertarian theology is a very significant one. It does not sound appealing to say that God will "give it his best shot," and pressing this libertarian point might lead someone otherwise inclined towards libertarianism to consider the soft determinist alternative.

The soft determinist alternative, though, has a problem of its own. To picture God as changing our preferences so as to change our choices seems to make him a puppeteer and ourselves his puppets. This is no more appealing than the claim that God will "give it his best shot" in answer to our prayers, and it is likely to raise questions about the adequacy of soft determinism to accord with our moral intuitions—puppets, after all, are not very convincing as free moral agents. It seems, then, as though the libertarian and the soft determinist both have problems with petitionary prayer involving requests about the free choices of human beings. The libertarian must somehow show that his view of free will fits the strong prayer promises made in 1 John 5:14, 15 and other passages, and the soft determinist must try to defuse the worries about a divine puppeteer.

The fourth application will address the concept of *evil*, specifically *moral evil*, that is, the morally wrong choices and actions of free agents. The most significant intellectual difficulty faced by the soft determinist theologian results from his joint affirmation of theological determinism and soft determinist free will. This is the problem of showing how God can be good and just when he is in ultimate control of all events, including the character-determined free choices of human beings. In other words, the soft determinist needs to argue that his views permit human beings, rather than God, to be responsible for moral evil. If it really is appropriate to say that soft determinist theology reduces human beings to puppets, then something must be wrong with that theology.[11] In contrast, the relation between free will and moral evil seems to provide a significant intellectual advantage to the libertarian theologian. This is because the libertarian maintains that it is not God, but human beings, who have ultimate control over human free choices, so that it is we who are responsible for moral evil.[12]

## The Freedom of Personal Integrity

### Preliminary Issues

The two definitions of freedom we have been considering each view the *person* as the locus of free will. The soft determinist definition makes the person virtually identical to his character, while the libertarian definition makes

11. For a recent argument in defense of soft determinist theology, see John S. Feinberg, *Theologies and Evil* (Washington, D. C.: University Press of America, 1979).

12. Alvin Plantinga is the best-known contemporary exponent of what I am calling libertarian theology. See, for example, Alvin Plantinga, "The Free Will Defense," in *God and Other Minds* (Ithaca, N. Y.: Cornell University Press, 1967), 131–55.

the person something more than his character, something that can at times transcend his character. In both cases there must be some connection between what the person is and what he freely chooses to do, which is just another way of saying that both definitions respect the *rationality condition.*

The *freedom of personal integrity* is closely related to the rationality condition. Its various versions are all accounts of what it is to be free to be the kind of person one wants to be, that is, to be free to translate one's values into action on a consistent basis. This concept of freedom therefore pays even more attention to the concept of the *person* than does the concept of free will, because ascriptions of the freedom of personal integrity depend on a clear and detailed analysis of personal identity.

The relationship between free will and the freedom of personal integrity can be confusing. The chief problem here is that accounts of personal integrity can be (and have been) presented as versions of soft determinist free will, which is not at all surprising given that the freedom of personal integrity requires a strong, even deterministic, link between character and choice. I think, though, that it makes more sense to treat free will and personal integrity as distinct concepts. The reason for this is clear enough: free will is the freedom of moral responsibility, and it is possible (even commonplace) to be morally responsible for one's actions and yet to lack the freedom of personal integrity. Free will is about the (minimum) conditions for moral responsibility; the freedom of personal integrity goes beyond that, asking what are the conditions for fully, even ideally, functioning personhood.

There is one more preliminary matter to discuss. The freedom of personal integrity can be viewed either as *absolute* or as admitting *degrees.* In the absolute sense, personal integrity requires that the person invariably act in accordance with his values. This is clearly an ideal standard rather than an achievable state. In the sense of admitting degrees, personal integrity requires that the person frequently or characteristically act in accordance with his values, with the possibility that the degree to which he does this may increase or decrease over time. This is an achievable and highly desirable state.

### Two Versions of the Freedom of Personal Integrity

One version of the freedom of personal integrity comes from an influential paper by Harry Frankfurt in which he argues that this freedom depends on the structure of the person's will.[13] He calls the freedom of moral responsibility (traditionally called "free will," as in this chapter) *free action,* and because of his views about the person's will he calls the freedom of personal integrity *freedom of will.*

13. Harry G. Frankfurt, "Freedom of the Will and the Concept of a Person," *The Journal of Philosophy* 68 (1971): 5–20.

Frankfurt says that an agent has both *desires* and *volitions,* volitions being effective desires, that is acts of will that translate desires into actions. The agent's desires may be first-order (a desire to do something) or second-order. There are two types of second-order desires. The first is simply a desire to have a particular first-order desire one lacks. The second, which Frankfurt calls a "second-order volition," is the desire that one of one's first-order desires will be the one which moves him to action. A *person* is an agent who has second-order volitions. In other words, a person is someone who cares about which of his possibly conflicting first-order desires will lead to action. If the person has *freedom of will,* then he is able to be, and succeeds in being, the type of person he desires to be, a person who acts only on those desires he wishes to act upon. In Frankfurt's terminology, he is one who can have the *will* (effective desire, leading to action) he wants to have. By contrast, a *wanton* is an agent who lacks second-order volitions. A wanton doesn't care about what will he has, he just acts on his strongest first-order desires.

According to Frankfurt, freedom of *action* is the freedom to do what one wants, to act on one's first-order desires. This is sufficient for moral responsibility, and it is possessed by both persons and wantons. It is distinct from freedom of *will* (i.e., personal integrity) which is possible for persons but not for wantons. Consider two drug addicts, one a person and one a wanton. Each acts freely on his first-order desire for drugs, but the similarity between them ends there. The addict who is a person will care about which of his first-order desires he acts upon; in fact, he may have a second-order desire to stop craving drugs. If he can act on that second-order desire, then it is a "second-order volition" and he has freedom of will; if he cannot act on it, then he lacks freedom of will. By contrast, the addict who is a wanton will not care which of his first-order desires he acts upon. If his strongest first-order desire is his craving for drugs, then he will act upon it without regret. He lacks freedom of will because he does not care what *will* (effective desire, leading to action) he has.

Frankfurt admits that people are usually much more complex than his account of the will allows them to be. An agent may fall prey to self-deception, or he may have a conflict between his second-order desires. If this confusion becomes so severe that it "prevents him from identifying himself in a sufficiently decisive way with *any* of his conflicting first-order desires, [it] destroys him as a person."[14]

Another version of the freedom of personal integrity comes from a paper by Gary Watson.[15] He calls it *free agency,* which is another term sometimes used to denote the freedom of moral responsibility. Watson's understanding

14. Ibid., 16.
15. Gary Watson, "Free Agency," in *Free Will,* ed. Gary Watson (Oxford: Oxford University Press, 1982), 96–110.

of free agency depends upon *valuing* and *desiring* being independent sources of motivation. Even though valuing (reason) and desiring (appetite) will often coincide, there is the possibility that a conflict will occur between them, such that what one values, what one rationally believes to be the best course of action, will be in conflict with what one desires to do. The agent who responds to such a conflict by translating his values into action is exercising free agency (personal integrity).

Watson says that an agent possesses both a *valuational system* and a *motivational system*. His valuational system (values) is that set of considerations which grounds his judgments about what is the best or most rational thing to do in any given situation. The *free* agent assigns values to alternative courses of action, and chooses accordingly. The agent's motivational system is that set of considerations which move him to action (what Frankfurt calls "will"). The possibility of *unfree* action arises because the agent's valuational system and motivational system may not be in complete harmony. Complete harmony between the systems would exist only when the judgments arising from the agent's valuational system completely determined his actions, a desirable state that Watson denies actually exists. The free agent is only partially free, for free agency (personal integrity) is never absolute except in the case of the traditional theistic conception of God in which the dependence of motivation upon evaluation is total.

Watson argues that a person's valuational system is the standpoint from which he views and judges the world, and that it is not possible for him to dissassociate himself entirely from this system. A person can disassociate himself from one set of principles only from the standpoint of another set with which he identifies. In effect, Watson is saying that *having a valuational system is a necessary condition for being a person*. Watson admits that real people are not necessarily as simple as his account suggests, for some are torn between conflicting value systems and wracked with ultimate conflicts and irresolvable tensions. Still, though, Watson says these grim cases "point to problems about the unity of the person" and he is "inclined to think that when the split is severe enough, to have more than one standpoint is to have none."[16]

### *Theological Application: Romans 7:14–25*

In this much discussed passage from his letter to the Romans, Paul uses the first person singular to describe an agent who struggles with a conflict between his devotion to God and the sinful element within him.[17] In the philosophical language of freedom, this agent—"Paul"—lacks the *freedom of personal integrity*, but he is still a *person* because the text makes it clear that he

---

16. Ibid., 106.
17. I will not take sides on just who or what it is Paul is referring to with his use of the first person singular; instead, I will simply examine on its own terms the experience Paul is describing.

has a valuational system (note v. 16, "the law"). Not only is Paul a person, the passage also indicates that he has *free will*, because he accepts responsibility for his failures to do what is good (vv. 15, 16, 19, 25).

This last claim requires some explanation. At some points in the passage Paul writes as if the sinful element within him was virtually an alien force, something distinct from himself (vv. 17, 20). If indwelling sin (v. 20) were really an alien force keeping Paul from doing good, then it, and not Paul, would be morally responsible. But, as I've noted, Paul accepts responsibility for his failures to do the good. The explanation of this is that Paul *identifies* with his valuational system and *disassociates* himself from the sinful element within him. That element is in fact a part of him—that is, it is a part of the person Paul as a locus of moral responsibility—but it is not a part of his *ideal self*, which of course is the Paul who possesses the absolute freedom of personal integrity. It is Paul's tension-ridden *real self* who has the freedom of moral responsibility but wishes it had the freedom of personal integrity.

It is important to understand that even though the Paul of this passage lacks the freedom of personal integrity, he does not suffer from the sort of pathological identity crisis Watson worries about.[18] To the contrary, it is because this Paul has such a clear identification with the law of God that he is driven to describe the sinful element within him as if it were not really a part of him at all. He is a slave to this element, "sold into bondage to sin" (v. 14), suffering from a "different law" which is "waging war against the law of [his] mind" (v. 23). In verse 24 he cries out for *freedom*—"Wretched man that I am! Who will set me free from the body of this death?" (NASB). This cry for freedom comes from the valuational core of the real Paul, a person who views the world from the standpoint of the law of God and who therefore longs to be free from his sinful tendencies.

Frankfurt gives us additional resources for understanding how the Paul of this passage can wish to do the good yet instead do the very evil he does not wish to do. When Paul asserts that he wishes to do the good, what he is saying, in Frankfurt's terms, is that he *has a second-order volition to do the good*. That is, he wants his first-order desires to do the good always to be his *will*, always to move him to action. By contrast, when Paul asserts that he does not wish to do the evil, he is saying that he *has no second-order volition to do the evil*. He has, of course, first-order desires to do the evil, even as he has first-order desires to do the good, but these conflicting desires are not

---

18. The language of the passage is so dramatic that one can imagine this Paul *never* acting on his valuational system. This, however, is not possible. For something to count as a person's valuational system, it is necessary that he act on it at least sometimes. To say that this Paul lacks the freedom of personal integrity is only to say that he finds himself unable to translate his values into action nearly as completely or as frequently as he would like.

equal in Paul's eyes. He *identifies* only with his first-order desires to do the good.[19]

What Frankfurt and Watson give the interpreter of Romans 7, and what they give us, is a set of intellectual tools for understanding the sort of freedom that the Paul of this passage believes he lacks and wants to have. In this section I have given only a small sample of the sort of help these tools can be, just as earlier in this chapter I gave samples of the theological helpfulness of philosophical discussions of the various other senses of human freedom.[20] I hope what I have written will be enough to convince any reader of this chapter that the study of the philosophical concept of freedom is worth the time of the Christian who wants a fuller understanding of human nature.

## Summary

There is a family of freedom concepts that can be classified into three categories, the *freedom of permission,* the *freedom of moral responsibility,* and the *freedom of personal integrity.* In this chapter I directed most of my attention to the second and third categories. The freedom of moral responsibility is what is often termed "free will," and is usually thought of as a necessary condition for moral responsibility. An adequate account of free will meets three conditions, the *ability condition* (the agent was able to choose otherwise than he actually did), the *control condition* (it was "up to the agent" what choice he made), and the *rationality condition* (the agent had "personal reasons" for the choice he made).

Any theological anthropology faithful to the biblical text will affirm human moral responsibility. This in turn requires that the theologian take free will seriously, adopting some account of it that meets the three conditions. There are two such accounts which theologians (and others) favor, *libertarian free will* and *soft determinist free will.* These competing definitions of free will can be contrasted in various ways, including their respective handling of the rationality condition. The libertarian maintains that a truly free choice requires that the agent have two or more options for which he has personal reasons, and that there be nothing in his character or circumstances that determines which option he chooses. The soft determinist equates free will with the agent's acting on his character-determined preference. In other words, a soft

19. See Walt Russell's chapter in this book (pp. 207–28) for another treatment of Romans 7. Russell believes that the tensions described in this passage are not normative for life in Christ, but represent the power of indwelling sin during the Mosaic era. Under the new covenant, God has promised the believer a larger degree of the freedom of personal integrity (e.g., see Jer. 31:31–34; Rom. 6:1–11, 8:1–17).

20. For another theological application of the freedom of personal integrity, see Eleonore Stump, "Sanctification, Hardening of the Heart, and Frankfurt's Concept of Free Will," *The Journal of Philosophy* 85 (1988): 395–420.

determinist free choice is to be understood as the agent's choosing to do whatever matters most to him at the time of choice. Adopting one of these accounts of free will can have a significant impact on the theologian's understanding of various subjects, including the four I addressed in this chapter—paradox, temptation, prayer, and evil.

The concept of free will addresses *minimal* conditions for the ascription of moral responsibility, and it is easy to think beyond this to *maximal* conditions for fully or ideally functioning personhood. This is the freedom of personal integrity, the ability to translate one's values into action on a consistent basis. This freedom is a highly desirable state which the "Paul" of Romans 7:14–25 lacked but wished to have. There is much more that needs to be learned about personal integrity, much more than the little I have included in this chapter. This should not be surprising. Theology and philosophy are always open-ended, requiring us human beings to search for a fuller understanding of what we are and what God wants us to become.

## Suggested Readings

Anglin, W. S. *Free Will and the Christian Faith*. Oxford: Clarendon, 1990. [A]

Bergmann, Frithjof. *On Being Free*. Notre Dame: University of Notre Dame Press, 1977. [B]

Boyle, Joseph M., Jr., Germain Grisez, and Olaf Tollefsen. *Free Choice: A Self-Referential Argument*. Notre Dame: University of Notre Dame Press, 1976. [I]

Craig, William Lane. *The Only Wise God*. Grand Rapids: Baker, 1987. [I]

Dennett, Daniel C. *Elbow Room: The Varieties of Free Will Worth Wanting*. Cambridge, Mass.: The MIT Press, 1984. [I]

Double, Richard. *The Non-Reality of Free Will*. Oxford: Oxford University Press, 1991. [I or A]

Edwards, Jonathan. *Freedom of the Will*. New Haven: Yale University Press, 1957. [A]

Franklin, R. L. *Freewill and Determinism: A Study of Rival Conceptions of Man*. London: Routledge and Kegan Paul, 1968. [I]

Kenny, Anthony. *Will, Freedom, and Power*. New York: Barnes and Noble, 1976. [I or A]

Pinnock, Clark H., ed. *The Grace of God, The Will of Man*. Grand Rapids: Zondervan, 1989. [B]

Simon, Yves R. *Freedom of Choice*. New York: Fordham University Press, 1969. [I] van Inwagen, Peter. *An Essay on Free Will*. Oxford: Clarendon, 1983. [A]

Watson, Gary, ed. *Free Will*. Oxford: Oxford University Press, 1982. [I]

Williams, Clifford. *Free Will and Determinism: A Dialogue*. Indianapolis: Hackett, 1980. [B]

Wolf, Susan. *Freedom Within Reason*. Oxford: Oxford University Press, 1990. [I or A]

Young, Robert. *Freedom, Responsibility, and God*. New York: Barnes and Noble, 1975. [I or A]

# A Response to David M. Ciocchi

*Nancy S. Duvall*

David Ciocchi's chapter takes on such a profound and complex issue, that of human freedom, that it is difficult to give a brief response. I will not attempt to address every issue but focus on two themes that seem to me to be related and central. The first theme deals with human freedom as a family of concepts and the second theme deals with freedom as an entity.

As I first read Ciocchi's chapter, I liked his presentation describing a *family* of freedom concepts because it suggested an awareness of the complexity of human freedom, and human freedom, to my understanding, is not a simple concept. However, a family involves relationships and it appeared that Ciocchi's chapter did not describe how these family concepts of freedom were related—was one more basic than the other? How did personal integrity influence moral responsibility? The discussion treated the three categories of freedom—permission, moral responsibility, and personal integrity—but without indicating any kind of relationship. My understanding of human freedom is that the categories are interrelated and in a hierarchical manner.

My lay (not philosophically trained) understanding is that freedom represents choice, just as responsibility is the "ability to respond." My sense is that as we have the ability to respond or make a choice, we are accountable. That ability or freedom to respond is what allows us to have a relationship to God. With no ability to respond, we are robot-like and therefore not able to love God. Ability to respond is what lays the foundation for relationship. To the degree that I am able to respond, I am responsible.

At the most basic level my responsibility is characterized by an evaluation of good or evil, whether my choice tends toward good results or evil results (ever since Adam and Eve ate from the tree of knowledge of good and evil [Gen. 2:17]). At a most basic level I am accountable for my choices.

There is an area where my choices may not impact others such as my preferences for food, or music. This seems to be the freedom of permission Ciocchi describes. There are a number of things that I am free to choose, *but* this freedom of permission may be limited for a higher value, that of caring for a brother and thus limiting my freedom for a higher good. Thus, in I Cor. 8:8–13 Paul warns against using my liberty in such a way as to become a stumbling block to another. In this instance the freedom of permission is limited because the moral responsibility of caring for my neighbor is more basic than my freedom of permission. At times one must limit a freedom to be consistent with a higher value. It appears that a moral responsibility is more basic than a personal freedom of permission.

The freedom of moral responsibility and the freedom of personal integrity are interrelated. Ciocchi's example of the freedom of personal integrity, "If I am able to live a life of consistently translating my values into action, then I have the freedom of personal integrity," has a built-in difficulty. It seems to assume that all values are equal and acceptable and all I need to do is be consistent with my personal values. However, the L.A. riots of 1992 provided examples that call into question Ciocchi's example. The media showed many film clips of people looting, some of whom literally said, "Society has deprived me; I'm just getting my fair share." Their view of fairness included the value of using whatever means were necessary to accomplish material equality. While they were consistent with their personal values, they were injuring the store owners and actually the public at large. In other words, while they were expressing the freedom of personal integrity according to Ciocchi, their moral choice was injuring others.

My second major comment on Ciocchi's presentation involves his treatment of freedom as absolute rather than a phenomenon of degree. For the most part, in his description of freedom, he writes as if it is an either/or phenomenon. In describing Mary's decision to go for a walk, he does indicate that her concern for her health may have mattered more to her than any of her personal reasons for other options, and thus indirectly allowed for some weighing of decisions. In his discussion of the freedom of personal integrity he indicates that it can be viewed as absolute or relative. But freedom is a matter of degree, at least in this life, and it is arguable that even Jesus limited his freedom out of love for and obedience to the Father (John 5:18; Phil. 2:6–8; Heb. 5:7–8).

I think that much of the difficulty of understanding freedom comes because we do not conceptualize it as a matter of degree, nor allow for individual differences. As I see it some people have more freedom than others, particularly in the area of freedom of personal integrity or "the freedom to be the self

God created me to be," as I would prefer to call it. The importance of the "degree of freedom" concept was brought to my awareness powerfully in my work with a profoundly depressed client. She claimed that she could do nothing: for example, she could not do house work, or cook for the family, or drive. I knew enough of the depth of her depression to recognize that she was mostly correct. *But* though there was a long list of what she could not do, I knew she still was responsible (had the ability to respond) for one or two actions. She could take her medication and she could come to therapy, even if someone else drove her. And I believed that if she would do what she could do, she would ultimately be able to do more. And time confirmed my prognosis.

The above example also highlights one more crucial issue. That involves the profound impact of past and present choices on future choices. A criminal on drugs may say that he committed a crime while he was on drugs and could not help what he did; he was not responsible. But he was responsible for taking drugs in the first place, and at the point of taking drugs was making a choice *and* giving up some degree of his freedom. A man and woman who engaged in premarital sex may say that they could not control their physiological responses after a certain point. They may be correct, but they were responsible for the events that led to that point—the kind of movies or other stimuli that they were around, such as the food or drink they had. I am stressing Ciocchi's statement that "much or most of the behavior of human beings is either freely chosen or the result of earlier free choices" and highlighting the impact of those choices. Our choices increase or decrease the degrees of freedom we experience.

A summary of what I have been saying is that we have varying degrees of freedom based on (among other things) prior experiences, level of maturity, self-awareness, and spiritual awareness, for various choices involving our relationship to others (moral responsibility), to ourselves (moral responsibility and personal integrity), and to our God-given freedoms (permission). We are accountable to God for our actions (choices) to the degree we have the ability to respond, and God is the only one who can accurately and perfectly judge our level of responsibility. We are constantly making choices and those choices have consequences for further choices. Scripture gives us principles for good choices that increase our freedom to choose as Christ would have us choose.

# A Response to David M. Ciocchi

*Walt Russell*

A cynic recently defined "a philosopher" as someone who talks about things he or she does not understand and makes it sound like it is your fault! Such is surely not the case with Ciocchi's sensitive and clear discussion of the hotly debated issue of human freedom. I commend him for both the clarity of his explanations to the philosophically unsophisticated and for his sensitivity in dealing fairly with views other than his own. His discussion of the issue of human freedom from a philosophical perspective is of tremendous value to those of us who have previously discussed these issues only within biblical categories. This is one issue that greatly cries out for an integrative and multidisciplinary treatment.

In this light, as a New Testament person, I would like to supplement Ciocchi's discussion in two manners. First, at the risk of clouding the issues with "party labels," I would like to correlate the two main views of libertarian free will and soft determinism with the post-Reformation historical labels. Secondly, I would like to discuss some key biblical texts that must be considered when reflecting on human freedom.

First, we must paste a few theological labels on the philosophical options. The view of "libertarian free will" (incompatibilism) asserts that humans have *categorical* freedom to choose in certain areas of human behavior. When this view intersected the issue of our salvation in Christ in the discussions in Europe in the late sixteenth and early seventeenth centuries, it was championed in the Netherlands by a Protestant theologian named Jacobus Arminius (1560–1609). In reaction to the Lutheran and Reformed views regarding salvation, Arminius argued that human beings have categorical freedom to repent and believe in Christ apart from God's unconditional predestination of them. As Ciocchi pointed out, this means that those who hold this view must "attempt to formulate divine sovereignty in some way that is neither apparently nor actually inconsistent with libertarian free will." Arminius's response (and those who have followed in this view) was to understand predestination in a *conditional sense* as God's predetermination of the destiny of individuals based on his foreknowledge of whether they would either freely accept Christ or reject him as their Savior. Thus, "Arminians" believe in predestination as the predecision on God's part to save those who choose to repent and believe in Christ, thereby preserving libertarian free will in this important area.

Those Christians defining human freedom in terms of any kind of determinism are generally labeled "Calvinists" because they follow the general teachings of John Calvin (1509–1564). Among Calvinists are those who agree with Theodore Beza (1519–1605), who popularized the doctrine of *supralapsarianism*, which holds that God's determination of the eternal destiny of every person is logically prior to his decrees to create mankind and to permit the fall. Also within the Calvinist family are those who believe in *infralapsarianism*, which views God's predestination of some to salvation and the rest to their just fate of condemnation as logically subsequent to both the creation and the fall of mankind.

Whichever logical view of God's predestinating decrees Calvinists hold, the onus is still upon them to resolve this view of God's sovereignty with a meaningful view of human freedom. While those who hold to a libertarian free will must nuance God's predestinating work, those who emphasize that work must nuance human freedom. The latter is what "soft determinism" (compatibilism) attempts to do when it emphasizes that the choices a person makes are determined by his character. From this perspective, apart from God's intervention, a sinner would freely choose to remain in sin and to reject God's offer of salvation because he or she freely *prefers* to do so. Hypothetically, human beings have the ability to choose freely, but as sinners their unregenerate character compels them to choose the sinful path. Only God's intervention in regenerating them can change their character so that they freely choose to believe in Christ. Therefore, in most deterministic perspectives, God's sovereign imparting of eternal life *precedes* the choice to believe in Christ.[21]

Having considered the two main views of human freedom in post-Reformation theological discussion, we turn now to a consideration of key biblical texts relevant to this topic. Numerous Old Testament proof texts supporting first human responsibility and then divine sovereignty are given by D. A. Car-

---

21. A very helpful book that continues this kind of discussion and lets Calvinists and Arminians make their own cases is David Basinger and Randall Basinger, eds., *Predestination and Free Will: Four Views of Divine Sovereignty and Human Freedom* (Downers Grove, Ill.: InterVarsity, 1986).

son in his fine book entitled *Divine Sovereignty & Human Responsibility* (New Foundations Theological Library; Atlanta: John Knox, 1981). Carson lists nine categories with 157 passages that attest to true human responsibility in the Old Testament (pp. 18–23) and four categories with 332 passages that underscore God as sovereign (pp. 24–35)! The clear teaching of the Old Testament is both that human beings are responsible and that God is sovereign.

The same dual emphasis can be seen in the New Testament where representative passages can be marshaled in support of both human responsibility and divine sovereignty:

| Human Responsibility/Freedom | Divine Sovereignty |
| --- | --- |
| John 3:16–19 | Ephesians 1:3–14 |
| Matthew 23:37–39 | Romans 8:26–39 |
| Acts 17:1–4 | Romans 9:6–29 |
| 1 Corinthians 9:16–17 | Romans 11:1–32 |
| Philemon 12–14 | Matthew 24:22; Colossians 3:12 |
| Revelation 20:11–15 | 1 Thessalonians 1:4; |
| John 5:24–29 | 2 Thessalonians 2:13–15 |
| 2 Peter 3:8–9 | 1 Corinthians 1:26–31 |
| Acts 18:5–6 | Acts 2:22–24, 37–40 |
| Romans 1:18–23 | Acts 13:42–49 |
|  | John 1:9–13; 5:19–21; 15:16–19 |

Seeing the biblical data does not resolve the tension between God's choosing and human beings' freedom because the tension appears to be woven into the fabric of Scripture. However, given the fact of God's sovereign choices in human history, it may be worthwhile to note the exact nature of his choices. Rather than emphasizing the unmerited choice of individuals for salvation (which may be true), the focus seems to be upon the calling to fulfill a privilege or an office.[22] In this sense the emphasis is upon the corporate or collective calling (N.B. the *we/us* in Eph. 1:3–14), rather than individual election. This does not contradict the fact of God's sovereign choosing, but it makes the group (rather than the individual) the dimension of the object of divine election, and thereby allows more room for individual human freedom.

---

22. See particularly the helpful discussion in Roger T. Forster and V. Paul Marston, *God's Strategy in Human History* (Wheaton, Ill.: Tyndale House, 1973) 117–49.

# Part 3

# Accounting for
# Human Complexity

*Christian Perspectives
from Anthropology and Psychology*

# 4

# Mind, Emotion, Culture, and the Person

*Perspectives from Cultural Anthropology and Scripture*

*Sherwood G. Lingenfelter*

Following the publication of Darwin's *Origin of Species* (1859), the study of anthropology diverged sharply from its roots in theology to a new evolutionary paradigm grounded in the scientific empiricism of the Enlightenment. Rejecting the notion that the origin, nature, and substance of man was to be understood primarily through the revelation of Scripture, scholars in the latter decades of the nineteenth century sought to explain humanity in naturalistic terms of physical and cultural evolution. For more than one hundred years cultural and social anthropologists have grappled with the issue of the relationship between mind, emotion, culture, and the person. The broad parameters of this discussion were set forth by such distinguished scholars as E. B.

Tyler,[1] J. G. Frazer,[2] L. Levy-Bruhl,[3] Lewis Henry Morgan,[4] and Emile Durkheim.[5] Setting aside the theological contributions to the subject, these men framed an empirical program of research to discover the natural laws of human physical, psychological, social, and cultural life.

Over the past half-century, the number of scholars exploring these issues has multiplied geometrically. The published descriptions of human societies and cultures has grown in even greater proportions. The establishing of the Human Relations Area Files at Yale University in the 1940s provided exhaustive documentation on hundreds of specific societies distributed over every geographical and cultural area in the world. Social and cultural anthropologists of diverse theoretical orientation have added literally thousands of additional studies from the peoples and the cultures of the world. From this vast body of empirical data anthropological theorists address the questions of the nature of the person, the human mind, and culture, contributing empirical description and analysis far beyond the scope of the traditional theological discipline of anthropology. The value of these contributions is the illumination they provide for what Scripture terms the "natural man." However, since they reject the concept of a "spiritual man," these studies yield little if any insight into the spiritual realm. The purpose of this chapter is to review the contributions of these scholars, and to explore how theological and socio-cultural anthropology may complement one another toward a more complete understanding of persons.

## Three Arguments:
## The Rational, Irrational, and Non-Rational Person

Richard Shweder[6] has written an excellent article reviewing the diverse contributions of anthropologists with regard to the subject of the mind of man and the ideas and actions of diverse peoples. Shweder declares that anthropologists and other scholars of the human mind have advanced an ancient dispute over the rationality or the irrationality of the human species. Shweder divides these scholars into two camps, the "enlightenment" scholars, who seek universals, natural law, and see human beings as rational creatures en-

1. E. B. Tyler, *Primitive Culture* (London: Murray, 1871).
2. J. G. Frazer, *The Golden Bough: A Study in Magic and Science* (London: Macmillan, 1890).
3. L. Levy-Bruhl, *Les Functions Mentales dans les Societes Inferieurs* (Paris: Akan, 1910).
4. Lewis Henry Morgan, *Ancient Society* (New York: n.p., 1877).
5. Emile Durkheim, *The Rules of Sociology Method* (1895; reprint, Chicago: University of Chicago Press, 1938).
6. Richard A. Shweder, "Anthropology's Romantic Rebellion Against the Enlightenment or There Is More To Thinking Than Reason and Evidence," in *Culture Theory: Essays on Mind, Self, and Emotion*, ed. Richard A. Schweder and Robert A. LeVine (Cambridge: Cambridge University Press, 1984), 27–66.

gaged in a process of progress and development, and the "romantic rebellion," who hold that human culture and thought fall beyond the scope of deductive and inductive reason, and that culture is a non-rational structure with cultural frames and expressive, symbolic components that shape the particular culture and history of a given society.

According to Shweder the enlightenment approach articulated by Tyler and Frazer assumes that people guide their lives by reason and evidence. Human reason, they argue, is characterized by a concern with empirical knowledge, and an attempt to articulate consistent beliefs and practices. These scholars assume that all people pursue rational goals, using inductive and deductive inference and constructing reasonable explanations of their world and experience. As Tyler and Frazer conducted extensive comparative analyses of peoples of the world, they concluded that primitive peoples showed less competence with regard to scientific canons of reason and evidence, and fell short of the development of the modern civilized mind. Both Tyler and Frazer characterized primitive thought as deficient in its canons of reason and evidence, and prone to magical, irrational thinking, and confused analysis of causality (i.e., a specific dream causes diarrhea). Tyler, Frazer, and (later) Piaget argued that the standards of scientific reason have been acquired by only a few civilized cultures. The primitive cultures were driven by more irrational or intuitive standards of thought than by the canon of scientific reason.

Shweder attributes the founding of the "romanticist counter point" to Levy-Bruhl.[7] Levy-Bruhl rejected the enlightenment ideal of the primitive as a confused scientist and argued instead that the primitive is "not a bad scientist; he is a good mystic; and the intellectual procedures of the primitive mind are not deficient applications of the rules of logic and science—they are alogical, not illogical, non-rational not irrational."[8] While most contemporary symbolic anthropologists have totally rejected Levy-Bruhl's idea of cultures as mystical, they have readily embraced the conception of non-rational, and scholars such as Geertz,[9] Schneider,[10] and a host of their students have argued that culture is conceptual structure, that is, systems of meanings, concepts, and symbols that establish cultural frames within which people organize their behavior and establish the standards for assessment and action in their social world. Such cultural systems are public systems rather than private and as such define the frames and premises upon which people determine the validity of their own and the behavior of others.

7. See n. 3.
8. Shweder, "Anthropology's Romantic Rebellion," 39.
9. Clifford Geertz, *Interpretation of Cultures* (New York: Basic Books, 1973).
10. David M. Schneider, *American Kinship: A Cultural Account* (Inglewood Cliffs, N. J.: Prentice Hall, 1968).

## Three Approaches:
## Universalism, Developmentalism, and Relativism

Anthropologists who differ with regard to the rational, non-rational or irrational characteristics of the mind and its relationship to culture also differ on the issue of the universality of mental and cultural attributes. Shweder declares that the issue of the modern vs. the primitive mind "divides enlightenment figures into two camps: Universalists and Developmentalists."[11] The Universalists argue that the intellectual processes of evidence gathering, analysis, and reason are available to all human beings and provide a common ground for moral virtues and other human adaptations. Developmentalists in contrast deny that all people have these capabilities in equal measure. They contend that, while human capabilities for rational thought are indeed universal, not all human beings or cultures have actualized their potential in these matters. Piaget[12] follows this line of argument with regard to child development and the achievement of scientific reasoning processes in the human being.

The Universalists explore human behavior and attempt to uncover those causes and patterns that have universal relevance for human life. Two key assumptions in this approach are the biological and the psychic unity of mankind. Because the human species everywhere has the same basic biological equipment, the Universalists argue that human economics, human social life, and human thought must indeed have some common biological ground. Those who embrace the psychic unity of mankind assert that the development of the human person is grounded in certain foundational psychic and social experiences (e.g., toilet training, weaning), linked to the prolonged dependency of the human child upon its parents and upon basic physiological and psychological needs such as food, water, shelter, protection, nurture, and positive affection from other human beings.

A Universalist may support any one of the three arguments (rational, irrational, non-rational) regarding the relationship of mind and culture. Leslie White[13] and Julian Steward,[14] the seminal thinkers of cultural materialism, view human beings as rational creatures who are motivated intellectually by their primary material needs. White argues that all human behavior focuses on the control and consumption of energy, while Steward sees human behavior determined by particular systems of production and ecological constraints. The structural anthropology of Claude Levi-Strauss[15] develops the hypothe-

11. Shweder, "Anthropology's Romantic Rebellion," 31.

12. J. Piaget, *The Construction of Reality in the Child* (New York: Basic Books, 1954).

13. Leslie A. White, *The Evolution of Culture* (New York: MacGraw-Hill, 1959).

14. Julian H. Steward, *Theory of Culture Change: The Methodology of Multilinear Evolution* (Urbana, Ill.: University of Illinois Press, 1955).

15. Claude Levi-Strauss, *The Savage Mind* (Chicago: Universy of Chicago Press, 1966).

sis of a universal structure of the human mind, through which human beings everywhere structure their cultural systems and their mythology. Freud's work on psychoanalysis and culture established the foundation for research on the pervasive presence of the irrational in human life and culture and on the universal psychological human responses that grow out of the fulfillment or lack of fulfillment of human emotional needs.

The Universalists who endorse the non-rational perspective embrace either a sociological or an ecological determinism producing universal human patterns of response. Scholars of social organization such as G. P. Murdock[16] and A. R. Radcliffe-Brown[17] argued for the universality of certain features of kinship and social organization which arise from economic and social functions, rather than rational human decisions.

While universalism was the dominant paradigm in anthropology in the early decades of this century, relativism flourished following the seminal works of Branislaw Malinowski[18] and Franz Boaz.[19] Malinowski developed the conceptualization of culture as functioning to meet basic human needs. Because all cultures function for need fulfillment in ways both meaningful and effective for the participants, Malinowski and his followers argued that each culture was of equal value and of relative significance in relationship to others. While Boaz and his students took a different tack emphasizing the unique historical development of each culture, the end result was the same; each culture was as valid as any other, because of its unique historical and ecological adaptations. In a similar vein, culture and personality studies of Ruth Benedict, Geoffrey Gorer, and A. Kardiner focused on the irrational dimensions of the personal psychological experience in distinctive cultures which provided foundation for relativistic expression of a national or cultural personality type.

The most extreme relativists are the symbolic anthropologists. David Schneider[20] contends that every culture must be understood in terms of its owns categories; the social concepts typically used by anthropologists, such as marriage and kinship, are western constructions and irrelevant to the analysis of Yapese or Balinese kinship. Schneider and Geertz propose that every cultural system is a unique construction of its participants, and as such the very foundational definition of persons can only be understood within the context of the specific society and culture. In discussing this perspective Shweder concludes:

16. G. P. Murdock, *Social Structure* (New York: Macmillan, 1949).
17. A. R. Radcliffe-Brown, *Structure and Function in Primitive Society* (1952; reprint, New York: Free, 1965).
18. Branislaw Malinowski, *Sex and Regression in Savage Society* (1927; reprint, New York: Meridian, 1955).
19. Franz Boaz, *The Mind of Primitive Man* (New York: n.p., 1911).
20. David M. Schneider, *A Critique of the Study of Kinship* (Ann Arbor, Mich.: The University of Michigan Press, 1984).

[T]he whole thrust of romantic thinking is to defend the co-equality of fundamentally different "frames" of understanding. The concept of non-rationality,
the idea of the "arbitrary" frees some portion of man's mind from the universal
dictates of logic and science, permitting diversity while leaving man free to
choose among irreconcilable presuppositions, schemes of classifications, and
ideas of worth.[21]

The romantic movement with its extreme relativism is anti-developmental in
its viewpoint and in the study of child development focuses primarily upon the
acquisition of information necessary for communication within that specific
context.

## Christian Critique: A Perspectival Approach on Being Human

One of the most significant insights from Shweder's article[22] is his conclusion that it is unnecessary to choose between an "enlightenment" and a "romantic" view of the human mind. Shweder suggests that we should be grate-
ful for the diverse perspectives of these social theorists and avoid the
temptation to expand one's preferred perspective to include the whole of the
human experience. Proposing that each perspective illuminates a part of the
whole of human experience, Shweder presents a matrix of possible and useful
interpretative approaches from which to answer the questions, what kind of
mental processes do human beings actually employ and how do anthropologists approach the study of these processes? Shweder's matrix plots two di-
mensional relationships between rational, irrational, and non-rational mental
processes, and universalism, developmentalism, and relativism in anthropological comparison.[23] This matrix is a useful one and I have adapted it for exploring not just mental processes but the larger questions of mind and culture
and the question of what it means to be human. In this chapter I shall add a
third dimension to Shweder's matrix: a contrast of the natural man and the
spiritual man, and explore how theological anthropology may enlarge upon
the pictures gained through naturalistically directed empirical research (see
fig. 1).

I will assume that each major theoretical position employed by anthropologists to study this subject contributes a legitimate, albeit particular, and restricted perspective upon the empirical data which they have studied. I agree
with Shweder that we must reject the temptation to argue that one particular
cell in the matrix explains all; rather, I contend that each perspective contributes a valuable picture of the human experience of the natural man, yet each
has its flaws of viewpoint and omission. Because of the limitations of space, I

21. Ibid., 48.
22. See n. 6.
23. Shweder, "Anthropology's Romantic Rebellion," 59.

Figure 1
Perspectives on Being Human

| Rational Relativist | Irrational Relativist | Non-Rational Relativist |
|---|---|---|
| Rational Developmental | Irrational Developmental | Non-Rational Developmental |
| Rational Universal | Irrational Universal | Non-Rational Universal |

shall not examine the weaknesses of each perspective, but rather will focus on the major fallacy of pervasive exclusive naturalism.

The fallacy of Shweder's work and of most anthropologists is the rejection of a dimension of the human experience other than that of the "natural man." From a Christian point of view, the missing dimension in Shweder's work is the "spiritual man." As Moreland argues in his chapter on dualism (pp. 55–79), the scientific propensity to reduce everything to the physical and to the natural must be rejected. From the revelation available to us in Scripture and the reinterpretation of empirical data in light of scriptural assumptions, we find a striking contrast between the spiritual man and the natural man, and our analysis of the question of being human must address this third dimension.

The agenda in this chapter is to discern first of all what anthropologists have contributed to our understanding of the person and character of the natural man. Once we have explored this in summary fashion we will then examine what Scripture has to say about how this "natural man" may be transformed through the redemptive work of Christ. But first we must acquire a relevant set of biblical concepts to aid us in our exploration.

## Some Relevant Biblical Concepts

The distinction between surface structure and deep structure is one that is widely discussed in cognitive anthropology. Surface structure refers to the non-rational cognitive systems of culture, the systems of classification, the symbols of social and religious significance, the belief systems that provide the integrating framework for cultural life. Each culture develops its own peculiar cultural frames which are used by participants to regulate public life. For example, according to David Schneider, "father" in America is defined by the cultural frames of "blood" and "law," while in Yap it is defined by the frames of "land" and "ancestral spirits."

Deep structure, in contrast, poses a "below the surface" cognitive and emotional structure, which is held in common by all human beings. Levi-Strauss' structure of the human mind or Melford Spiro's psychic unity of mankind are variant conceptualizations of deep structure. That emotional dimension of persons which drives them to irrational behavior resulting in obsession and repression is part of the psychic deep structure of human beings. Spiro argues that one's concept of "father" is not driven so much by cultural frames as it is driven by oedipal struggles between the father and the child for the affection of the mother.

Two biblical concepts that appear analogous to these technical terms are "mind" and "heart." As I read Scripture those passages that address issues of the mind seem to focus upon surface structure issues, the elaboration of human thought and human notions to produce human conceptualizations and interpretations of life and reality. In his epistles Paul develops a theology of the natural mind that is consistent with what anthropologists describe in surface structure behavior. In Romans Paul describes how those who rejected the knowledge of God were given over to a depraved mind (Rom. 1:28). Paul declares that the sinful mind is hostile to God, incapable of submission to God's law (Rom. 8:7). The Gentile lives in the futility of his own thought (Eph. 4:17), and their unspiritual mind puffs them up with idle notions (Col. 2:18). The natural man, the unbeliever, is corrupted in both mind and conscience (Titus 1:15). The natural man has an "alienated mind" intent upon its own designs and corrupted by rebellious and evil behavior (Col. 1:21).

The deep structure of the human psyche is perhaps captured in the biblical concept of "heart." Throughout Scripture the heart is spoken of as the seat of human emotions. The writer of Ecclesiastes depicts the heart as filled with schemes to do wrong, full of evil, and points to the irrationality, the madness that grows out of the seat of human emotions. As Freud and Spiro noted so graphically, the obsessional and the magical thought of human beings grows out of deep-seated anger, fear, and hurt. Jeremiah (17:9) describes the heart as "deceitful above all things and beyond cure. Who can understand it?" In the Gospel of Matthew, Jesus places the issue of spiritual defilement directly with the heart, the seat of human emotions: "For out of the heart come evil thoughts, murder, adultery, sexual immorality, theft, false testimony, slander" (15:19).

Building, then, from the concept of mind and heart as elaborated in Scripture we will reconsider the insights of the cultural, psychological, and social anthropologist as they apply to the "alienated minds" and the "rebellious hearts" of the natural man. We must move beyond the anthropological dimension to the theological dimension to understand the spiritual man. The characteristics of the "reconciled mind" and the "renewed heart" can only be understood from Scripture. In the discussion that follows I will attempt to show how the careful research of the anthropologist illuminates better for us the characteristics of the alienated mind and the rebellious heart. From these studies we are better able to discern how the word of God penetrates "to dividing soul and spirit, joints and marrow; it judges the thoughts and attitudes of the heart" (Heb. 4:12).

## The Rational Paradigm of Persons and Cultures

Over the past three decades cognitive anthropologists have gained significant insights into the operations of human cognition from the perspective of the rational paradigm (see fig. 2). The work of Noam Chomsky has provided seminal insights into the generative grammatical structure of sentences in human language. Levi-Strauss[24] has explored the everyday systems of classification and the principles of deep structure in human cognition. Berlin and Kay[25] have explored universal patterns of lexical development with particular reference to the basic color lexicon (four elementary colors), but also spawning a series of further investigations on patterns of folk botanical classification, kinship classification, and numerous other domains.

One of the most intriguing studies is that of Howard Gardner, educational psychologist of Harvard University, on the characteristics and attributes of human intelligences. Gardner[26] proposes seven distinctive frames of human intelligence that exist as organismic potentials in all members of the human species. These potentials are inherent in each person, yet vary genetically in terms of individual competence and potential for development. The particular competencies proposed by Gardner include linguistic, spatial, logical-mathematical, bodily kinesthetic, musical, interpersonal, and intrapersonal-for-self. Gardner argues that these competencies occur in genius forms and in idiot savants in human populations as well as in their normal forms of cognitive development. Musical and logical-mathematical genius are well known in Western culture, as are the idiot savant expressions of the same competencies. Gardner presents convincing evidence for the existence of these separate "computational or information processing systems" as characteristics of the human species. Gardner also suggests that different cultures emphasize differ-

24. See n. 15.
25. B. Berlin and P. Kay, *Basic Color Terms: Their Universality and Evolution* (Berkeley: University of California Press, 1969).
26. Howard Gardner, *Frames of Mind: The Theory of Multiple Intelligences* (New York: Basic Books, 1983).

ent competencies and structure developmental process to facilitate competency development to the maximum level possible in individual participants within the culture.

The cultural materialists like the cognitive anthropologists are searching for cultural universals. One of the most eloquent spokesman is Richard Adams[27] who argues that all human activity is ultimately reducible to action for the consumption of energy. Adams shows how human social organizations are structured to organize human production, consuming energy and consuming the products produced through it. Concepts of property, labor, and political power have at their roots the human organization of the consumption of energy. In a parallel vein, Marvin Harris[28] contends that the means of production and the ecological constraints on human life are deterministic of culture and social life. Harris argues that the sacred cow in India and the profane pig in the Islamic and Jewish world are products of the organization of production and ecological considerations in those productive systems. The mental structures of human life are epi-phenomenal to the material structures that are basic to human survival.

## Figure 2
### Rational Persons and Their Culture

|  | The natural/ rational person "Alienated minds" | The spiritual/ rational person "Reconciled minds" | Scripture |
|---|---|---|---|
| Universalism | Cognitive universals | Redeemed Cognition |  |
|  | Intelligences — Howard Gardner | Spiritual wisdom and understanding | Col. 1:9 |
|  | Processes-Berlin and Kay | Know the mystery of God, namely, Christ | Col. 2:2 |
|  | Structures — Levi-Strauss, Chomsky |  |  |
|  | Materialists Universals | Redeemed material life |  |
|  | Energy and structure — Adams | Wealth and property subject to Christ — Gonzales |  |
|  | Material and ecological forces — Harris | Labor and ecology subject to Christ | Col. 1:15–17 |

27. Richard N. Adams, *Energy and Structure: A Theory of Social Power* (Austin: University of Texas Press, 1975).

28. Marvin Harris, *The Nature of Cultural Things* (New York: Random House, 1964).

| Develop-mentalism | Stages of human development | Intellectual and spiritual development | |
|---|---|---|---|
| | Human reason — Piaget | Human will —obedience to God | Col. 1:23 |
| | Stages of moral development | Redemption of moral and spiritual character | |
| | Moral reasoning — Kohlberg | Transformed hearts and minds | Col. 3:1, 2, 5, 10, 12 |
| Relativism | Functionalism (need, choice) | Liberationism | |
| | Rational choice and decision making — Firth, Barth | Spiritual freedom, subjection to Christ | Rom. 14; 1 Cor. 10 |
| | Rationalism and cultural context | World view transformation | |
| | Rational interplay of culture and thought — Cole and Scribner | New canons of relevance — Hiebert | |
| | Ethno science — Goodenough Frake | Biblical transformation — Hiebert | |
| | Cultural systems of classification | Revelational systems of classification | |

The developmentalist perspectives on the rational man focus on human cognitive and moral development. Piaget[29] has been most influential in the study of child development, proposing that the intellectual capacities of a child grows through stages beginning with a concrete, context-bound thinking stage and culminating in abstract generalized thinking. Piaget proposes a process of self-construction through which the child learns to reflect, reason, and construct a body of abstract knowledge. By the time children reach adolescence, they are able to free themselves of the limitations of surface content (e.g., color, shape) and the spatial temporal appearances of objects, reasoning in reference to the abstract. Shweder[30] notes that intense investigation of Piaget's theory has led researchers to question his "operational stages" of reasoning and his assumptions regarding the limited reasoning capacity of young

29. See n. 12.
30. Shweder, "Anthropology's Romantic Rebellion," 50.

children. Shweder also observes that "the evidence suggests a strong tendency, even among adults, for human problem solving procedures to be local and content specific rather than abstract."[31]

Kohlberg[32] defines a similar "stage" process for moral development. Like Piaget, he assumes that some human beings acquire the highest level of rational reasoning processes and are therefore capable of making better moral judgments than those who have yet to achieve these intellectual skills. With regard to cross-cultural variation and moral thinking, Kohlberg attributes variation to the inadequate development of rational reasoning in some cultures.

The relativist conceptualization of the rational man picks up many of the themes that have been elaborated by the Universalist and the Developmentalist but place much greater emphasis on cultural diversity. One version is the functionalist theory, articulated by Malinowski, which states that human beings create cultural systems to meet their basic physiological, economic, social, and emotional needs. While these needs are universal, the cultural responses for satisfying them are multiple and diverse. Raymond Firth, one of the most famous students of Malinowski, elaborated the idea that choice and variation are endemic to cultural systems. Observing how every social structure has a dynamic dimension or organization that is in constant flux and change, Firth described human beings as rational decision makers who respond to their changing circumstances and world by making reasoned choices rather than following some rote formula of their culture. Frederick Barth (1966) has argued that cultural change becomes institutionalized as people's patterns of choice and decision making shift to a new consensus.

The rational decisions that people make, however, cannot be divorced from the cultural context in which they have been socialized and through which they relate to one another. Cole and Scribner[33] have demonstrated that tribal people have developed the logical skills relevant to their overall cultural system. People make reasoned decisions within the context of culturally defined parameters, processes, and choices. Each human group creates a rational adaptation to the demands of their own social and ecological environment. As a consequence, social and cultural systems are relative, yet based upon universally present rational capabilities.

Some cognitive anthropologists have spent considerable time deciphering and describing cultural systems of classification and analysis. Ward Goodenough's analysis[34] of Trukese kinship terms precipitated an extended pro-

31. Ibid., 51.

32. L. Kohlberg, *The Philosophy of Moral Development*, vol. 1 (New York: Harper and Row, 1981).

33. M. Cole and S. Scribner, *Culture and Thought: A Psychological Introduction* (New York: Wiley, 1974).

34. Ward Goodenough, "Componential Analysis and the Study of Meaning," *Language* 32 (1956): 195–216.

gram of research and discussion on the universal or relative "logical structural components" that comprise kinship categories around the world. Others began to apply the "componential" approach to other systems of classification. Charles Frake's diagnosis of disease among the Subanun of Mindinao is one of the most well known efforts of this kind.[35] D'Andrade[36] has applied the componental methodology to trait psychology, American beliefs about illness and other cultural constructions of reality. Studies in the genre describe the rational systems of classification and analysis that produce seemingly endless cultural elaboration and diversity.

## The Rational Paradigm in Biblical Perspective

As we reflect upon the insights of the universalist, developmentalist, and relativist perspectives of the rational paradigm, we must ask how a biblical world view might alter the analysis and interpretation of data by these scholars. Missing from the discussion of the cognitive attributes of persons is that of the spiritual dimension of human life (see fig. 2). None of these scholars consider spiritual competence nor spiritual intelligence as a significant dimension of the person. There is ample evidence in the ethnographic literature as well as in Scripture for a particular spiritual competence as well as the other competences described by Gardner. Every culture has its spiritually competent men and women who communicate with the spirit world and who are especially attuned to spiritual experience.

The wide spread occurrence of "spiritual genius" in world cultures is routinely dismissed or ignored by anthropologists. Scripture teaches that much of that spiritual competence is attuned to the forces of darkness; the power of the gospel serves to rescue people from that darkness into the kingdom of the Son (Col. 1:13). However, the reconciled mind is one that knows the mystery of God as expressed in the Lord Jesus Christ (Col. 2:2). Believers are granted a gift of spiritual wisdom and understanding (Col. 1:9) that sets them apart from others in the same culture, called to a life "worthy of the Lord" and pleasing to him in every way.

The work of Adams, Harris, and others on the subject of the material basis of culture is not only provocative, but illuminative of many of the driving forces at work in the "alienated mind" and the resulting cultures and societies created by them. Christians as well as non-Christians are participants in such materialist systems and subject to the same constraining pressures. The es-

35. C. O. Frake, "The Diagnosis of Disease Among the Subanun of Mindinao," *American Anthropologist* 63 (1961): 113–32.

36. R. G. D'Andrade, "Trait Psychology and Componential Analysis," *American Anthropologist* 67 (1965): 215–28; idem, "A Propositional Analysis of U.S. American Beliefs About Illness," in *Meaning and Anthropology*, ed. R. Basso and H. Selby (Albuquerque: University of New Mexico Press, 1976).

sence of the gospel is that believers are no longer subject to those constraints and deterministic forces. As Gonzales[37] has illustrated so well, fellowship in the early Christian community involved a significant redefinition of the values of wealth and property. *Koinonia* in the early Christian community meant much more than fellowship: it involved the sharing of goods for those who had need. The material aspects of the Christian life were subject to the authority of Christ. Wealth and property were not truly one's own to do with as one pleased (according to Roman law) but rather they belonged to Christ and the believer served as steward of the material resources given to him by God. While the anthropologist illuminates for us the driving material forces that have determining power on the "alienated minds" and the cultures of the nations, neither Adams nor Harris considers the possibility of the redeemed man nor of a restructured community of *koinonia* in subjection to the lordship of Jesus Christ. However, Adams and Harris are correct that the means of production and the ecological forces at work in the world are powerful and pervasive and the church must constantly be on guard to protect its *koinonia* from the conforming and unredeemed agendas of materialist systems.

As noted, there are some serious reservations about the accuracy of Piaget's analysis of stages of human development, and those same reservations are applicable to Kohlberg's analysis. However, more important than the scientific deficiencies of their argument is the complete exclusion of the spiritual dimension in the developmental process of human intellect and moral life. Social psychologists have excluded the component of "will" in their analysis of intellectual and moral development. Scripture refers frequently to a place of human will in spiritual and moral development. For example, Paul challenges the Philippians to "continue to work out your salvation with fear and trembling, for it is God who works in you to will and to act according to his good purpose" (Phil. 2:12–13). Again to the Colossians Paul reminds them that their reconciliation to Christ is contingent upon their continuing in faith. It is the action of the human will first to believe God and then to obey him that leads to salvation and subsequent moral and spiritual development. The important place for the will is spelled out in some detail in the third chapter of Colossians. Paul reminds these people that they have been buried with Christ and raised again to a new life. As a consequence, they are to set their hearts on things above, set their minds on things above, put to death their earthly nature, and clothe themselves with compassion, kindness, humility, gentleness and patience. Each of these action items are based upon spiritual will, enabled in the believer by the work of the Holy Spirit. The moral qualities described in Colossians 3 do not stem from the achievement of certain reasoning pro-

---

37. Justo L. Gonzales, *Faith and Wealth: A History of Early Christian Ideas on the Origin, Significance, and Use of Money* (San Fransico: Harper and Row, 1990).

cesses as described by Kohlberg, but rather in the act of faith and the will to obey God on these matters as set forth in his Word.

Following Gardner's discussion of human intelligences,[38] Christian maturity demands the exercise of our spiritual intellect as well as our logical/mathematical intellect. The spiritual intellect enables the believer to discern morally and spiritually—a power not generally attributed to logical/mathematical intellect. Paul defines maturity in Ephesians (4:13) as "attaining to the whole measure of the fullness of Christ." Other dimensions of spiritual maturity include standing firm in the will of God (Col. 4:12), training oneself to distinguish good from evil (Heb. 5:14), and developing perseverance of faith (James 1:4).

The anthropologists researching cultural systems of classification and analysis have contributed valuable and well documented studies that help us understand how the "alienated mind" serves to create a meaningful, helpful, and rational world for its participants. Once again, the denial of the spiritual man and the possibility of "reconciled minds" effectively eliminates the possibility of understanding what happens to human beings following conversion. In fact, after conversion people transform their systems of classification in response to new spiritual knowledge and power obtained through the Scriptures. Very soon after exposure to the Word of God, people begin to re-examine and re-think their systems of classification, particularly as they relate to critical issues of life such as illness, food, fertility, and social conflict. The power of the Holy Spirit leads to a restructuring of the forces of power in the natural and supernatural world for these people. The freedom that one obtains in Christ releases people from the regulations and prohibitions regarding food, illness, and other culturally defined strictures (Rom. 14; 1 Cor. 10). People are no longer subject to cultural systems to which they have been in fact in bondage, but rather they are now subject to Christ and called to a new spiritual and social life.

Paul Hiebert[39] describes this as a world view transformation; people reinterpret their lives and experience through the person of Christ and the perspective of the gospel, developing new canons of relevance and relationship. People reinterpret their world around a new hermeneutic, the person and work of the Lord Jesus Christ. As a consequence, their choices and decisions are no longer couched wholly in the context of their culture, but in reference to the eternal work of God and the redemptive work of Christ in their life. The rational person begins to interact through cultural eyes and concepts with

38. See n. 26.
39. Paul Hiebert, *Anthropological Insights for Missionaries* (Grand Rapids: Baker, 1985); idem, "The Missiological Implications of an Epistemological Shift," *Theological Students Fellowship Bulletin* (May-June 1985): 12–18.

the eternal and universal Word of God and, responding in obedience to this
Word, to act as an agent of transformation within community and culture.

## The Non-Rational Paradigm of Persons and Cultures

While it is dangerous to generalize about broad trends in anthropological
theory, the latter decade of the twentieth century has been dominated by
what Shweder calls the "romantic rebellion." These scholars (see fig. 3) have
rejected the human being as a rational person attempting to construct rational
solutions to a problematic world. Across the discipline scholars have discovered overwhelming evidence that in spite of human attempts to solve their
problems rationally, they are driven by social constraints and elaborated communication systems which shape both their public and private worlds. Douglas and Wildavsky[40] have argued eloquently that decisions made in America
with regard to environmental, nuclear, and other social risks are not predominantly the product of scientific reason, but rather the logical outcome of the
social environments in which the people debating these issues live and work.
On the issue of environmental risk, Douglas and Wildavsky show how Americans participate in the social environments of the bureaucracy, the marketplace, and, what they term, the border. Those in America who trust the bureaucracy and resonate with those values see government regulation and
government planning essential to the management of social risk. Those who
trust the market place argue for the long term effectiveness of open competi-
tion for the resolution of development and environmental issues. Many Americans, however, trust neither the bureaucracy nor the marketplace and constitute border social environments. Organizations such as the Sierra Club take a
stance against both the bureaucracy and the marketplace and their values are
shaped by their unified commitment on an agenda of environmental protection. Douglas and Wildavsky show how rationality within these contexts is relative to the agendas of trust and distrust. Decisions about social risk are non-
rational based upon the trust frames within which each of these interest
groups operate.

Douglas[41] goes further to argue that these social environment distinctions
are universal. Douglas proposes that the values of every social environment
are determined at least in part by factors of grid and group. *Grid* refers to the
degree to which social roles are elaborated or unelaborated within a social setting and individual behavior is highly structured by rules (as in a bureaucracy)
or relatively unstructured and autonomous (as in an open market or "swap

40. Mary Douglas and Aaron Wildavsky, *Risk and Culture: An Essay in the Selection of Technical and Environmental Dangers* (Berkeley: University of California Press, 1982).
41. Mary Douglas, *Cultural Bias,* Occasional Paper #35, Royal Anthropological Institute of
Great Britian and Ireland, London.

meet"). *Group* refers to the degree to which the value for the survival of group is weak or strong within a particular social environment. Weak grid and weak group produce the competitive marketplace of western societies while strong grid and strong group produce the bureaucratic social environment (such as Presbyterian or Episcopalian churches). The border social environments are either strong grid and weak group (such as university faculty organizations and multi-staff megachurches), or strong group and weak grid (such as the Amish and the Plymouth Brethren). Social groups such as Sierra Club and other more extreme environmental activist groups place very high value on group unity and emphasize very weak grid relationships.

The non-rational paradigm is also expressed in developmental research. Ochs and Schieffelin[42] argue that the socialization of children is contextual and varies significantly from one culture to the next. Examining the process of acquiring language, they demonstrate how white middle class children, Kaluli children, and Samoan children are socialized in very different ways by older members of their society, yet all become competent speakers of their languages. Each of these societies orchestrates the ways in which children participate and learn the form and function of language. The process of language acquisition is part of the larger process of gaining social competence. The essence of their argument is that the development of the child is framed within a very particularistic context and that linguistic knowledge is integrated with socio-cultural knowledge and generative (producing a restricted range of responses) in the same way as grammar is generative. Their research supports in a developmental perspective the arguments of the symbolist, namely, that cultural frames are relative and distinctive to each and every cultural system. The work of Howard Gardner[43] on comparative studies of education offers a similar conclusion in reference to the development of the seven intellectual competencies described earlier. Gardner argues that each cultural system is selective in identifying particular competencies for elaboration and development. While all human beings have common intellectual potential, the nature of contextual socialization raises some competencies to much higher levels than others. One of his most compelling illustrations is that of the Suzuki method of teaching musical competency in Japan and America.

The relativist expression of the non-rational paradigm has the broadest following in contemporary anthropological thought. Shweder[44] notes that "the most significant romantic development to emerge within cognitive anthropology during the past twenty years is perhaps the definition of culture as ar-

42. Elinor Ochs and Bambi B. Schieffelin, "Language Acquisition and Socialization: Three Developmental Stories and Their Implications," in *Culture Theory: Essays on Mind, Self, and Emotion*, ed. Richard A. Schweder and Robert A. LeVine (Cambridge: Cambridge University Press, 1984), 276–322.

43. See n. 26.

44. Shweder, "Anthropology's Romantic Rebellion," 45.

bitrary code." Led by Clifford Geertz,[45] David Schneider,[46] and Victor Turner,[47] scholars have focused on cultural definitions, social discourse, ritual elaboration, and the construction of symbol systems to describe these non-rational constructions of reality.

### Figure 3
### Non-Rational Persons and Cultural Systems

| | Natural, non-rational man | Spiritual, non-rational man | Scripture |
|---|---|---|---|
| | "Alienated mind" | "Reconciled mind" | |
| **Universalism** | Deterministic Social Environments | The Kingdom of the Son | Col. 1:13 |
| | Grid/group — Douglas | Kingdom values | |
| | Unconscious socially determined decisions | Transformed social relations | |
| **Develop-mentalism** | Contextual socialization | Scripture socialization | John 6:45 |
| | Particularistic development—Ochs, Scheffelin | Biblical context for development | 2 Tim. 2:15–17 |
| | Culturally defined | Culturally defined competencies | |
| | Competencies—Gardner | Kingdom agendas | |
| **Relativism** | Elaborated symbol systems | Transformed symbol systems | |
| | Cultural frames—Geertz, Schneider | Refocused cultural frames | Eph. 4:17; Col. 2:16 |
| | Normative cultural relativism | Kingdom norms, pluralists context | Col. 2:18; 1 Cor. 10:31–33 |
| | Particularist determinism | Free from the law of sin and death | Titus 1:15; Col. 2:20–23 |

45. Clifford Geertz, "From the Native's Point of View: On the Nature of Anthropological Understanding," in *Culture Theory: Essays on Mind, Self, and Emotion,* ed. Richard A. Shweder and Robert A. LeVine (Cambridge: Cambridge University Press, 1984), 123–36.

46. See n. 10.

47. Victor Turner, *The Forest of Symbols* (Ithaca, N. Y.: Cornell University Press, 1967).

The work of Clifford Geertz, researching the concept of person in Java, Bali, and Morocco, is exemplary of this tradition. Geertz argues that the Western conception of person "as a bounded, unique, more or less integrated motivational and cognitive universe . . . is, however incorrigible it may seem to us, a rather peculiar idea within the context of the world's cultures."[48] He first describes how the Javanese sense of person is arranged into "two sets of contrasts, at base religious, one between 'inside' and 'outside' [belonging or not belonging, Muslim or non-Muslim] and one between 'refined' and 'vulgar.'"[49] The Balinese, in contrast, engage in a "systematic attempt to stylize all aspects of personal expression to the point where anything idiosyncratic, anything characteristic of the individual merely because he is who he is physically, psychologically, or biologically, is muted in favor of his assigned place in the continuing and, so it is thought, never changing pageant that is Balinese life."[50] The Balinese person is "dramatis personae not actors,"[51] for the Balinese all the world is indeed a stage and the players perish, but the play does not. The Moroccan pattern offers again a third perspective of looking at persons. Geertz suggests that Moroccans define persons "as though they were outlines waiting to be filled in."[52] This outline marks a public identity in tribal, territorial, linguistic, religious, and familial terms—a framework enabling people to negotiate the content of interpersonal relationships in each of the social contexts in which they engage in practical relations.

Geertz and other symbolic anthropologists embrace what Shweder calls a "normative cultural relativism." According to this position there are no transcultural standards or values by which particular cultures can be evaluated. Further, they argue that the cultural patterns elaborated in each of these symbol systems define how people think, feel, and live out their particular lives. Some, such as Rosaldo,[53] claim that the culture dictates how people think and feel even in their subconscious minds.

## The Non-Rational Paradigm in Biblical Perspective

The conclusions of the symbolists are in fact consistent with some of the claims that Paul makes with regard to the thinking of the Gentiles. For example, the apostle insists that the Ephesians distance themselves from the Gentile mode of life and the futility of Gentile thinking (Eph. 4:17). He describes a

48. Geertz, "From the Native's Point of View," 126.
49. Ibid.
50. Ibid., 128.
51. Ibid.
52. Ibid.
53. Michelle Z. Rosaldo, "Toward an Anthropology of Self and Feeling," in *Culture Theory: Essays on Mind, Self and Emotion*, ed. Richard A. Shweder and Robert A. LeVine (Cambridge: Cambridge University Press, 1984), 137–57.

cultural elaboration common in the Gentile world among the Colossians, and attributes it to an unspiritual mind that "puffs him up with idle notions" (Col. 2:18). The perspective of the symbolist—people creating arbitrary frames that have normative and determining effects on their social and cultural lives— seems consistent with the notion of alienated mind and corrupt conscience as described in Scripture.

What is utterly neglected in the non-rational paradigm is the notion of the spiritual man and the "reconciled mind." While I endorse wholeheartedly Douglas's notions of grid and group and the deterministic social elaboration arising out of those particular social arrangements, she fails to understand how the believer has been rescued from the dominion of darkness and brought "into the kingdom of the Son he loves, in whom we have redemption, the forgiveness of sins" (Col. 1:13, 14). I interpret being rescued from the dominion of darkness as being liberated from the bondage of deterministic social and symbol systems that are part of the non-rational man. The believer is a new creation (2 Cor. 5:17) empowered by the Spirit to embrace and follow kingdom values proclaimed by the Lord Jesus Christ in the Gospels and to live transformed social lives as outlined for us in the Epistles.[54]

Christian parents, regardless of their cultural setting, embrace in common the Old and New Testaments as the standard for faith and practice, and their children undergo not only the contextual socialization common to their cultural tradition, but also a scriptural socialization that teaches them to live according to kingdom values within their local cultures. The work of the Holy Spirit in human development (John 6:45) is utterly ignored by secular developmental scholars and sometimes even by Christian developmental scholars. Scripture declares without question that all human beings have not only the seven competencies proposed by Gardner, but also a potential spiritual competence which is engaged by the human will and by a faith response to the Word of God. The spiritual man is no different from the natural man in the fact that it is necessary for him to develop cultural competencies; however, with the reconciled mind the agendas of the spiritual man are no longer cultural agendas but kingdom agendas (2 Tim. 3:14–17).

The evidence for highly diverse, elaborated symbol systems in the cultures of our world is incontrovertible. However, people who become Christians within any of these particular cultural contexts experience spiritual liberation, and, when discipled in the Word of God, undergo significant transformation of their symbol and social systems. The cultural frames, which (the symbolic anthropologist argues) arbitrarily determine the course of social and cultural life, are re-focused by the gospel. The believer is set free from the non-rational customary practices of the society, such as table manners and dress codes, or

---

54. Sherwood G. Lingenfelter, *Transforming Culture: A Challenge for Christian Mission* (Grand Rapids: Baker, 1992).

child training practices. These things, which Shweder calls symbolic expressions of non-rational choices, are irrelevant to the believer (Col. 2:16). Rather, the believer is called to focus his eating and drinking for the glory of God; he or she is free to pursue kingdom values in the pluralist context of any and every culture (2 Cor. 10:31–33). The believer is freed from the bondage of the particularistic symbolic and social system in which he or she was converted (Col. 2:20–23).

In sum, the reconciled mind, while still alive and subject to the non-rational social and cultural world, is empowered by the Spirit of God and by the Word of God for kingdom living. While the unique expressions of the church that grow out of this transformation may show the continuation of aspects of the non-rational paradigm, being rescued from the dominion of darkness assures the believer of special access to revelational truth, available primarily through faith and obedience rather than the power of rational discourse.

## The Irrational Paradigm of Persons and Culture

The third major paradigm in anthropological thought is that of the irrational mind shaping the person and the culture (see fig. 4). The conception of the irrational focuses on two distinctive dimensions: first, a degraded intellectual performance and secondly, thought driven by emotional need. Some anthropologists argue that human beings are naturally prone to faulty reason, false belief, and irrational practices. They argue that most people have a primitive mentality most of the time. Their data gathering strategies are deficient, their deductive reasoning skills are inferior and they have faulty inductive inference procedures.[55]

### Figure 4
#### Irrational Paradigm of the Person

|  | Natural man "Rebellious heart" | Spiritual man "Renewed heart" | Scripture |
|---|---|---|---|
| Universalism | Degraded intellectual performance | Heart to know God | Jer. 24:7 |
|  | Faulty reason, false belief, irrational practice | Noble heart receives the word | Luke 8:11–15 |
|  | Obsessional and magical thought | Heart of flesh | Ezek. 11:19 |
|  | Spiro, Freud, Tversky | Fruit of the Spirit | Gal. 5–6 |

55. R. Nisbett and L. Ross, *Human Inference: Strategies of Shortcomings of Social Judgments* (Inglewood Cliffs, N. J.: Prentice-Hall, 1980); A. Tversky and D. Kahnemann, "Judgment Under Uncertainty: Heuristics and Biases," *Science* 185 (1974): 1124–31.

| Develop-mentalism | Primitive vs. Scientific mind | End not science, but to know God | |
|---|---|---|---|
| | Deficient cultures — Tyler, Frazer | Intuitive understanding of truth (faith, hope, love) | |
| | Primitive—intuitive vs. Modern—rational | Maturity is spiritual intuitive | Eph. 4:13; Col. 4:12 |
| Relativism | Irrational processes | Intuitive expression of spiritual truth | |
| | Differing concepts of persons—Gorer, Whiting | Pluralistic world and expressions of the church | |
| | Elaborated personal character | "A new self" in the image of the creator | Col. 3:9–10 |

A second perspective on the irrational mind is provided by Melfred Spiro.[56] Spiro argues that some cultural propositions are emotionally motivated and emotionally driven. As such they become obsessional and "magical" ideas and practices. Usually such ideas are driven by unconscious emotional thought or need. These thoughts usually are constructed as defenses against painful emotions which produce great anxiety in the person. Spiro attributes accusations of witchcraft, such as that which surfaced in Salem in New England in the seventeenth century as obsessive, irrational cultural propositions to which the public gives assent. Spiro concludes that all cultures are driven in some degree by irrational, emotional motivations which enter into public discourse and become part of accepted cultural propositions, such that they even explain what other scholars argue are non-rational cultural frames.

The classical expression of the irrational mind was phrased by Tyler and Frazer in developmental terms. Contrasting primitive thought with the scientific interest of Europe, Tyler and Frazer concluded that these deficient cultures had failed to develop the scientific reasoning skills essential for civilized society. Horton[57] picks up this same theme in his recent work on traditional African thought systems. Horton contrasts the African reliance on intuitive

56. Melfred E. Spiro, "Some Reflections on Cultural Determinism and Relativism With Special Reference to Emotion and Reason," in *Culture Theory: Essays on Mind, Self, and Emotion*, ed. Richard A. Shweder and Robert A. LeVine (Cambridge: Cambridge University Press, 1984), 323–46.

57. R. Horton, "African Traditional Thought and Western Science," *Africa* 37 (1967): 159–87.

and emotional concerns with the data gathering strategies of the scientific method and formal logic. The intuitive bent of African thinkers is seen as irrational, creating deficient science and inaccurate information.

The culture and personality studies of Benedict, Gorer, and Whiting and Child explain the elaboration of personal character and the diversity of cultural systems on the basis of human responses to deep emotional needs, and intuitive thinking and response to those needs. Relativists in their orientation, these scholars support the proposition that cultural diversity is as much a product of the irrational processes of emotion and intuition as they are of non-rational self-construction and communication.

## The Irrational Paradigm in Biblical Perspective

The biblical concept that connects most directly to the irrational paradigm is that of the "heart." Scripture depicts two kinds of hearts, the rebellious heart and the renewed heart. As we have discussed earlier, the rebellious heart is madness, full of evil, deceitful, and beyond human understanding. Scripture resonates solidly with Spiro's conclusion that obsessional and magical thought are driven by emotional need stemming out of heart desires and motives. This is not to say that people do not have capacity for rational thought (i.e., the rational paradigm), but rather that the power of human desire is so great that people are often blinded by their desire, and even when not blinded, often set aside reason in lieu of desire.

The place of the intuitive and emotional for all of these anthropological thinkers plays either a neutral role producing elaborated cultural differences, or a detrimental role inhibiting cultural development or producing obsessional and magical beliefs and practices. All of them fail to see the redemptive power of the work of Christ and the transformation that occurs when the heart is redeemed and renewed. In both the Old and the New Testament, the Word of God describes a transformed heart as a crucial dimension of salvation. When Ezekiel speaks of the promised return of Israel, they are not only restored to the land, but promised the gift of "an undivided heart and . . . a new spirit" (Ezek. 36:26). In writing to the Galatians Paul speaks of the flesh in contrast to the Spirit which comes from God. Among the works of the flesh are the obsessional behaviors described by Spiro: sexual immorality, idolatry, witchcraft, rage, drunkenness, orgies, and the like. The fruit of the Spirit in contrast is "love, joy, peace, patience, kindness, goodness, faithfulness, gentleness, and self-control" (Gal. 5:19–23). The renewed heart and the new spirit, which transform the life of the believer, directly address the obsessional magical thought and faulty belief and practices of the nations and peoples.

At the same time the Bible does not teach that rational reason is the outcome of faith in Jesus Christ. The end of the Christian faith is not science, but rather to know God. The knowledge of God does not come from reason

alone, but also from an intuitive, heart understanding of the truth. Paul declares this most eloquently in 1 Corinthians 13, where he concludes, "and
now these three remain, faith, hope, and love. But the greatest of these is
love." Faith, hope, and love are dimensions of intuitive rather than rational
reason. The believer must come to an intuitive understanding of the truth and
accept Scripture by faith if he is to come into a knowledge of God.

Maturing personally and maturing culturally involves for believers the renewed heart and the spiritual intellect. Jesus sums it up in the Gospel of Matthew calling disciples to "take my yoke upon you and learn from me, for I am
gentle and humble in heart, and you will find rest for your souls" (Matt.
11:29).

The perspective of the relativist within the irrational paradigm—cultural
diversity arises out of irrational processes—must also be taken into consideration by the believer. We remain in the fallen world and believers respond to
the gospel within the context of their personal, emotional, and cultural needs.
Obsessional beliefs and practices persist and impose themselves into the life of
the church and the believer. An intuitive, heart response to spiritual truth will
result in pluralistic expressions within the life and the body of the church. The
key truth of the gospel is that once we become followers of Christ we obtain
a "new self" in the image of the Creator (Col. 3:9–10). With this new self the
common social and cultural distinctions that divide us and that perpetuate the
pluralistic world become secondary. This is not to say that they will go away,
because even as Paul wrote these words there were indeed Jews and Greeks,
barbarians and Scythians, and slave and free. The pluralist world continued
long after Paul and continues even today. The essence of his message then is
not that pluralism will disappear, but rather that pluralistic distinctions fade in
light of the new self created in the image of the Creator. When people become
one in Christ they respond first to him and then to one another across cultures
in unique and distinctive ways. The community of the church, the unity of the
body of Christ, transcends the temporal and social divisions of the unredeemed world.

## Summary and Conclusion

The approaches of anthropologists have been presented in terms of rational, non-rational, and irrational paradigms of mind and culture. In each of
these paradigms anthropologists have adopted universalist, developmental, or
relativist perspectives on the nature of the person and cultural systems.
Throughout the chapter I have argued that the anthropological insights are
of significant value, but are limited primarily to understanding the natural
man. We understand the natural man from a biblical perspective as "alienated
mind" and "rebellious heart." At this point it is helpful to take stock of the
picture that has developed of the human person through the multiple per-

spectives of these theories and the theological perspectives derived from Scripture.

The first and most important conclusion is that there are indeed universals in the human experience, and that these universals may be described through empirical research and divine revelation. From our discussion, we have identified two major factors that dominate the life of persons: the human mind, with its multiple intelligences and rational and non-rational expressions of thought, and the human heart, with its wide range of desires, will, and emotional responses that constitute the intuitive and irrational in human life and experience. Human communication, social life and cultural expression, interpersonal relations and spiritual responses grow out of the complex interactions between the mind and the heart in what we call a "person."

The complexity of the human mind with its multiple intelligences is essential to understanding the nature of human thought. The logical-mathematical intelligence is only one of the seven or more competencies biologically present in persons, existing in complementary relationship to linguistic, spatial, bodily kinesthetic, musical, interpersonal, and intrapersonal-for-self competencies. All human beings recognize the law of non-contradiction as a part of their logical-mathematical competence. However, the other competences interplay with the logical-mathematical, so that contradiction is not only endemic in human thought, but essential to human life. Human beings engage in rational and non-rational activity as a functional outcome of their multiple competencies and the complex relationships that they have with others. Only a small minority of human beings have logical-mathematical skills developed to such a high level that it dominates their personalities.

Beyond the multiple competencies of the mind, the powerful force of emotion and will in human beings exerts significant force in human thought, social and cultural expressions, and behavior. The evidence presented here suggests that the normal state of the person is "chaotic" in the sense that it encompasses contradictions arising from the powerful opposing forces of mind and heart. Human beings are at one moment rational, and at another non-rational, and in a third moment irrational in terms of their responses to social, cultural, and spiritual stimuli.

With regard to the developmental processes that characterize the person, it is now clear that the development of logical reasoning is only one aspect of human intellectual skills, and there is much more to be learned about the development of other mental competencies. Further, secular and Christian scholars have ignored the effect of conversion on the development of natural as well as spiritual competencies. I believe that the radical transformation that conversion has on "emotion and will" must have a significant effect on the development of mental competencies. It is impossible to separate the irrational intuitive forces of emotion/will from the exercise and development of mental competencies. The mind and the heart—the intelligences and the emotion/will—of the person respond in continuous dialectic interplay like the alternating current in our electrical power systems. Transformation of the heart through the conversion of the believer and the entrance of the Holy Spirit must exact a positive force on the development of mental competencies. To my knowledge no one has done significant research on this subject.

Finally, it is also clear that relativism does indeed adequately express much of what we find in the creative development of cultures and societies. Values and beliefs are indeed constrained and shaped by forces of social environment and economic life. Systems of different types are generally effective for meeting basic biological and social human needs. However, all are prisons of disobedience, to which God has given over human beings so that he might have mercy on them all (Rom. 11:32).

The kingdom of God is anti-structural to the kingdoms of darkness. The kingdom principles of Scripture overturn the material, social, and spiritual logic of human life. The kingdoms of darkness are driven by the programs of Satan, whereas the kingdom of the Son is driven by the program of God. Using the analogy of the computer, the hardware and operating systems are the same for the kingdoms of darkness and the kingdom of the Son. The key distinction of the two originates in the program and the programmer. Satan's programs for the kingdoms of darkness permeate persons and cultures and turn them to his agendas of destruction. God's person and program brings salvation to the individual and the transforming power of his Spirit and his grace into the community and the culture.

The chapter has argued that anthropologists miss a fundamental dimension of the human person and cultural expression when they reject the conceptualization of the "reconciled mind and the renewed heart." Through reconciled minds and renewed hearts humans are released from the prisons of their cultures and transformed in heart and spirit for new relationships within their culture and in the broader context in the universal church of Jesus Christ.

## Suggested Readings

Cole, M., and S. Scribner. *Culture and Thought: A Psychological Introduction*. New York: Wiley, 1974. [I]

Gardner, Howard. *Frames of Mind: The Theory of Multiple Intelligences*. New York: Basic Books, 1983. [A]

Gonzales, Justo L. *Faith and Wealth: A History of Early Christian Ideas on the Origin, Significance, and Use of Money*. San Francisco: Harper and Row, 1990. [I]

Heibert, Paul. *Anthropological Insights for Missionaries*. Grand Rapids: Baker, 1985. [B]

_____. "The Missiological Implications of an Epistemological Shift." *Theological Students Fellowship Bulletin* (May–June 1985), 12–18. [B]

Lingenfelter, Sherwood. *Transforming Culture.* Grand Rapids: Baker, 1992. [B]

Shweder, Richard A. "Anthropology's Romantic Rebellion Against the Enlightenment Or There is More To Thinking Than Reason and Evidence." In *Culture Theory: Essays on Mind, Self, and Emotion.* Edited by Richard A. Shweder and Robert A. LeVine. Cambridge: Cambridge University Press, 1984. [A]

# A Response to Sherwood G. Lingenfelter

## David M. Ciocchi

Sherwood Lingenfelter's chapter is a fine example of the integration of faith and learning. It combines the author's competence in his own academic discipline, anthropology, with his reflections about the implications of biblical teaching for assessing the conclusions of anthropological research. In his chapter Lingenfelter accomplishes his goal of showing how theological and socio-cultural anthropology can complement one another, thereby giving us a more complete understanding of what it is to be human. I find myself in complete or nearly complete agreement with what Lingenfelter has to say, so my response to his chapter will consist of reflections aimed at supporting or enlarging upon some of his points. I will write from the perspective of my own discipline, philosophy, using the "linguistic" and "logical-mathematical" types of intelligence which have for so long had pride of place in the academic culture of the university. My response will not make any significant use of the other types of intelligence Lingenfelter mentions, but it should be of some use nonetheless.

In his celebrated essay *On Liberty,* English philosopher John Stuart Mill developed a utilitarian argument in favor of unrestricted liberty of thought and discussion. His central contention was that we can only discover and appreciate truth in a social setting that encourages a frank, critical review of the arguments for and against every possible position. In some fields, such as politics, no party is likely to have a corner on the truth; instead, each party will have a part of the truth and will need to have its truths recognized and its errors exposed by members of the other parties. Although Lingenfelter is not writing about political philosophy, he does take a position fully consistent with Mill's warning about the possibility of competing positions each containing a part of the truth. After reviewing the major theoretical positions taken by anthropologists, he writes that "each perspective contributes a valuable picture of the human experience of the natural man, yet each has its flaws of viewpoint and omission." It seems clear enough that Lingenfelter implicitly accepts Mill's claim that the fullest possible approach to the truth requires looking for aspects of the truth wherever they may be found. No single anthropological theory can give us all there is to know about human beings.

Not only can no single anthropological theory tell the whole human story, Lingenfelter also argues that *all* the standard theories leave out part of that story by ignoring the spiritual dimension of what it is to be human. He says that anthropologists are guilty of "the major fallacy of pervasive exclusive naturalism" and that they must reject "the scientific propensity to reduce everything to the physical and to the natural." The results of this pervasive naturalism are rather grim, including such things as (1) scholars overlooking the existence of a spiritual competence even though the ethnographic literature gives plenty of evidence for it, and (2) a professional inability of anthropologists to understand what happens to human beings following conversion.

One way of addressing this myopic naturalism of anthropologists is implied by Lingenfelter's talk about the "alienated minds" and "rebellious hearts" of unbelievers. Presumably, many anthropologists are non-Christians who simply do not want to see and believe certain things. If they were to experience conversion, they would undergo a world view transformation that would likely have a profound impact upon the way they do their professional work. Scholars with "reconciled minds" and "renewed hearts" are less likely than their unbelieving colleagues to neglect the spiritual dimension of man. A clear implication of this is that the discipline of anthropology could be improved if more anthropologists were converted to faith in Christ, strange as that may sound to those accustomed to the dominance of scientistic naturalism in the academic world. Lingenfelter probably believes this himself, and he certainly believes that faith in Christ allows us to see the "spiritual man" that so many anthropologists miss due to their philosophical love affair with the "natural man."

Another way of addressing the naturalism of anthropologists is by taking a philosophical approach to their basic beliefs. In a broadly philosophical sense, *naturalism* designates the belief that "nature"—that is, the universe—is the sum total of reality. Everything that exists or could exist is *natural,* that is, is an aspect or part of the natural order. Given the prestige of science, the "natural" is usually taken as synonymous with the "physical," that is, with that which is at least in principle accessible to scientific investigation. This philosophical naturalism by definition rejects the *supernatural,* for there can be nothing which is not itself natural. There can be no God in the biblical sense, hence no Holy Spirit to effect the changes we observe in people who undergo conversion to Christ. If there is a "spiritual" dimension to man, for a naturalist that dimension *must* be understood in natural terms, it *must* be something that does or in principle could reveal its secrets to diligent scientists. When anthropologists who embrace philosophical naturalism overlook the "spiritual man," they are simply being consistent with their basic beliefs about the nature of reality. We need not only more Christian anthropologists—we need more good philosophical arguments against naturalism and in favor of biblical theism. A better supply of such arguments could help prepare anthropologists (among others) to believe in Jesus Christ.

Along with claiming that naturalistic anthropologists neglect man's spiritual dimension, Lingenfelter charges social psychologists with excluding the component of "will" in their accounts of human moral and intellectual development. He tells us that the moral qualities listed in Colossians 3 are not the result of achieving one of Kohlberg's stages of moral reasoning, but rather they result from the act of faith and the will to obey God. He believes that the moral, intellectual, and spiritual development of human beings is dependent ultimately on their willingness to open themselves to such development by submitting in faith to God.

It may be that social psychologists who exclude the notion of "will" from their theories are, like naturalistic anthropologists, simply being consistent with their basic beliefs about the nature of reality. That is, they may not believe that there *is* any such thing as "will," and they may believe instead that various determining factors such as cultural and economic conditions account fully for the moral and intellectual development of human beings. In fact, I do not believe that there is any other way to make sense of their exclusion of will from their theoretical vocabulary. There are deep *philosophical* differences between these thinkers and Christians such as Lingenfelter who take biblical revelation seriously.

Believers in biblical revelation generally regard each human being as a free agent who has the freedom to "will" or "choose" in such a way as to be a legitimate subject of moral praise and blame for the life he lives, including his history of moral, intellectual, and spiritual development. In other words, Christians have a very strong sense of human *moral responsibility,* and are apt to be suspicious of theories which suggest that human beings are *no more than* the products of their social and economic environments. Lingenfelter's concerns about social psychology fall squarely into this category of biblically informed thought.

# A Response to Sherwood G. Lingenfelter

*Walt Russell*

I highly commend Lingenfelter for the very lucid and helpful path that he has cleared for us as we make our way through the maze of diverse anthropological viewpoints and perspectives. As an outsider to the field of anthropology, you may feel as bewildered as I do when you try to understand some of the amazing tangle of competing anthropological paradigms. Lingenfelter's chapter will at least help you understand that bewilderment may be the most appropriate response within such a complexity of perspectives! I commend him for orienting us non-anthropologists.

Additionally, I commend Lingenfelter for the comfort that he gives to those of us within the field of biblical studies who have been fearful—either rationally, non-rationally, or irrationally!—of the relativism of many anthropologists. His commitment to the absolutes of the Scriptures combined with his appreciation of the genuine aspects of relativism within cultures are heartwarming indeed. His integrative perspective and his submission to the authority of God's Word are exemplary to all who desire to do Christian integration within their fields. Moreover, his personal and methodological commitments to historic Christian orthodoxy free us to enjoy the many wonderful insights that anthropology can give us into persons within cultures. His work is especially timely with the recent influx into biblical studies of integrative works combining exegetical and anthropological insights.

As a respectful and appreciative outsider to anthropology, I have been helped in my orientation to this field of study by a chart in Bruce J. Malina's very stimulating book, *The New Testament World: Insights from Cultural Anthropology* (Atlanta: John Knox, 1981), p. 8. In this chart Malina lays out the various perspectives that we can have in viewing persons. All people are 100 percent the same in *nature*—the area of the "objective," of physical "sensations"; 50 percent the same, 50 percent different in *culture*—the area of the "social," of group-sharing "conceptions"; 100 percent different in *person*—the area of the "subjective," of unique, "perceptions." "From this point of view, human beings are individualized or personalized representatives of human nature immersed in particular cultures. It also means that all human knowing is simultaneously *objective, subjective,* and *social.*"

While the perspective of people's nature is viewed as the domain of the sciences, it is also the domain of theology and philosophy. All three of these disciplines offer insights into various aspects of "our nature" as human beings. This would also encompass the dimension of persons Lingenfelter calls "the deep structure"—cognitive and emotional structures held in common by all human beings. Those working within the fields of science, theology, and philosophy must allow for the complementary insights from those working from the social and personal perspectives. Secondly, the perspective of people's culture is the domain of the social sciences like anthropology and sociology. Lingenfelter also refers to this dimension as "the surface structure." Notice that one must be careful in extrapolating beyond the perspective of the *social* dimension of persons (their surface structure) to the perspective of their *nature* (their deep structure). Such an extrapolation may exceed the boundaries of the social perspective. Lastly, the realm or perspective of people as individual persons is the domain of fields like psychology. Since this perspective of persons emphasizes the uniquenesses and differences of individual personhood, one must also be sensitive to how the social dimension influences these individuals and cautious about too much extrapolating beyond this perspective to the nature of all human beings.

In interacting with specific points within Lingenfelter's chapter as a New Testament person, I will restrict myself to two brief points of a supplementary nature. First, in one of his earlier sections entitled "Some Relevant Biblical Concepts," he speaks of Paul's theology of the "natural mind." Essentially, this terminology designates the faculty that produces human conceptualizations and interpretations of life and reality as exercised by those alienated from God. In Romans 1:18–32 Paul gives us a cosmic view of how the Gentile cultures of the world move from alienated or pagan thinking about God to alienated and darkly pagan cultural patterns. These Gentile patterns are contrasted by Paul with the unique Jewish alienation in Romans 2:1–3:8. In particular, the Gentile peoples of the world (broadly considered as one entity) are "pagan" because they choose to suppress the truth revealed about God through the created world and through their consciences (1:18–20). This suppression begins a downward spiral of "exchanges" that result in "giving overs" by God: *idolatrous exchange* (1:21–23) leads to the *giving over to religious or cultic im-*

*morality* (1:24–25) which leads to the giving over to the *homosexual exchange for heterosexual sexuality* (1:26–27) which results in not acknowledging God and the *giving over to pervasive immorality in every area of life* (1:28–32). Paul speaks of this downward spiral of Gentile thinking and cultural patterns in a similar fashion in Ephesians 4:17–24. As Lingenfelter points out, anthropology gives us significant insight into these cultural patterns of those who are alienated from the life of God.

Secondly, Lingenfelter speaks of the "world view transformation" that should take place when we Christians realize that we have been delivered from the spiritual and social bondage of our depraved cultural systems. As those so delivered, we Christians should be the most flexible of human beings culturally because we now interpret the world no longer wholly within the context of our own culture. Rather, we now interpret the world in reference to the eternal work of God and according to his redemptive-historical plan centered in the Lord Jesus Christ. This perspective frees us to be appropriately relativistic (i.e., flexible) regarding non-rational customary practices of whatever society we are within in order to do loving deeds that preserve the unity among Christians (e.g., 1 Cor. 8, 10; Rom. 14:1–15:13). In addition, we are freed to do expedient acts that will help win non-Christians within any cultural group (1 Cor. 9:19–23; 10:23–33). However, doing these loving and expedient deeds is predicated upon a healthy critique of one's own culture according to the transcultural standards of God's Word. Such a critique has been particularly difficult for us Western Christians because of our long-standing numerical superiority within Christianity. We have wrongly assumed that *our* cultural patterns were equivalent to the *biblical* patterns. We must seek to understand better the alienated elements of our pervasively individualistic and existential world view in light of the redemptive-historical world view revealed in the Scriptures.

# 5

# On Being Human

## A Psychoanalytic Perspective

### Nancy S. Duvall

The question of whether psychology in general, and the psychoanalytic perspective in particular, should be viewed as (1) an enemy of the Christian faith, (2) a practical complement to one's faith, or (3) a truly integrative discipline that interfaces with Christianity is a significant question for serious Christians. This issue is particularly pertinent in the light of Freud's well known anti-religious attitudes. As the founder of the psychoanalytic movement, did he set a tone that indicates Christianity and psychoanalytic thinking are inherently antagonistic? This chapter will explore the psychoanalytic perspective, looking at some of Freud's concepts, Freud's attitude toward religion, the historical developments since Freud, and psychoanalytic revisions, and then address the issue of the interface of psychoanalytic thinking and Christianity.

## Freudian Concepts

Though Freud wrote voluminously and changed some of his theory as his thinking evolved, certain concepts were foundational. His emphasis on the unconscious and related defenses profoundly affected the psychological world. We now recognize that his awareness of the unconscious was not completely original—others had recognized it before him—but Freud emphasized the unconscious to a degree that made it impossible to ignore. In discussing the unconscious, he described a number of ways by which individuals avoid feelings, thoughts, and motives that would be painful. A major defense is repression, which Freud ultimately came to describe as being involved in all defenses. Repression is the process of keeping out of awareness ideational content, feelings, and motives that would cause pain if acknowledged. Another major defense is projection, whereby we attribute to others ideas, feelings, and motives that we would rather not acknowledge in ourselves. In projection we experience those mental contents as if they were in others, rather than in ourselves. For example, I am not jealous of John, he is jealous of me. These Freudian ideas and descriptions of how individuals function are not so radical now, but in Freud's culture where duty, rationality, and responsibility were emphasized, they were not popular. The question is, Are they accurate descriptions of how people function and how they handle pain?

Scripture not only asserts that the heart is deceitful and wicked (Jer. 17:9), but strongly affirms that we can not know all of ourselves without God and others. Furthermore, the Bible gives wonderful examples of repression and projection. Freud could not have asked for better examples than David and Saul. David had so powerfully repressed his adultery with Bathsheba and his complicity in Uriah's death that when Nathan came before King David and told his parable of how the rich man was unwilling to take from his own flock and therefore he took from the poor man, David's anger became heated. He was indignant at the treatment of the poor man whose ewe was taken from him, but did not recognize the similarity with his own sin until Nathan spoke his pointed words: "You are the man." (2 Sam. 12:1–12). In that moment Nathan brought David's unconscious guilt to light, and David later repented as recorded in Psalm 32.

Likewise, one can find no better example of projection than Saul's accusation that David was jealous of him and wanted to harm him. David had two opportunities to kill Saul (1 Sam. 24:4–7; 26:8–12) and did not. Furthermore, David was sorrowful that he had even cut off a piece of Saul's robe in his first opportunity to kill Saul. The one who actually threw spears to kill was Saul, and his attempts on David's life were very literal projections (1 Sam. 18:11). Later, Saul told his son Jonathan to put David to death (1 Sam. 19:1). Freud did not invent the phenomena of repression and projection; he merely described the way we function.

Another foundational concept for Freud is the instinctual nature of human beings. Instinct or drive was that which energized or activated the person. Freud's definition hints at the dilemma that he faced:

By an 'instinct' is provisionally to be understood the psychical representative of an endosomatic, continuously flowing source of stimulation . . . The concept of instinct is thus one of those lying on the frontier between the mental and the physical . . . [Instincts] are to be regarded as a measure of the demand made upon the mind for work. What distinguishes the instincts from one another and endows them with specific qualities is their relation to their somatic sources and to their aims. The source of an instinct is a process of excitation occurring in an organ and the immediate aim of the instinct lies in the removal of this organic stimulus.[1]

An instinct was on the boundary, "the frontier between the mental and the physical." Freud seems to have vacillated on this point. At times the instinct was described as more physical or biological; in his later works it seems to be more mental. On the whole, and especially in his earlier works, Freud seems to have identified instincts more with the physical and especially as related to sexual drives. In the definition cited, he stresses their somatic sources and aims and the emphasis is on the biological. He came from a philosophical setting that emphasized physics and chemistry, and accordingly he employed a kind of reductionism to describe everything in the most basic physical terms. Later in his life he struggled to describe the more mental aspects of psychological functioning and seemed to gravitate toward the more mental side of the frontier.

For Freud the most basic need was satisfying the instincts, and a person—by now being described more scientifically as "object"—was important as the means of gratifying the instinct. Instinct was more basic than relationship and relating to others was the means of satisfying the instinct. Thus this model of personality is called a drive model—*drive* being a synonym for *instinct*—because drive is the foundational concept. Freud defined a person as most basically driven by instincts, classified in 1920 as two kinds, sexual and death instincts. These instinctual assumptions come into direct conflict with Christian anthropology and values. The Christian sees this drive/instinctual model as very limiting and in no way reflecting the *imago dei*. This instinctual foundation of Freud, emphasizing the more mechanistic and biological aspects, is a major difference from a Christian perspective which would emphasize mankind's distinction from animals and allow not only for psychological processes, but spiritual ones.

Freud had several ways to describe the functioning of a human being and, after having utilized what he called a topographic model (that of the unconscious, preconscious, and conscious), decided that a better description would be what he termed the structural model. This structural model is familiar as

1. Sigmund Freud, "Three Essays on the Theory of Sexuality." The standard edition of the complete psychological works of Sigmund Freud, ed. James Stracney (London: Hogarth, 1953), 7, 168.

the Id, Ego, and Superego. The Id represents the more directly instinctual; its task is to provide for the discharge of tension or excitement that builds up. The Ego is the part of the person that mediates reality and relations with the Id and with the Superego; it is the executive functioning of the personality. The Superego is that which represents morality, values, and goals taken in from others; it is the assimilation of the parents' standards. Unresolved conflict between the Id, Ego, and Superego might manifest itself in neurosis. Early in his career Freud focused his attention more on the Id.

As time went on, Freud and his followers directed themselves more to the functioning Ego, and with the further passage of time there has been more focus on how values and experiences are taken into one's mental world to become part of one's intrapsychic structure, a more technical term for the internal mental world of the Id, Ego, and Superego. *Intrapsychic* refers to what is within the psyche rather than what is external. It should be noted that the terminology for Ego in German was *das Ich,* which could stand for something like the whole person, or it could represent the way a person functions. Freud's translator into English tended to translate *das Ich* more like the second meaning, emphasizing the various and multifaceted ways of functioning rather than any central agency or self.

Freud stressed awareness of developmental issues, and a crucial one for Freud was the Oedipal conflict, where the child has to work out the relatedness to both parents. There were different versions for boys and girls, but the one that was emphasized and that gave its name to this issue was the boy's relationship to his mother and father whereby he was sexually attracted to his mother, but out of fear of being castrated by his father gave up his sexual interest in his mother and assumed a male identification with his father.

Another seminal idea from Freud involves what he discovered in the therapy setting, the phenomenon of transference, whereby one relates to someone not on the basis of who that person truly is, but on the basis of some significant (usually parent) figure. Under the carefully regulated conditions of therapy, where the client could not know the real Freud, they would relate to him in ways that clearly were not relevant to him, but reflected more the client's expectations based on past experiences. If the client's father had been authoritarian and critical, the client would begin to experience Freud in a critical and authoritarian manner. These distortions that the therapist elicited would ultimately become the material for interpretation and insight and ultimate healing. Transference became the phenomenon that would illustrate and show in the ongoing relationship with the therapist what the client's intrapsychic world was like.

Another important conceptualization was first described by Freud but only fully developed by others after him. It had to do with not just relating to "objects" (persons) in the external world, but those "objects" coming to be represented in the internal (mental) world. Thus the term *internal objects* would later be used to describe those internal representations that are formed on the basis of exposure to the external world. Freud had recognized that we take on values from others and these values in turn become for us a conscious (and often unconscious) regulator which he termed the Superego. Freud hinted that this phenomenon of internalizing happens not only with values, but with the phenomenon of what others are like. After living in the world I will come to have a generalized view of others (typically unconscious) and thus I will come to have an "object representation" of how people are. If I have been treated as if I am merely there to be taken advantage of, used, abused, and mistreated, then I will come to expect others to treat me that way regardless of whether they do or not. Likewise I will come to have a "self representation" or view of myself, often unconscious, which may or may not be accurate. If I have been treated as dumb, I may consciously or unconsciously think of myself as stupid. The description of this internal world was to be more fully described by Freud's followers.

## Freud's Attitude Toward Religion

In the process of developing what he considered a new science, that of the psychological, Freud thought he had a new method of viewing phenomena and he rather enjoyed taking his newly discovered tool of psychoanalysis and using it as a perspective from which to view and analyze the world, literature, culture, and religion. In 1907 he published a paper on "Obsessive Acts in Religious Practices," where he noted a resemblance between obsessive acts and both neurosis and religious observances. Three years later he did a study of Leonardo di Vinci in which he claimed that the God concept is psychologically nothing more than a magnified father. In *Totem and Taboo* (1913) he espoused his theory of the origin of religion largely based on contemporary anthropological views, which have for the most part been repudiated since Freud's time.

In the fall of 1926 Freud described to his friend Oskar Pfister the topic of a pamphlet of his that was shortly to be published: "The subject matter—as you will easily guess—is my completely negative attitude towards religion in any form and however attenuated."[2] He was speaking about *The Future of an Illusion*, which would deal with his psychoanalytic critique of the nature and function of religion. Here he would describe religion as an "illusion" and as a defense that was developed to help people deal with the crushing supremacy of nature. Although technically careful to define *illusion* as a wish and not necessarily a falsehood, he by and large used *illusion* in a very negative sense. In

2. Heinrich Meng and Ernst Freud, ed., *Psychoanalysis and Faith: The Letters of Sigmund Freud and Oscar Pfister*, trans. Eric Mosbacker (New York: Basic Books, 1963), 109–10.

general, Freud argued that most people need religion to cope with their fears of the power of nature, that all religion takes the form of a universal neurosis with its origin being in the form of a father complex, that all religious dogmas are illusions, and that, as scientific knowledge increases, the need for religion will decrease. Freud's view of man emphasized the biological, instinctual, and highly mechanistic view with no real room for spiritual issues or relatedness to God except as a defense measure against the powers of nature. With these kinds of foundations it is little wonder that there have been great tensions between psychoanalysis and Christianity.

However, from its inception psychoanalysis and its founder Freud had a rather profound friend in Oskar Pfister, a Swiss pastor and theologian. Pfister was a student of Freud and yet a very thoughtful and committed theologian. He was offered the chair of Systematic and Practical Theology at a prestigious university, but chose to remain in the pastorate. Pfister maintained a very warm friendship to Freud and to his family throughout his lifetime. While he was very appreciative of the help gained from psychoanalysis, he was also very critical of Freud's handling of religion. The reason that Pfister was so responsive to psychoanalysis was that he found that it helped him as he in fact tried to help others. In his book *Christianity and Fear*, Pfister wrote:

> I tried forthwith to apply these discoveries to my Ministry, and found to my joy that I could now discover facts and render help in a way which since then has not failed . . . What caused my analytic labours to become the fulfillment of a long-standing dream was that while they dealt with real life they were also connected with a practical activity which in my own sphere became identified with my task as a pastor. In hundreds of instances which I had attacked in vain by methods grappling directly with the conscious—in vain because the religious ethical conflict was situated and did its work on the unconscious—I am now achieved the cures I had so long desired.[3]

While Pfister found the understandings of psychoanalysis helpful in his ministry, he was no blind and subservient disciple. In response to Freud's *The Future of an Illusion* Pfister published *The Illusion of a Future*, where he astutely criticized Freud's view of religion. One of the strong points of the critique was that Freud based his conclusions on observations of primitive religions and pathological individuals. Pfister also pointed out that Freud seemed unaware of his own metaphysical assumptions, which were reductionistic and mechanistic in nature. Pfister also noted that when Freud "attempted to strangle the religious illusion he erected the messiahship of science."[4] Pfister

3. Oskar Pfister, *Christianity and Fear*, trans. W. H. Johnston (London: Allen, 1948), 23–25.

4. Quoted in John E. G. Irwin, "Pfister and Freud: The Recovery of a Dialogue," *Journal of Religion and Health*, 12 (1973): 320.

was also critical of Freud's attempt to describe mankind and reality based exclusively on the limiting and sometimes deceptive approach of empiricism. Pfister took a larger view, noting, "In my opinion the world of spiritual order . . . stands more securely . . . than the whole deceptive world of the senses."[5]

Though these two men had rather different metaphysical assumptions, approaches to life, culture, and God, and though they differed rather radically on religion, yet they had in common the desire to help people who were suffering. Freud directly acknowledged that in one of his letters to Pfister: "In itself, psycho-analysis is neither religious or non-religious, but an impartial tool which both priest and layman can use in the service of the sufferer."[6]

With his view that, "I do not believe that psycho-analysis eliminates art, philosophy, religion, but it helps to purify and refine them,"[7] Pfister became first in a line of persons that believe psychoanalysis is not in itself antithetical to Christianity, but something that can be used to bring one to a more mature religious experience. He was able to distinguish Freud's very observant descriptions of the way people function from Freud's metaphysical assumptions, and thus was able to utilize the helpful aspects without accepting Freud's view of the nature of human beings.

## Historical Developments Since Freud

With the rise of Hitler and his anti-Jewish attitudes and with World War II imminent, Freud and his daughter Anna moved to London. In general, there was a dispersal of psychoanalysts from Germany and Austria to England and the United States. The death of Freud in 1939 and the trauma and isolation of World War II occasioned a decrease in unity, communication, and interchange of theory among psychoanalysts. The post-war era saw new developments take place. Freud's daughter Anna continued her father's interest in Ego development and defenses. In the United States Heinz Hartmann, who had immigrated from Germany, continued exploring the role of the Ego, adding that it not only mediated defenses but regulated adaptation in many areas that did not necessarily involve defenses. The Ego was responsible for adaptation in a broad sense, not just mediating between the Id and the Superego.

Hartmann also made an important distinction between "ego" as a set of functions and "self," a representation, an experiential construct, an internal image built up in a similar way to the way we internalize images of others. By identifying "ego" as a set of functions, Hartmann meant that the ego was the name for that which regulated reality, for example, remembering, planning, handling frustration, judging, mediating, handling anxiety. The "self" was

5. Ibid., 321.
6. Meng and Freud, *Psychoanalysis and Faith*, p. 17.
7. Ibid.

much like a self concept, only in Hartmann's theory it might not be completely conscious. This distinction between ego (functioning) and self would pave the way for a later development in which psychoanalysts would explore not only conflict between the Id, Ego, and Superego but the development of the self.

With Anna Freud and Heinz Hartmann, the newer developments and elaboration began to be termed Ego Psychology because the emphasis was on the development of the Ego functions, such as relationships with others (how I treat others, how intimate I am, how much distortion or defense is in the relationship). Margaret Mahler, who began her career as a pediatrician in Vienna, should be mentioned in connection with this psychoanalytic school. She initially studied abnormal and, later, normal children to see how they developed psychologically. Thus psychoanalysts began to explore not only by clinical insights, but by observation of normal developmental issues how we become psychologically separate or individual. Mahler's focus was on how the infant, who is biologically united to the mother until birth and thereafter psychologically united, comes to be not only biologically separate, but psychologically individuated. Her suggested developmental model of separation-individuation has been an extremely helpful model, but even here more recent research from people like Daniel Stern are indicating major modifications. Stern, a psychiatrist and researcher of infant development, emphasizes the strong relational component that seems to be inherent from birth. His research indicates that infants are differentiated from their mother almost from birth and equipped for communication with their caregivers. Infants are strongly relational from birth.

Psychoanalysts like Anna Freud, Hartmann, and Mahler reflect the Ego Psychology school of analysis, claiming to be the natural outworking of Freud's emphasis on drive theory and Ego development. They focus on Ego development, indicating that relationship with others is one of the functions of the Ego.

But this school was not the only line of psychoanalytic theory that developed in the post-war era. A woman analyst, Melanie Klein, had moved to England and begun to make some radical shifts in emphasis. Though claiming that she was naturally following Freud, she began to note that the infant's needs were not primarily for instinctual gratification, but for contact, emotional contact. The other person (object) was not there just to gratify needs; rather, there was an inherent need for relatedness. She did clinical work with children as well as adults and in her role as therapist she was noting the profound need for contact, connection, relatedness.

A Scottish analyst, Ronald Fairbairn, also stressed these very powerful relational needs and indicated that the conflict over dependency versus independency was even more basic than the Freudian Oedipal conflict. Like Klein, he was emphasizing developmental issues prior to the Oedipal conflict and again emphasizing the importance of early relational needs. Fairbairn even termed his theory an Object Relations Theory.

Donald Winnicott, who had been a pediatrician for many years before becoming an analyst and who knew firsthand infant development, highlighted the crucial importance of the mothering relationship in the psychological development of the infant. If this relationship was adequate in meeting the infant's needs ("good enough," in Winnicott's phrase), the child would grow up in a healthy way; if the relationship with the mothering one were seriously inadequate, the child would develop a "false self," one that went about the business of living and interacting, but seriously cut off from one's "true self," that which one was meant to be.

As the reader can see, psychoanalysts such as Klein, Fairbairn, and Winnicott came to focus on issues prior to Oedipal ones. They concentrated on the earlier developmental issue of the infant and the mother or mothering one. Their therapy tended to bring out not only sexual issues but those of dependency. Their clinical work tended to focus on the internal world that had been internalized. In general these therapists represent what we may call an Object Relations school of psychoanalysis.

One now sees the pattern of the historical development of psychoanalytic thinking. With the advent of Hitler, the center of psychoanalysis in Vienna was dispersed, some analysts going to England and the continent, others to the United States. During and after World War II the Ego Psychology School of Psychoanalysis developed in the United States and the Object Relations school developed in England. As scientific and professional communications reopened after the war the two schools of thought enriched one other. The two approaches reflected different emphases: "while ego psychologists conceive of object relations as one of the functions of the ego, the object relations theorist stresses that all aspects of ego functioning become organized *within* the self-representations in healthy development and cannot really be separated from it."[8] Ego psychologists emphasized instincts and indicated that relating to others is one of the many functions of the ego. Object relation theorists emphasized the centrality of relationships and said the ability of the ego to function develops out of good relationships.

A third major development occurred as Heinz Kohut (who followed in the Freudian and Ego psychology tradition) began to focus, not only on the functioning of the ego, but also on the self. Kohut based his work on Hartmann's distinction between self and ego, but went farther than Hartmann by recognizing that the self is not just a representation, an internal image. Rather, the self is an active agent. It develops out of interpersonal interactions, but it is

8. Althea J. Horner, *Object Relations and the Developing Ego in Therapy* (New York: Jason Aronson, 1979), 8.

more than a self concept or self image. The person is no longer primarily bio-logically driven, though the instinct (or drive) as energizer is still there. Over-all, Kohut's main emphasis is on the development of the self and indeed the-oretical and clinical issues based on his emphasis are called "Self Psychology."[9]

## Psychoanalytic Revisions

Morris Eagle has described a number of recent developments in psycho-analysis and critiqued them. Amidst the vast number of new contributions, formulations, and reformulations from research and, in general, the mush-rooming of information and ideas, Eagle has found a radical shift. He writes in his introduction:

> In the last number of years the very face of psychoanalytic theory has changed radically. Some of what were once thought to be the very foundational propo-sitions of psychoanalysis have been markedly reformulated. It is not at all certain that all these alterations are consistent with classical psychoanalytic thought as developed by Freud and his early followers. Indeed, when one takes a compre-hensive look at the range of reformulations one is not at all clear as to what re-mains of traditional psychoanalytic theory.[10]

Eagle goes on to argue that the more recent findings and formulations really are a radical revision of the more traditional Freudian concepts.

What Eagle describes as a reformulation of the Freudian paradigm seems to be the cumulative shift from psychoanalysis as a drive-structured model of personality to a much more relational one, influenced by Object Relations Theory and the emphasis on the self. While theorists work for an integration of models, it is clear that the highly biological and indeed mechanistic view espoused by Freud can no longer contain all the clinical observations, research and theoretical developments.

Freud's claim that instincts are the foundation of personal life has been rad-ically reassessed. For many psychoanalysts the evidence is clear that interest in and involvement with others is not simply and primarily a way to get biolog-ical needs met (though it may serve that function). Instead, relatedness and connectedness to others is an independent and crucial need in its own do-main; in fact, relatedness is the primary need, the foundational one.

One of the earliest empirical studies to explore instincts and relational is-sues involved the research by Harry Harlow,[11] who investigated whether sim-

9. Heinz Kohut, *The Restoration of the Self* (New York: International University Press, 1977).

10. Morris Eagle, *Recent Developments in Psychoanalysis* (Cambridge, Mass.: Harvard Uni-versity Press, 1987), 3.

11. Harry Harlow, "The Nature of Love," *American Psychologist* 13 (1958): 673–85.

ply gratifying the instincts (e.g., the need for food) would be sufficient for the growth of rhesus monkeys. He had some of the monkeys fed by a mechanical arrangement whereby all of their needs for nourishment were met. Other monkeys were similarly fed but the feeding apparatus had a terry cloth covering so that the monkeys could have some kind of physical contact. The monkeys fed by the completely mechanized bottle were strange monkeys, exhibiting what appeared to be abnormal behaviors, and when they were mated, these monkeys did not evidence parenting behaviors and were even destructive to their offspring. Given a choice, the monkeys preferred the terry cloth "mothers" for some kind of contact.

Through a series of experiments Harlow and his researchers began to give strong evidence that even monkeys need physical contact, nurturance, being related to. This kind of empirical information seriously challenged Freud's drive theory and, along with clinical observations both in therapy and observing normal ( and abnormal) development in children, began to suggest the critical importance of relatedness or bondedness. Persons like pediatrician Terry Brazelton and developmental psychiatrist Daniel Stern have studied infant development and confirmed how exquisitely infants orient to parenting ones, and not just for instinctual gratification.

A second major shift from Freud's earlier theorizing is that his structural model of Id, Ego, and Superego no longer seems adequate, nor does a conflict among them describe all abnormal behavior. While the terms *Id, Ego,* and *Superego* have some descriptive utility, they do not capture the more central issue of some unifying entity. Freud himself seems occasionally to have utilized *das Ich* (the Ego) to represent the whole person, but the emphasis was on the functioning ego, the ego as a set of operations. When Heinz Hartmann made the distinction in terminology between *ego,* a set of functions, and *self,* a representation or image, he set in motion a clarification that would eventually evolve into "self" as an entity that is the center or core of the person. Psychoanalysts who followed after Hartmann defined *self* as "self-representation" or self image, emphasizing that the "self-representation" may not be entirely conscious, but more like an unconscious self-image. Eventually Heinz Kohut began to emphasize not only the self image of a person but the self as an entity, a center of initiative and a recipient of impressions. Kohut's self psychology, as it is called, has introduced into psychoanalysis something akin to the soul, though self psychology has focused more on the nurture and development of the self than the given nature of the self.

A third critical revision since the time of Freud is that pathology (abnormal behavior) cannot be fully accounted for by a model that merely describes conflict between Id, Ego, and Superego. Rather, pathology must take into account what are described as developmental deficits. In essence, this model is based on a theory derived from a developing body of knowledge of how mental life grows and develops. Pathology is based not merely on conflict but on the developmental level of mental capacity to handle conflict. It may occur because some coping mechanisms necessary to handle psychological issues, such as anxiety or loss, may not have come into existence and therefore may not be available for use. The ability to deal with reality and anxiety regarding the future and the ability to handle depression and loss are mature functions and are not automatic. They are learned over time and, object relations theorists would add, in the context of healthy relationships. Such ability as learning to tolerate frustration is actually quite a sophisticated achievement. If I never have any frustration (but who hasn't?), I will not learn to tolerate it; if I am frustrated too much, too quickly, too often, I may be overwhelmed and not learn ways to cope with it. How many people in our culture escape their frustrations with drink, drugs, sex—anything that will distract them from physical and/or emotional pain? One psychoanalyst describes maturity as the ability to handle emotional pain truthfully, without denial or defense. Too many people in our world are arrested at developmental levels where they do not have the resources to cope, and therefore repress, distort, and defend.

Related to developmental deficits are the use of defenses, designed to protect us from being overwhelmed emotionally, but ultimately causing their own form of problems. Ever since the fall, when Adam and Eve hid behind fig leaves and Adam attempted to put the blame on God ("The woman you put here with me—she gave me some fruit from the tree, and I ate" [Gen. 3:12]), people have been using psychological defenses to hide, and these are utilized until such time as the person can develop the capacity to cope with stress in a truthful manner. Dealing with truth is not always a matter of mere logic, but of managing anxieties so that one does not have to use denial (pretending it is not there), projection (putting into someone else thoughts or feelings that one does not want to acknowledge), splitting (keeping apart good and bad aspects because it is simpler and easier to deal with only one aspect), and a variety of other defenses. Increasingly, the evidence indicates that in areas where emotional issues are involved in the thought processes (as opposed to, say, symbolic logic), processing one's thoughts and feelings in a truthful manner is a highly complicated process that is learned (internalized) from others. Pathology may involve being arrested at a developmental level such that one cannot cope at a mature level, thereby using defenses and mechanisms that distort truth.

In addition to the revisions of psychoanalytic developmental theory, there have been new developments in the relationship between psychoanalysis and religion. Ana-Maria Rizzuto is a psychoanalyst who was asked to utilize her knowledge in teaching Catholic seminary students about pastoral care. She developed the class and then ultimately did extensive clinical research on how people come to have not only a cognitive understanding, but a representation (internal image that may not be fully conscious) of God. She was very aware that she was studying a subjective experience and not religion or theology in its more objectified aspects. In her book, *The Birth of the Living God*, she writes not about God or religion, but about how we come to have some relationship with God. Her contribution is significant because she indicates that no one—at least no one in a Western culture—can grow up without some relatedness to God, whether that is consciously formulated or not, whether that relationship is basically truthful and healthy or distorted and unhealthy. She acknowledges God as within the arena of very significant relationships in our lives.[12]

In 1984 William Meissner, a Catholic psychoanalyst, published *Psychoanalysis and Religious Experience*.[13] Like Rizzuto's work, this book makes no claims about God in any objective sense but focuses on religious experience.

Rizzuto and Meissner are in some ways like latter day Pfister's, believing that psychoanalytic theory and practice have something to offer in understanding our relatedness to God, self, and others.

## Summary of Psychoanalytic Developmental Theory

In spite of a wide variety of theoretical differences, or differential emphases, among psychoanalysts, there is a common core of thought that represents psychoanalytic developmental theory. This common core stresses (1) the developmental stages of growth, (2) the context of a relationship, and (3) the corresponding development of the internal world (e.g., self representation, object representation, God representation). The emphasis is not on symptoms or behaviors. It is not exclusively on instinctual expression. Nor is it predominantly conceptual or predominantly conscious. Rather, the emphasis is on intrapsychic phenomena—the inner world—and not primarily on external interpersonal relationships. Still, it is of the interpersonal relationship between the therapist and the client that provides information about the internal and intrapsychic world. Thus, the emphasis of psychoanalysis is also on changing the experience of the intrapsychic world which reflects not only cognitive but emotional connections.

Of crucial importance in psychoanalytic developmental theory is that of the relationship to the mother or caregiver. While there is a recognition of genetic and constitutional differences in individuals and a recognition of maturation processes, psychoanalysts place great stress on the mothering relationship, maintaining that out of this maternal matrix self and ego functions emerge

12. Ana-Maria Rizzuto, *The Birth of the Living God* (Chicago: University of Chicago Press, 1979).

13. William Meissner, *Psychoanalysis and Religious Experience* (New Haven: Yale University Press, 1984).

and develop. In Winnicott's terminology, if the relationship with the mothering one is "good enough," the development of the self and ego functions will emerge in the natural maturational processes. The mothering one must have empathy to be attuned to the particularities of her child. If the mother matches well the needs of the child, he or she will grow psychically and take on more and more of his or her own psychological functioning. The complexity of this mothering process recognizes the highly intricate interaction, and a mother who might be quite adequately matched for one child may not be so well matched for another child.

Applying the psychoanalytic concepts to psychotherapy would involve utilizing the therapeutic relationship to elicit how one interacts with others as a guide to what the client's internal world is like, how a client relates to herself, and how she relates to others and to God. Historically this phenomenon of eliciting information about the client's distortion has been labeled "transference." This therapeutic relationship is also utilized to lead to new levels of psychological developments where defenses and distortions are not utilized. The therapist has to be very skilled to discern where the client is developmentally and has to utilize his/her therapeutic skills to interpret distortions and defenses and *also* provide empathy and caring that lead to new levels of growth. The therapeutic relationship not only elicits distortions, but also has some real and new aspects that provide what the client may not have received in earlier parenting. In some ways there may be a re-parenting. Although it is not the only source of God's provision, therapy may provide a very specific enactment of Psalm 27:10: "Though my father and mother forsake me, the LORD will receive me." A number of Christian clients have commented on the incarnation experience in therapy as they have experienced Christ's love through the therapist. For some it is Christ's love; others experience it as the LORD receiving them in those areas where the mother or father abandoned them.

## Psychoanalysis and Christianity

With this background and updating, it is now appropriate to address the issue of the relationship between psychoanalytic theory and Christianity, and to assess the degree to which insights from psychoanalytic theory clarify our understanding of humanness. Do psychoanalysis and Christianity have to be opposed? Are they two very different ways of helping hurting people, or are they different facets of one truth?

To me it is clear that psychoanalysis and Christianity do not have to be antagonists. To be sure, they have been cast in these roles, especially when Freud's initial observations and theory have been extrapolated to a metaphysical level. But such a man as Oskar Pfister was able to utilize aspects of Freud's theory to help him be more effective in his pastoral ministry. He was critical of Freud's inferences from exclusively pathological populations and of his underlying metaphysical assumptions which exalted science and empiricism as a religion. Pfister was willing to utilize the practical truth manifest in this new psychoanalytic theory, without completely accepting the philosophic assumptions or philosophic statements about the nature of man. He recognized that this new way of looking into man led to "the inner man," places that were not as accessible to normal awareness. He would have recognized that the psychoanalytic understanding of defenses illustrated in King David's repression of his sin with Bathsheba or Saul's projection of his anger at David, was a helpful and practical description that did not require him to deny the Christian view of man's nature. Pfister could distinquish between therapeutic insights and premature extrapolation about the nature of human beings. We might say, then, that without denying the truth he knew from Scripture, Pfister put into operation that wisdom of Cervantes, "Where the truth is, in so far as it is truth, there God is."[14]

A second significant aspect of the relationship between psychoanalysis and Christianity is that the psychoanalytic theory is fluid, but that with increasing knowledge, research, verification, and correction, it will approach truth.[15] Just as in physics, where classical physics was held to be "the truth" until Einstein opened new realms, some of Freud's evolving theory lasted only a brief while, but its insufficiencies became apparent. As Morris Eagle observed, contemporary psychoanalytic theory has changed radically from Freud's original assumptions about the nature of humankind. This more contemporary version of psychoanalytic theory has a much different emphasis and the principles being gleaned from it are ones that can be utilized not only to help hurting Christians, but also to highlight and emphasize profound Christian insights into human nature. In the past the relationship of psychoanalysis and Christianity may have been utilized in complementary ways, each in its own way being used to help persons in need and pain, but increasingly the two fields seem to enhance and illuminate each other.

With the revisions in psychoanalytic theory, its foundational premises are approaching and supporting a Christian view of mankind. One central element is that of relationship. Psychoanalyst Steven Mitchell indicated that relationship is replacing drive (or instinct) as the foundational principle of psychoanalytic theory, that a person's most basic need is for relatedness. For the Christian, this need is expressed toward other human beings and God. Indeed God was the one who said, "It is not good for the man to be alone" (Gen. 2:18). The opening lines of Augustine's *Confessions* illustrate the need for

14. Quoted in John D. Carter and Bruce Narramore, *The Integration of Psychology and Theology* (Grand Rapids: Zondervan, 1979), 14.

15. Assuming scientific realism. For more on this, see J. P. Moreland, *Christianity and the Nature of Science* (Grand Rapids: Baker, 1989), chaps. 4 and 5.

God-relatedness: "Thou hast formed us for Thyself, and our hearts are restless till they find their rest in Thee."[16] Christians understand that these relationship needs can never be fully satisfied until man's estrangement from God is healed by the work of Christ. At the same time psychoanalysis can help us understand difficulties in relationship with God, as well as with humans. Thus psychoanalytic theory helps one understand difficulties in relationship, what caused them, and ways to help; but Christianity offers the fulfillment of relational needs as well as the moral norms necessary to define what those relationships (e.g., family relationships) ought to be.

A second new emphasis, seen largely in the development of Heinz Kohut's Self Psychology, is the recognition of something close to the soul in its more historical terminology. The self is beginning to be recognized as more than a self concept or self image, more as an agent or center of activity. Historical scholarship is also reinvestigating the roots of Freud's theories and his use of the German language. Bruno Bettelheim argues that Freud himself had references to the soul that were eliminated in the English translations.[17] While neither Freud nor Kohut imply anything like *imago dei* or a Christian view of the soul, contemporary psychology and psychoanalysis are considering more than behaviors and instincts. Hints of something more than biology, something unique to each individual, something given rather than exclusively a product of nurture, are emerging in theoretical discussions.

Given these important changes, psychoanalytic anthropology is congruent with a Christian view of man. Furthermore, the kind of phenomena that psychoanalysts view as disruptive (leading to psychopathology) and curative (leading to healing) are basic to the fall and to redemption. Sin and its consequences, leading to separation from God, are foundational to the Christian message. Psychoanalysts are finding that separation anxiety, the fear of being alone and alienated, is absolutely foundational for understanding psychopathology.

At the risk of overstatement, one might say that all defenses and distortions are designed to eliminate pain, particularly the pain of being alone, unconnected, or unrelated. This is why therapy involves helping persons be connected emotionally to another and learning how to be related to self and others. Therapy is thus establishing true connectedness and not a false blotting-out-of-pain through drugs or denial. It involves being connected to the self one was created to be and not a false self. Psychoanalytic theory is discovering critical and profound developmental issues and offering some insights into reestablishing, or in some instances establishing for the first time, needed contact and connections.

16. Augustine, *Confessions* 1.1., in *Basic Writings of Saint Augustine*, ed. Whitney J. Oates (New York: Random House, 1948).
17. Bruno Bettelheim, *Freud and Man's Soul* (New York: Knopf, 1983), 70–78.

Psychoanalytic theory profoundly highlights critical issues, but in itself cannot go far enough because the separation from God needs to be healed by acceptance of the work of Christ for complete relational needs. Psychoanalytic therapy may do ground work of healing relationships so that one's relationship with God is enhanced. This kind of therapy may reflect only a complementary relationship with Christianity by helping one's human relationships. But if in clarifying relationships it also clarifies and fosters the relationship with God, the therapy may be truly integrative. For person's with separation fears, the only complete healing is expressed in John 3:16 and Romans 8:38–39. Integrative psychotherapy is that which helps the person get to the place where they can appropriate healing in relationship with God as well as others. Contemporary psychoanalytic theory vividly describes the importance of relatedness and the consequences of pathological separation; Scripture highlights the relational God and the healing of separation through God's grace toward us.

The view presented here is that the truths gleaned from psychoanalytic study about personality functioning, psychopathology, and development ultimately support the truth gleaned from Scripture about the nature of human beings. These truths, whether from psychoanalytic study or from Scripture, if utilized can enhance one's relatedness to God as one eliminates distortions and defenses, as one becomes the soul/self God created one to be, as one relates to God in truth. In many ways psychoanalytic principles can be utilized to glorify God if one accepts Irenaeus' statement, "The Glory of God is a human being fully alive."

## Summary

This chapter addresses the relationship of the psychoanalytic perspective and Christianity, looking at basic concepts, Freud's attitude toward religion, historical developments and revisions since Freud, and the current interface between psychoanalytic thinking and Christianity. Originally some Christians utilized the psychoanalytic theory by distinguishing the practical, clinical helps from Freud's metaphysical assumptions. With increasing research, clinical observation and therefore revisions of psychoanalytic theory, the description of humankind coming to light is much more compatible with a Christian anthropology than Freud's original view.

## Suggested Readings

Bishop, Leigh C., and Samuel B. Thielman. "C. S. Lewis on Psychoanalysis: Through Darkest Zeitgeistheism." *Journal of Psychology and Christianity* II (1992): 44–56. [I]

Carter, John D., and Bruce Narramore. *The Integration of Psychology and Theology*. Grand Rapids: Zondervan, 1979. [B]

Eagle, Morris. *Developments in Psychoanalysis: A Critical Evaluation.* Cambridge: Harvard University Press, 1987, particularly chapters 1 and 2. [A]

Irwin, John E. G. "Pfister and Freud: The Recovery of a Dialogue." *Journal of Religion and Health* 12 (1973): 315–17. [I]

Lewis, C. S. "Morality and Psychoanalysis." In *Mere Christianity.* New York: Macmillan, 1960. [B]

Meissner, W. W. *Psychoanalysis and Religion Experience.* New Haven: Yale University Press, 1984. [A]

Rizzuto, Ana-Maria. *The Birth of the Living God: A Psychoanalytic Study.* Chicago: University of Chicago Press, 1979. [A]

Sorenson, Anita Lehmann. "Psychoanalytic Perspectives on Religion: The Illusion has a Future." *Journal of Psychology and Theology* 18 (1990): 209–17. [I]

Westerndorp, Floyd. "The Value of Freud's Illusion." *Journal of Theology and Psychology* 3 (1975): 82–89. [I]

# A Response to Nancy Duvall

## Keith J. Edwards

In her chapter on psychoanalytic theory, Duvall has provided an exceptionally clear and distinct summary of a complex, and often difficult, body of literature in psychology. In the years since Freud began to write about the inner lives of his patients, psychoanalytic theory has been controversial. In the past twenty years, it has fallen out of favor with psychologists in university psychology departments throughout the United States. Many research psychologists treat psychoanalytic theory as a relic of the past, having only historical significance for the contemporary scholar. But despite the disdain of the ivory tower, research-oriented, psychological establishment, psychoanalysis has remained a viable theoretical perspective and clinical orientation among a large contingent of practicing clinicians. Duvall has drawn together the major writers who have transformed Freud's original formulations into the contemporary fields of psychodynamic and object relations theories. In my response, I would like to focus on the importance of interpersonal relationships and comment on the process of integration which her chapter demonstrates.

### Relationships and Growth

Throughout her review of psychoanalytic psychology, Duvall clearly indicates that the need for human relationships is at the core of the human personality. This emphasis on human relatedness is one of the enduring contributions of Freud and other psychoanalytic theorists who have come after him. It follows that the method of treatment employed by psychoanalytic thera-

169

pists would give a central role to the therapeutic relationship. As I understand it, the therapeutic relationship has two functions.

The first function of the relationship between the patient and the therapist is to evoke the patient's characteristic style of relating so the patient can increase self-awareness and reduce the use of defensive distortion. The thoughts, feelings, or behavioral impulses the patient has toward the therapist is viewed as evidence of the person's internal psychological world. The therapist serves as a guide to help the patient achieve deeper self-understanding by making observations and interpretations of the patient's experience in the therapy setting. The relationship is the "laboratory" for this therapeutic work. Through her encounter with the therapist, the patient gains insight into her interpersonal dynamics. This insight is presumed to enable the patient to engage in less defensive distortions, perceive herself and others more accurately, and lead a more effective life.

The second function of the therapeutic relationship is to provide a context within which the person will experience healing and growth. As patient and therapist work together, the therapist becomes an emotionally significant person in the patient's life. The relational attachment the patient forms with the therapist gives the therapist power to influence and transform how the patient thinks, feels, and behaves. The therapist enables the patient to achieve more mature levels of functioning by performing reparative parental functions in the therapeutic relationship.

The importance of interpersonal relationships as the context in which people learn about themselves and grow has important implications for the work of the church. If we accept the central premise of Duvall's chapter, then people need to be involved in meaningful relationships within the church if they are to grow psychologically and spiritually. We need to go beyond the passive listener role created by the worship and teaching formats that dominate church experience, if we want the church to have a significant impact on people. We must create ways in which people can be involved in each others lives in on-going relationships. Those relationships must build trust and openness so that believers can begin to move beyond the "false self" of performance-based spirituality to experiencing the healing power of incarnate truth in relationship with one another. If we are going to encourage people toward a model of fellowship in which there is "confessing our faults to one another" (cf. James 5:16), then the truth of "no condemnation" (Rom. 8:1), must characterize our relational community. Psychological defenses are used out of fear and the antidote is love. As Scripture says, "perfect love drives out fear" (1 John 4:18). Growth to maturity in Christ is not possible without such love.

The essential witness of the early church was to be relational. Jesus told his disciples that the mark of discipleship would be love: "By this all men will know that you are my disciples, if you love one another" (John 13:35). When

Christian ministry embodies this relational dynamic, the power of the gospel becomes evident. When our ministry programs place believers in the role of passive listeners and the major activity is cognitive analysis, we have the form of religion but not the power. Someone has said that the church has a tendency to be like a Sunday afternoon football game with twenty-two players on the field in need of rest and 50,000 fans in the stands in need of exercise. We need to create ecclesiastical structures that involve believers in an active, relational community.

One other important emphasis in Duvall's chapter, which has important implications for ministry, is the developmental model of maturity. Individuals who have experienced severe trauma early in their lives are going to require a different form of ministry than those who have had a nurturing childhood. We cannot have a one-size-fits-all approach to Christian ministry. If the church is going to minister to the whole body of Christ then we have to meet people at their point of need. To do this we must understand human needs. The material reviewed by Duvall provides a very useful framework for such understanding.

## The Task of Integration

The relationship between Pfister and Freud described by Duvall in her chapter is an illustration of how the task of integration can proceed. The basis for such integration was the concern both men had with the real, material world of human experience. As Duvall says, "they had in common the desire to help people who were suffering." In practice, this meant they both had a willingness to listen to and observe other people in an attempt to understand them. Freud was endowed with God-given human abilities to observe, comprehend, and describe what he observed. His formulations were provocative and they enabled others, like Pfister, to look at old problems in new ways. Pfister's willingness to consider Freud's ideas transformed his work with people and made him more effective.

As Duvall has demonstrated, there are many ideas in the psychoanalytic literature that can help us understand human nature. This understanding can guide us into more effective service of others. In order to achieve this understanding, we need to be willing to spend time studying significant writers who may have little or no interest in, or even hostility toward, the things of God. This task is not without risk. We need the guidance of the Holy Spirit to lead us into truth. We need to have an adequate understanding of the Bible, theology, and the philosophy of knowledge to be able to critically evaluate, in light of God's truth, what secular writers are teaching. I see Duvall's analysis of psychoanalytic theory as a model of this type of informed dialog.

# A Response to Nancy Duvall

## Klaus Issler

Change is inevitable—and apparently this dictum applies to theories as well. I was pleased to learn that psychoanalytic theory is still being revised and has not remained in the exact form given to it by its founder. Many of us were exposed in a college psychology course to its original overly-sexual orientation. And, as believers, we were disturbed by Freud's fairly anti-Christian views. It was encouraging to learn that some of the original concepts of the theory are still useful in pastoral counseling and that new areas of study are providing additional insights into personality growth and functioning.

It is interesting to note that an accent on healthy relationships has become the foundational principle of psychoanalytic theory. Such a focus on relationships as a critical context for mature development is a welcome emphasis. Western psychological tradition has had, in large measure, an overly individualistic flavor. For example, Lawrence Kohlberg's earlier work in moral education was identified with moral dilemma discussions. The purpose was to prompt moral stage advancement for each student based on the analysis of hypothetical moral dilemmas. A moderate level of stage change resulted (typically one-third of a stage) from these kinds of discussions, yet moral reasoning involved only one component of a more holistic concept of moral maturity.

A new direction emerged in the seventies. Kohlberg and his associates realized that moral reasoning and moral action must be linked. The concept of a "just community" emerged as research was undertaken in prisons and high schools. In contrast to the earlier moral dilemma discussions, decisions were made by groups regarding actual practices of the group. Research uncovered identifiable phases for moral development for groups. Movement along these phases was documented over a multi-year period. Kohlberg concluded that the most effective means for moral development involved experiencing life within a community that actively pursued corporate decision-making about group life and behavior.

This harmonizes well with the biblical focus on growth taking place in relationship with God and within a body of believers. To the question, "Teacher, which is the greatest commandment in the Law?" Jesus replied: "'Love the Lord your God with all your heart and with all your soul and with all your mind.' This is the first and greatest commandment. The second is like it: 'Love your neighbor as yourself.' All the Law and the Prophets hang on these two commandments" (Matt. 22:36–40). God is a "Being in fellowship"—Father, Son, and Holy Spirit. We have been created as social beings: to fellowship with him and with each other. The true evidence of our growing discipleship is how we love one another (John 13:34–35).

A basic dilemma in Christianity may unconsciously prevent us from pursuing close friendships which are the basis for fulfilling many of the "one another" passages (e.g., "admonish one another," Col. 3:18; "carry each other's burdens," Gal. 6:2). In *Friendship: A Study in Theological Ethics*,[18] Gilbert Meilander suggests that our dilemma stems from two contrasting kinds of love that we experience: *agapē* and *philia*. Christian love (*agapē*) is a universal love, given to all, even enemies (e.g., Matt. 5:46–47). It is also self-less, sacrificial, and steadfast (e.g., 1 Cor. 13:5–8). But friendship love (*philia*) is a preferential kind of love given only to a few. It must be mutual and it expects love to be returned. It is a kind of love that may change over time; it will ebb and flow with the changing dynamic of the relationship.

Meilander offers one helpful perspective to bring these two diverse streams together. He writes:

> Life is a journey, a pilgrimage toward community in which friends love one another in God and time no longer inflicts its wounds on friendship. Along the way, friendship is a school, training us in the meaning and enactment of love. Friendship is also a foretaste of the internal reciprocities of love which have yet to be fully realized.[19]

Let us then facilitate these rare gifts of close relationships to teach us how to love as we grow in maturity in Christ.

"All truth is God's truth" affirms that truth is unified and harmonious no matter whether God allows believers or unbelievers to uncover it. Within its limited sphere of focus, a contemporary psychoanalytic theory contributes to our understanding of the complexity of personality development.

18. Gilbert Meilander, *Friendship: A Study in Theological Ethics* (Notre Dame, Ind.: University of Notre Dame Press, 1981).
19. Ibid., 66.

# 6

# The Nature of Human Mental Life

*Keith J. Edwards*

Susan was sitting on the sofa talking with her psychologist about some of the problems she was having with her husband, who didn't seem to understand her. Her therapist responded in an understanding way and commented that many couples experienced similar problems. As the students in my Abnormal Psychology class watched this filmed segment of an actual interview, nothing seemed out of the ordinary. However, it did seem a bit strange that the married woman on the screen had a teddy bear in her hand.

The discussion about the woman's marital problems went on for a short time more when there was a sudden change in the woman's voice and demeanor. She clutched her teddy bear close to her face and looked down, her voice seemed much younger, and the conversation shifted to the relationship between the client and the therapist. Susan was now expressing fear of what the "doctor" was going to do with her, uneasiness with the interview, and a desire to see her "mommie." It was quite a sudden and unexpected transformation. What had happened?

Susan was suffering from a multiple personality disorder (MPD). She had changed from a married woman of 35 to a child of 7, literally, in the blink of an eye. She actually had several distinct personalities, any one of which might emerge in a given situation. Her therapist was engaged in the process of trying to understand the characteristics of each of Susan's personalities so he could begin to help her toward the reintegration of these various, dissociated parts of herself.

In Susan's case 6 of her 7 personalities are adult women. One of them is quite violent and two of them quite unconventional. In one of her unconventional personalities, Susan as "Heather" has been known to go to bars and pick up strange men and spend the night with them. Since Susan loses consciousness when Heather takes over, she has no recollection of her behavior. She only knows about Heather and her actions from the reports of others, including her distraught husband. Susan experiences the changes of consciousness when switching from one personality to another as automatic and outside of her control. She has learned, through self-observation and the observations of others, what situations might trigger a personality switch. Thus, she has achieved some degree of control over this process by controlling her circumstances. Since she often has little control over the behavior of others, this strategy doesn't work very well. Her situation reminds me of the former television series, "The Incredible Hulk," where a mild-mannered doctor who, when he encountered conflict or threat, would change into the ferocious, well-muscled, marginally socialized green giant.

The multiple personality disorder is one of the most fascinating evidences of the complexity of the human mind. Distinct personalities with their own voice tone, body movements, and emotional make-up can inhabit the same person. While such disorders are rare, they do raise some interesting questions about the nature of the human mind, the nature of consciousness, and the coherence of the self. People suffering with MPD like Susan also present a challenge to our conceptions of personal responsibility, personal growth, and free will. Susan's internal psychological world consists of separate, compartmentalized personalities which have been so dissociated (disconnected) that there is little or no shared awareness among them. Direct exhortations to Susan to stop her immoral behavior as "Heather" are not helpful. As was noted, Susan doesn't even remember what she, as "Heather," has done. Furthermore, the transition between personalities is not experienced as under volitional control. Working with people like Susan requires patience and understanding of the powerful psychological processes that operate outside of her awareness (unconscious forces) that underlie her disorder.

To a lesser degree than is true of MPD patients, all of us have psychological forces in our personalities that we experience as automatic, intrusive, unwanted, and disturbing. Feeling angry with people we love, experiencing fear when we are asked to speak to a group, having intrusive sexual thoughts, and being depressed about a mistake we have made in the past are all more or less common to human experience. For most of us, these experiences are temporary episodes which we manage to live through and get on with our lives. For some, such experiences occur with such frequency and/or intensity that they become major stumbling blocks to experiencing any inner peace or sense of well being. Patterns of dysfunctional thinking, feeling, and/or behaving resist the afflicted person's best efforts at transformation. They desire to experience the freedom we are to have as children of God through faith in Jesus Christ, but the pain will not go away. In addition to their psychological problems, they begin to feel like spiritual failures as well because of their persistent dysfunction.

How is it that sincere people of faith continue to be afflicted with various psychological problems? Is there something we can learn about the human psyche that will help us understand how such problems are established and maintained? The purpose of the present chapter is to try to provide such understanding. A major premise of the chapter is that we can work more effectively with people if we understand the structure and functioning of the human brain since it is the brain that mediates the functioning of the mind in the physical world. What I would like to do in this chapter is review some areas of psychology that illustrate the complexity of human consciousness. In the process we'll review some recent research on individuals with brain malfunctions that show how brain structure relates to subjective awareness. We also want to consider what implications these findings have for faith, spiritual maturity, and the practice of ministry intended to facilitate faith and maturity. An integrated Christian world view cannot afford to overlook these issues. In order to accomplish these things we need to first review some basic physiology of brain structure and function.

Before beginning it may be helpful to state how I approach the study of a discipline like psychology from a Christian perspective. I assume our understanding of human nature will be enriched by our study of the work of cognitive neuroscientists. For whatever is the essence of our spiritual nature, we experience and express our spiritual reality in time and space through our material being.[1] Scripture says "faith comes by hearing." I take this to mean that the words of Scripture must be transmitted in material ways to the self mediated by a brain. Further, it is in the exercise of faith by means of our material being that faith is consummated. Paul writes in Romans 10:9, "if you confess with your mouth, 'Jesus is Lord,' and believe in your heart that God has raised him from the dead, you will be saved." Exercising faith is a physical process as well as a spiritual one.

Spiritual growth is a process that intimately involves changes and transformations in our material being. The apostle Paul emphasized such transformations in terms of both the body (1 Cor. 9:24–27) and the mind (Rom. 12:1–2). When we come to a saving faith in Christ we are spiritually new creatures

---

1. In writing this chapter, I have adopted the substance dualism perspective on human nature advocated by Dr. Moreland in his chapter (pp. 55–79). This position, and the language of my chapter, makes a clear distinction between the brain and the mind.

(2 Cor. 5:17), but much of our physical brain remains unchanged. Memories of past experiences and learnings are stored in the neurons of the brain. If we have had particularly traumatic emotional experiences in the past, especially in childhood, this painful history will be recorded in our brain's memory system. The processes of transformation required to reduce the destructive impact of early trauma, such as childhood sexual abuse, involves experiences that activate and modify these memories. There must be, as David Seemands has so eloquently said, "a healing of the memories."[2] For it is through the memory structures of the brain that the past continues to influence our present experience.

If we have pathology in the organic or functional organization of our brains, then these factors will affect our spiritual lives as well. Much of the controversy about the legitimacy of psychology in the Christian church seems to me to stem from an unnatural dichotomy between our spirits and the rest of creation. The incarnation of our spirits makes psychology relevant to the practice of faith. Contrary to some critics, psychology is not a recent humanistic heresy. The ancient sages of the Old Testament revealed an inspired understanding of the human psyche.[3] Modern neuropsychology has added a new dimension to an ancient perspective. One of the constructive outcomes I have experienced from studying neuropsychology and human functioning has been an increased sense of compassion for myself and others who struggle with the very real remnants of a dysfunctional past that resides in our brain's memory structures. My study has also enabled me to be more effective in helping others overcome destructive patterns and experience, more fully, the "peace that passes understanding." It is my hope that as a result of studying this chapter you will have a deeper appreciation for the wonder of God's creation (Ps. 19) and a more profound sense of humility (cf. Gal. 6:1) as we seek to encourage others to faith and maturity in Christ.

## Brain Structure and Functioning

One of the fastest growing areas in psychology today is cognitive neuroscience. The theory and research in this area is providing a deeper and more precise understanding of the brain mechanisms that underlay the human mind. Such study has important implications for understanding what it means to be human. We will begin our exploration of the nature of mental processes by considering some of the major structural features of the brain. The brain is a complex organ and we can only give some basic general descriptions of structure and functioning in this section. Almost everything one can say

2. D. Seamands, *Healing of the Memories* (Wheaton, Ill.: Victor, 1965).
3. J. Coe, "Why Biblical Counseling is Unbiblical or Speaking Psychology Gently to the Church," paper presented at the Christian Association for Psychological Studies, Anaheim.

about the brain must be qualified since generalizations rarely apply to all people. But there are some general principles of brain function that will be useful to know. The human brain can be divided into three distinct components or systems. The three components are the brain stem, the limbic system (the midbrain), and the cerebral cortex. One of the important aspects of this model is that it highlights the fact that the brain is not a single, unitary structure. Rather, the brain consists of numerous, interconnected structural components which function interdependently and mediate the activities of the mind.[4]

### The Brain Stem and Action

At the base of the skull, just at the top of the spinal column is an elongated structure known as the brain stem. The brain stem is the inner and most primitive layer of our brain complex. It mediates reproduction, self-preservation, and vital functions such as the circulation of blood, breathing, sleeping, and the contraction of muscles in response to external stimulation. The brain stem is sometimes referred to as the "reptilian brain" because all vertebrates from reptiles to mammals share this portion of the anatomy. We can think of the brain stem as the source of physical action. Many of the functions mediated by the brain stem are determined by instinct. The brain stem is also responsive to impulses from the limbic system and neocortex. Thus it is possible to bring functions mediated by the brain stem under a certain degree of voluntary control.

### The Limbic System and Emotion

The limbic system is the next layer and covers the top of the brain stem. Its function seems to be the generation of emotions that play an important part in motivation and memory. Two structures within the limbic system that are especially central to emotional experience and memory are the amygdala (a small, almond-shaped structure) and the hippocampus. Scientists can surgically stimulate the limbic system of laboratory animals and create spontaneous outbursts of fear and aggression. Tumors in this region can cause abnormal emotional behavior including extreme acts of violence.

The limbic system reacts very rapidly to incoming impulses from our senses. Neuroanatomy research has established that sensations travel directly to the amygdala in the limbic system before the same information reaches the highest level of the brain, the cerebral cortex. The amygdala mediates an appraisal of the emotional significance of the sensations and sends signals to activate other brain structures that generate the felt emotion. Emotions are early warning signals that focus our attention, stimulate further, more conscious mental activity, and motivate us to action.[5]

4. D. L. Watson, *Psychology* (Belmont, Calif.: Brooks Cole, 1992), chaps. 2–8.

The appraisal of sensations mediated by the emotional system is rapid and operates outside of conscious awareness. Because of this, emotions are most often experienced as involuntary and unavoidable. The rapid, preconscious appraisal process detects immediately whether the sensations signal something strange or familiar, good or bad, strong or weak, active or passive. But the question arises, "Who is doing this preconscious appraisal?" Based on current understanding of the operation of the emotional system it appears that the "appraisals" mediated by the limbic system are a joint result of instinct and experience.

The research on infants implicates genetic endowment as one causal factor in emotional experience. Babies have a repertoire of facial and motor expressive responses from birth. These are accompanied by feelings that precede learning experiences. Infants born blind and deaf have expressive patterns equal to normal children. From the earliest phases of life, a child possesses both the capacity to experience the primary quality of feelings and the ability to manifest them through expressive motor behavior such as facial expressions, voice tone, crying, visual tracking, and the cycling of the hands and the feet. The emotional system appears to be innately responsive to a variety of experiences that are common to infants in interaction with their primary caregivers, usually the mother and the father. The emotional system is very responsive to concrete sensations that accompany human interaction such as pleasure, pain, voice tone, facial expressions, body posture, movement, touch, smell, color, shapes, rhythms, and images. The famous pediatrician T. Berry Brazelton has noted that babies have a series of expressive motor responses that seem employed exclusively in interaction with others. Thus the emotional system, from birth, is primarily activated in relationships with others and is central in the attachment between the infant and others.[6]

The infant's earliest feelings are not very differentiated. As the infant grows in his or her cognitive capacity for symbolic thought (e.g., the ability to maintain some notion of mother even when she is not in eye sight [a phenomenon referred to as object constancy]), he or she begins to develop increasingly differentiated emotional experiences. A crucial process in the child's development is the differentiation between "me" and "not me." For example, for the child to be able to experience the emotion of guilt, he or she must possess some degree of self-awareness. As the child grows, cognitive and emotional development proceed together. The quality of early emotional attachments has a profound effect on the developing child because of the responsiveness of her emotional system to human relationships and her limited cognitive capacity. In her chapter in this volume (pp. 151–68), Dr. Duvall stresses the cen-

5. L. S. Greenberg and J. D. Safran, *Emotion In Psychotherapy: Cognitive Processes and Emotional Disorders* (New York: Guilford, 1987).
   6. V. F. Guidano and G. Liotti, *Emotions in Psychotherapy* (New York: Guilford).

tral role of relationships in the development and treatment of psychological problems within psychodynamic theory. The central role of the emotional system in the attachment process identified here supports her analysis from a neuropsychological standpoint.

### The Cerebral Cortex and Thought

The cerebral cortex is the large convoluted mass of brain tissue that surrounds the limbic system. It is divided into two halves, called hemispheres. As a broad generalization, we can say that the left hemisphere of the cerebral cortex mediates language and speech (in right-handed individuals) and the right hemisphere mediates nonverbal processes including imagery and subtle visual and auditory pattern discrimination. The two hemispheres of the neocortex are connected by an enormous band of more than two hundred million axons called the corpus callosum, which transmits electrical impulses between the two hemispheres. The left hemisphere sends and receives impulses from the right half of the body and the right hemisphere sends and receives impulses from the left half of the body. So if a person has a stroke that causes brain damage to the motor area in the left hemisphere, they would experience paralysis on the right side of the body and vice versa. This feature of the brain-body connection is known as contra-lateral control.

The hemispheric processing of visual information is a little more complex. Since our subsequent discussion of human consciousness will describe studies using visual perception, it is important to understand how the two hemispheres process visual stimuli. Imagine a person looking at a dot projected on a screen. If two words are momentarily flashed on the screen, one on each side of the dot, and the person continues to fixate on the dot, then the word to the right of the dot is projected to the left hemisphere and the word to the left of the dot is projected to the right hemisphere. Because the corpus collosum and another interconnection, called the optic chiasm, transmit impulses between the two hemispheres, the person would perceive the two words as a single phrase projected on the screen.[7]

The cerebral cortex uncommitted is uniquely designed to support what are referred to as the "higher mental processes." In fact, of all mammals humans have the largest amount of uncommitted gray matter at birth, a phenomenon that accounts for our vastly superior ability to learn and adapt. Our capacities for symbolic mental processes like language and imagery, which enable us to engage in abstract reasoning, creative thinking, and verbal and symbolic expression, are mediated by the cerebral cortex.

Endowed by our Creator at conception with innate capacities (Ps. 139:13–16) that insure our survival after birth under the care of our parents, we begin

---

7. Michael S. Gazzaniga, *The Social Brain: Discovering the Networks of the Mind* (New York: Basic Books, 1985).

to acquire memories of our experience which then further shape and are shaped by our ongoing interaction with the world. Within the limits of genetic endowment, humans have a tremendous capacity for learning, adaptation, growth, and change enabled by the magnificent brain God has given us.

The impact of experience on the child's developing brain is most profound early in life. As the child matures patterns of behaving, thinking, and feeling become more fixed and stable as natural development and life experience affect memory structures. A young child whose loving parents are sensitive to his or her unique gifts and talents and who is encouraged to constructive activity will have a secure base on which to build his or her life. On the other hand, a child who is harshly punished, criticized and ridiculed, or sexually violated by trusted adults will carry an emotional vulnerability throughout his life because of the nature of the memories such early trauma creates and the impact these memories have on subsequent thinking, feeling, and behaving. Scripture is replete with admonitions to parents to act responsibly in the nurture of the children God gives us. Jesus gives special consideration to children (Matt. 19:14; Mark 9:37) and pronounces harsh judgment on anyone who causes a child harm (Mark 9:42). The impact early traumatic experiences have on the child's vulnerable brain system is consistent with these biblical teachings.

## Psychologically Significant Mental Processes

Having identified the main components of the human brain and the primary functions they serve, we can turn to a more focused discussion of psychological processes that the brain system mediates. I have identified three characteristics of brain functioning that will be important throughout the remainder of the chapter. One is that the physical brain consists of a diversity of components that operate as separate, interactive systems in the mediation of consciousness. The second is that, from birth, the child's brain is dominated by emotional and perceptual processes and that this feature, together with the child's long period of limited conceptual capacity, makes childhood a time of psychological vulnerability for the mind. The third is that emotions are mediated by a brain system whose functioning is programmed from birth, that is sensitive to non-verbal stimuli, especially those experienced in relationships with other people, and is capable of learning and differentiation over time. We will now consider some significant mental processes that the brain mediates.

### Sensation, Perception, and Consciousness

Sensations are the most basic level of information in the mental system. Sensations are space and time patterns of neuronal firing that result from the excitation of external and internal sensing organs and are transmitted to the brain by the nervous system. Sensations are present in all organisms in the phylogenetic scale including protozoans. Sensations can affect an organism directly by eliciting a reflex response or by activating higher level mental processes.

Perceptions are interpretations of the meaning of sensations. The meaning is derived from an interaction of the sensation with memories of previous experiences. Whereas sensations may directly stimulate a reflex reaction, perceptions form the basis of adaptive learning and purposeful behavior. This is so because they incorporate memories of previous experience to interpret current sensory input. Sensations and most perceptions do not enter conscious awareness, but we can make ourselves aware of them by a conscious introspective process.

Sensations are essential to the maintenance of our physical and mental health. Perceptions are mental translations of sensations and are the building blocks of consciousness. We could say that sensations represent our experience and that perceptions are the meanings we give that experience. This can be illustrated by the phenomenon of language. If we hear the same phrase in two different languages, we will have the sensation of hearing sounds. Our perception of the meaning of the phrase in each case will depend on our prior experience with the languages spoken.

The brain's emotional system is particularly responsive to sensations. As was noted above, we begin life with a capacity to experience instinctually a certain basic set of feelings in response to certain sensations. The physical sensations a child experiences when interacting with her adult caregivers stimulate emotional responses that facilitate bonding between the parent and the child. Memories of these early emotionally ladened experiences become the core of our personalities and the mental grid through which we will interpret the rest of our life. As the child acquires the capacity for language and higher levels of abstract thought, the emotional memories are associated with verbal propositions to form conceptual-emotional belief complexes about the self and the world. Beautiful scenery, a warm bath, soothing music, vigorous exercise, the company of a cheerful friend, or the encouraging words of a passage of Scripture can all influence our belief complexes.

### Emotions and Memory

It is evident by now that emotions and memories are two very important psychological phenomena. Within the human brain, emotions play a very important role in memory. We often remember the feeling tone of an experience long after we have forgotten the content. An event that has strong emotional overtones is remembered with much greater clarity and detail than unimportant events. The recent movie, *JFK*, tells a version of the story of the assassination of John F. Kennedy. Most people born before 1950 can recall, in great detail, what they were doing on the day the president was shot in Dallas. Because of the emotional impact this event had on them, they remember more about that day than the day before the assassination. The Post Traumatic Stress Disorder (PTSD) is another example of the vividness with which people record emotionally significant events. Vietnam War veterans have been particularly subject to this debilitating problem because of the unusually traumatic nature of the land war in Asia.

The Post Traumatic Stress Disorder also illustrates another feature of emotionally significant memories. The original emotionally traumatic experience can be reactivated by sensations or perceptions that remind the person of the original event. Victims of such traumas find it very difficult to inhibit these flashback experiences or moderate the emotional response once it starts. This is because of the automatic, preconscious mediation of the memory structures. Once activated, the emotional experience may further stimulate the recollection of thoughts and images of the initial traumatic event, causing the person to feel like they are reliving the trauma.

Under normal life circumstances, if an initial, automatic emotional response proves unnecessary, it can be quickly overridden by conscious, rational analysis. Suppose you were walking along the sidewalk and became momentarily frightened by the sudden sound of a low flying helicopter. You would quickly calm down when you saw the chopper fly safely over you and proceed out of sight. For a Vietnam veteran suffering from PTSD, the sound of the chopper might trigger an emotional reaction and related memory flashbacks too strong to be moderated by conscious appraisals. Under such circumstances his emotional reaction may appear to an observer to be "irrational." But it is more accurate to say that the emotional reaction reflects the "rational" appraisal of the automatic, emotional memory system which may be at odds with the "rational" appraisal of the conscious, conceptual system. Sometimes the information that triggers the emotional reaction never reaches conscious awareness and the person is at a loss to explain the emotional reaction. This is often seen in the symptoms of an adult sexually molested as a child. Subtle interpersonal mannerisms of a spouse may trigger emotional reactions that neither partner understands. Failure to understand the causal connection with the sex abuse can result in serious misunderstandings, marital problems and divorce.

Emotions are one of the most misunderstood and underestimated brain functions. Emotions have been variously viewed as irrational, subjective, dangerous, sinful, and related to the flesh. Yet Scripture clearly recognizes the distinction between emotions and sin. Paul writes in Ephesians 4:26 that we should be angry but "not sin." We need a better understanding of emotions and their function if we are going to have an adequate model of human nature. Emotions are concrete experiences with specific informational content. To feel something means to know something. Emotions, feelings, or "vibes" are identified with the tacit or intuitive level of knowing. Emotions are the "royal road" to understanding a person's deeper, core beliefs which may not be consciously recognized. Emotions are often the first or only clues to dysfunctional memories which must be made conscious if the person is to change the memories and experience healing.

### Consistency: The Organizing Principle of Memory

One of the notable features of our memory systems are their structure. This structure is called a memory schema. A schema is a representation of diverse mental elements and the meaningful relationships among those elements. Consider the following example. A child wakes up on Christmas morning and runs down to the tree to unwrap her presents. She sits on the soft carpet and there is a fire in the nearby fireplace. The bright colors of the gift wrap, the Christmas music playing on the stereo, and the smell of breakfast wafting in from the kitchen, all add to the emotional intensity of this special moment. When such an experience is stored in memory, the elements and associations are stored as a unified whole, as a memory schema. In the future, when one element of this schema is represented in consciousness, the other characteristics of the episode will tend to be recalled. A person's self-concept is one example of an emotionally laden memory schema.

A key feature of sensations, perceptions, and thoughts that affects whether or not they are linked together in a schema is their degree of similarity or consistency. There are a vast array of features that will affect the degree of similarity and hence, the degree to which mental events will be linked in a memory schema. When two or more events enter consciousness, the mental system will experience a state of tension or dissonance until the events are associated into the most homogeneous schema possible. This process is analogous to the state of tension we experience when we first look at the pieces of a puzzle. As we examine the various pieces the degree of "fit," consistency, guides our perception of what goes together. When we cannot find a way to fit pieces together in a "consistent" whole, we will experience tension and frustration. As we build the puzzle into a more coherent whole, the state of tension decreases until the moment when we experience the satisfaction of seeing the unified whole. The principle of consistency and the dynamic of dissonance are important for understanding how emotional schemas are formed and how they are changed. Memory structuring is a goal-oriented process guided by the principle of consistency and motivated by the tension of dissonance.

Since time is one of the most powerful factors influencing perceived relationships, memory schemas tend to be episodic in nature, like a stored video tape. A person's degree of knowledge and conceptual skill will also affect perceptions of consistency and logical relatedness. Young children create explanations for events in their lives that are very different from adults. Again, turning to sexual abuse victims for an illustration, one of the debilitating effects of such abuse is that the children virtually always conclude they are somehow responsible for the sexual encounter and so they connect toxic emotions like shame and fear of punishment to the memory of the abuse episodes. An important part of the process of recovery involves accessing and changing these shame schemas.

The associations evident in memory schemas are not fixed. Changing memories requires a change in the way the person perceives the elements of the schema and their relationships. Without minimizing the spiritual realities of conversion, we can understand the powerful psychological effects faith in Christ and our new knowledge about God and his love will have on our thoughts and feelings in terms of the principles of consistency and dissonance. Such a major change in our beliefs will have a major impact on our memory schemas. The result is a renewing of the mind (Rom. 12:2).

In working to influence others, we have maximum impact for change if we can induce questioning (dissonance) or novel ways of viewing old problems or induce new ways of feeling that are inconsistent with prior beliefs (belief is another word for a memory schema). Changing a person's beliefs requires activating their related belief schemas. You can tell if you have activated a core belief schema by the emotional intensity the person experiences. Important, emotionally ladened self schemas are most likely to be activated (elicited) in the context of important interpersonal relationships. Much of the power of the therapeutic relationship discussed by Nancy Duvall in her chapter (pp. 151–68) can be understood in terms of the consistency and dissonance principles of memory and the responsiveness of our emotional systems to interpersonal relationships.

Another important way to activate significant emotional schemas is through the use of stories, metaphors, and illustrations and the inclusion of novel or unexpected information. Effective speakers and writers use these techniques to impact their listener or reader. This principle is powerfully illustrated in the story of Nathan confronting David about his sins of adultery and murder recorded in 2 Samuel 12. He used the story about the stolen lamb to activate David's beliefs about fairness and justice. Prior to Nathan's confrontation, David was obviously not seeing himself in the story. His strong judgment of the thief in Nathan's story showed he was clearly emotionally involved. When Nathan says to him, "You are the man!", the impact on David's emotions and beliefs is immediate and powerful and the subsequent change is dramatic. That David responded so fully in repentance rather than becoming defensive or having a nervous breakdown can be understood in terms of core emotional beliefs about God and his love that were evident throughout David's life. Scripture says that David was a man after God's own heart (1 Sam. 13:14; Acts 13:22). Since memory schemas (beliefs) are hierarchical, his core relational, emotional schemas about God guided his response to Nathan. To not repent and seek God's forgiveness would have been inconsistent with

David's emotional attachment with God and would have been a threat to his core identity.

### Self-Awareness

One of the most significant aspects of human consciousness is the capacity for self-awareness. Self-awareness is the conscious process of interpreting our own subjective experience. It is a process of turning our attention to our internal states and becoming aware of our thoughts, feelings, and sensations. It is often referred to as introspection. It is a doubling of awareness in consciousness where I both have a subjective experience and become aware of the nature of that experience. For example, when I was a teenager I was always quite nervous when I would ask a girl out for a date for the first time. As I dialed the telephone, I would be aware of my nervousness, fear, and uncertainty of her feelings toward me. I'd talk to myself—a unique feature of self-awareness—to calm down and maintain the courage to ask for the date. When she answered the phone, I'd make the request for a date and then wait for the answer. If it was no, then I'd be aware of negative thoughts and feelings about myself and about her as I sat and struggled with feelings of rejection.

As I observed myself having these reactions, I would experience having feelings about my feelings. I would judge myself as weak, inept, and neurotic because I was having the feelings of rejection. I would replay the experience sometime later in my mind, usually as I was trying to go to sleep, and experience the rejection feelings again. More often than not other similar experiences of rejection would come to mind and the feelings of self-rejection would intensify. The negative thoughts and feelings would be so automatic and intrusive that the only way I could get to sleep was to redirect my focus of attention to some other thing like counting sheep or the next day's activities. We can control the content and intensity of our self-awareness to a certain degree by how we direct our focus of attention.

Visualization is a form of self-awareness that has become very popular in sports like golf and tennis. It is well established that you can improve your skill in either of these sports by effective use of visualization. The popular book, *The Inner Game of Tennis,* teaches these techniques. Visualization has also been used extensively in psychological treatment. These techniques have been controversial in the Christian church. The use of visualization techniques by secular psychologists and New Age gurus is one of the reasons critics say Christians should not be involved in psychology. But this is a case of rejecting a technique because of guilt by association. As has been argued here, visualization is a form of symbolic thought that is a natural result of our brains capacity for such cognition. The real issue in the controversy is the content of one's thoughts, not the process itself. In fact, we are told in Scripture to use our capacity for thought and visualization in order to experience the peace of God (Phil. 4:8–9).

Our capacity for symbolic, self-representational thought provides a way in which the effects of trauma such as childhood abuse can be transformed. Visualization allows the victim to access those early memories and transform them by self-reflective, conscious experience. The skill of the helper is crucial in this process. Merely accessing painful memories, without simultaneously providing new symbolic experiences and insights, can be more destructive than helpful. In fact, most victims have learned to cope with their abuse primarily by not thinking about it because they have been unable to experience new insights needed to achieve healing.

Self-awareness is an abstract, symbolic form of cognition that allows us to access, experience, and change emotional memories. Self-awareness is a mental process that can have a profound effect on our state of being. It is central to the process of self-direction and self-control. It is the process through which faith enters our consciousness and begins to transform our mind (Rom. 12:2).

Having considered some basic processes of the mind, we will now consider some research on consciousness that indicates the degree to which consciousness can become divided. The research was done with a special group of people who have had their corpus callosums severed for medical reasons. Persons who have had this operation are called split-brain patients.

## Some Research on Consciousness

In the previous sections we have emphasized a number of important mental processes which are mediated by our brains. The research described in the next section illustrates that complex mental processes can occur outside of conscious awareness and result in significant behaviors, emotions, or perceptions. The studies described illustrate the possibility of a state of divided consciousness that challenges our understanding of self-awareness and our subjective sense of possessing a unified consciousness. The research has been done with split brain patients.

### The Split Brain

The corpus callosum connecting the two halves of the cortex can be surgically cut. Severing this connection as well as a smaller, more anterior structure called the anterior commissure isolates one hemisphere of the brain from the other. The corpus callosum can be surgically severed in mammals with surprisingly little effect on functioning. What psychological effects there are of such surgery were first observed by Roger Sperry and Ronald Myers at California Institute of Technology in the late 1950s. They discovered that when all the interconnections between the two half brains were severed in cats, the right brain literally did not know what the left brain was doing. The phenomena is described very nicely by a former student of Sperry's, Dr. Michael Gazzaniga :

[If] a cat learned while the right eye was open but the left eye was closed that every time it pushed a panel with a triangle on it, it would receive some liver pate, it did not know that fact subsequently when the left eye was open and the right was closed. The information learned by the right brain did not transfer over to the left brain. In study after study, animals with sectioned neural interconnections between the hemispheres behaved as if they had two separate brains, hence the term "split brains."[8]

Split-brain studies in humans became possible when a professor of neurosurgery at Caltech decided to cut the corpus callosum of a patient whose seizures were uncontrollable by any other means. The surgeries were successful and the degree of seizure control exceeded expectations. Gazzaniga notes that when this operation is done for people with severe epilepsy, the patient's behavior, affect, and general personality are virtually unaltered.[9]

Post-surgical testing of the patient with the severed corpus callosum revealed a fascinating aspect of split-brain phenomenon that could not be observed with animals because animals cannot talk. The split-brain patient could report those things flashed to his right visual field (left hemisphere) but reported no awareness of having seen anything when the same things were projected to his left visual field (right hemisphere). When the patient was questioned after something had been exposed to his left visual field he denied having seen anything. The same phenomena were observed when the patient was blindfolded and objects were placed in his right and left hands. Things put in the right hand were easily named, things put in the left hand could not. The difference in conscious awareness between the two hemispheres was fascinating. A few of those studies will be described below. The observations reported by the researchers are interesting in themselves but are especially of interest to us as we consider what it means to be human. The experiments to be described demonstrate the mental capacities of these separate brains and clearly raise questions about the common-sense notion that our mind consists of a unified, indivisible consciousness.[10]

*Out-of-awareness perception resulting in behavior.* While it has been noted that the left hemisphere is dominant for language some split-brain patients do have limited language capacity in the right hemisphere. In a study reported by Gazzaniga one such patient had the word *bike* flashed to his right visual field. He reported not seeing anything. The experimenter then asked him to draw a picture of the word with his left hand which is controlled by the right hemisphere. The patient said he didn't know what to draw. The experimenter coaxed him to let his left hand try to draw something. Then, under guidance

8. Ibid., 29.
9. Ibid., 41.
10. Ibid., 77.

of the right hemisphere, the left hand picked up a pencil and drew a picture of a bicycle. The conscious, verbal patient had no idea what the left hand was drawing.

Consider the fascinating dual "selves" in this example. The dominant left hemisphere possesses the verbal "self" who interacts with the experimenter to cooperate with the demands of the situation. The "self" of the right hemisphere has perceived the word, associates the object with its verbal label (bike), and comprehends the experimenters verbal instructions. But he could only express himself through the action of drawing. In this particular patient, the right hemisphere mediated perception of the bike and comprehension of the word "bike," but the perception was not available to the verbal system in the left hemisphere. So the patient reports not having seen anything. When asked to draw something, he reports being confused because he is not aware of having seen anything that could be drawn. He wants to comply with the request but he does not have the knowledge to do so in awareness. Yet the left hand, directed by the non-verbal consciousness of the right hemisphere, was able to respond accurately to the experimenter's request. Even as his own left hand drew the correct picture verifying the right hemisphere's perception and linguistic comprehension, the conscious self of the left hemisphere remained confused and could only hazard a guess as to what was seen based on his interpretation of his own crude drawing.

This is a fascinating example of a divided consciousness involving parallel processing that is a challenge to our sense of being a unified self. The activity directed by the right hemisphere was in response to the verbal request of another human being and involved performing a conceptual matching task and a complex visual-motor task to depict an object whose name had been seen in the left visual field for a brief moment.

*Out-of-awareness perception resulting in emotion.* Out-of-awareness perception can also have an impact on our emotional state. Gazzaniga used a complex visual tracking machine to show a film to the left visual field of a split-brain patient. It was a film about safety and had some physical violence in it. While the patient was not aware of seeing anything, the content of the film clearly had an impact on her emotional state. She became uneasy and fearful in a normally secure and familiar testing situation. Although she was conscious of her emotional state, she could not account for its origin because she was cut off from awareness of what had been seen by her mute right hemisphere by virtue of her commissurotomy.

What is also of interest in this particular experiment is that, although the right hemisphere could not communicate the content of the scene that had been seen, the resulting feeling tone was available to conscious awareness. It is also worth noting that the right hemisphere was able to mediate comprehension of the possible meaning of the violent film for the self, as indicated by her emotional response, without any verbal, conscious mediation. The connections between the right hemisphere and the limbic system would account for this process. It is a clear example of emotion resulting from direct visual perception of a potential threat. As was noted earlier, much of our emotional experience, especially early in life, is the result of such direct experience without conscious, verbal mediation.

Perceptions of threatening stimuli not only automatically activate emotions, but also arouse our physiological systems that support the fight or flight response as well. The result is that we experience action tendencies along with the emotions and physiological arousal that are seemingly automatic. In the split-brain patient, the degree of emotional upset triggered by the film suggests that her right hemisphere could mediate comprehension of the threat in the film but could not provide the conceptual moderation of her experience. In fact, she reported feeling fearful and expressed a desire to get away from the experimenter. She could not explain any of these reactions, especially the reaction to the experimenter whom she knew well and liked very much.[11]

*Out-of-awareness perception by an intact brain.* The previous research studies reported controlled observations with split-brain patients. The same left hemisphere localization of verbal, self-aware consciousness can be demonstrated using anesthesia. In a procedure called the Wada test, a fast-acting anesthetic is injected in such a way that the drug is delivered to one hemisphere and not to the other. The technique allows one hemisphere to be put to sleep temporarily while the other remains awake. Gazzaniga was able to observe and test a patient who had his left (verbal) hemisphere anesthetized. After the anesthesic was injected, no consciousness was associated with the left brain as indicated by a paralyzed right hand. The left hand was mobile because the right brain was awake. Gazzaniga placed a spoon in the speechless person's left hand and asked him to remember it.[12]

After the drug wore off the patient was asked to name the object placed in his left hand. The patient looked puzzled and did not have conscious awareness that anything had been placed in his hand. His only experience was that of being "asleep" for a period of time. He had no conscious recollection of the just transpired events.

When it was clear that the patient could not recall the object on his own, even though he had an intact corpus callosum and could, theoretically, "go get" the requested information from the right hemisphere, he was shown a group of objects, one of which was the spoon. Upon viewing the objects he had a flash of awareness of familiarity and correctly identified the spoon as the one placed in his left hand.

11. Ibid., 76.
12. Ibid., 81–84.

I find this sequence of events to be totally fascinating. It is an unambiguous demonstration of how experience, processed perceptually with the left brain temporarily out of action, remains inaccessible to verbal consciousness, even in the intact brain. Verbal exhortations by the experimenter to remember the object and motivated searching by the subject did not produce the correct identification. It took another concrete experience (seeing the group of objects), which facilitated the perception of familiarity by the right brain, and the attention of the now conscious and connected left brain for the person to recognize the object.

### The Brain and the Mind

One of the most widely debated issues in philosophy has been the nature of the mind as distinct from the brain. The dualist position described in detail by J. P. Moreland in his chapter (pp. 55–79) maintains that the mind is a distinct, nonmaterial entity. The mental properties of the mind, while dependent upon and interacting with the physical substructures of the brain, are nevertheless distinct mental entities. On the other hand, most contemporary cognitive neuroscientists, who tend to be monists, view the mind as "the emergent properties of sufficiently complex and appropriately organized matter which qualitatively transcends a simple summation of the elementary properties of the constituent parts."[13] In other words, the brain, with its complex of 100 to 200 billion neurons, its different parts and their interconnections, is assumed to be the material substance that gives rise to the emergent functioning of the mind. The term *mind* is the label they use to describe the complex functioning of the material brain.

While I endorse the dualist view of the mind and brain, it is clear that, in either view, the brain is essential to the functioning of the mind. The brain mediates between material reality and subjective existence, the subjective sense of being a self. The working brain helps anchor the mind in the empirical world. The brain's capacity to carry out the neurophysiological processes that underlay consciousness and facilitate the storing of memories of prior experiences are essential to learning and adaptation. A healthy, functioning brain is essential for full expression of our selves. When physical brain structures are injured or diseased, there is a corresponding impairment of mind functioning. This reality becomes painfully evident when we see an aging loved one begin to suffer from Alzheimer's disease. Impairment of the person's memory functioning is especially painful to witness as the person fails to recognize life-long partners, leaves food cooking on a dangerously hot stove, wanders away from home and gets lost, neglects personal hygiene, and cannot carry on a satisfying conversation because of the impaired memory. Mental ill-

---

13. E. J. John, "A Model of Consciousness," in *Consciousness and Self Regulation*, ed. G. E. Schwartz and D. Shapiro (New York: Plenum, 1976), 1–50.

nesses that have significant organic, neurochemical causes, such as some schizopherenias and manic depressive disorders, are also very disruptive of the functioning of the mind. Brain tumors or lesions can cause dysfunction ranging from dizziness to violent acts such as murder. In each of these instances the brain damage or disease is referred to as organic brain dysfunction since it has physical (organic) causes. The health of the physical brain affects mind functioning.

Some forms of organic brain dysfunction can be treated with more or less success. Medical interventions, either using surgery or medications, may correct or minimize the organic problem restoring the mind to more healthy functioning. An antipsychotic medication can help relieve a schizophrenic from debilitating hallucinations and lithium can stabilize a manic depressive's mood swings. Such treatments are not without their own problems since most psychotropic medications have temporary and/or permanent side effects. Psychological and educational interventions can also help individuals cope more effectively by providing self-understanding, promoting self-acceptance, and facilitating coping skills. There is potential relief from the pain and suffering of organic brain dysfunction and medical and psychological researchers are making great strides in this area. The main point, for our purposes, is that medical science has advanced our understanding of the biological basis of some mental illnesses which in earlier times were identified as moral or spiritual problems. Proper diagnosis and treatment has enabled people with problems caused by impaired brains to be treated effectively with compassion and enabled them to experience a degree of restoration of their mind.

It is also true that the functioning of the mind can be impaired by psychological brain dysfunction. I mean by the term *psychological brain dysfunction* mental dysfunction for which there is no identifiable organic pathology. We would more commonly refer to such dysfunction as "psychological problems," or "emotional problems." I am using the term *psychological brain dysfunction* to emphasize the mediational role of the physical brain in maintaining the psychological problems.

Such a suggestion is controversial among Christians. The controversy arises because of our thinking about self (moral) responsibility. We tend to believe that if a person has a physically healthy brain, then any mental problems are character flaws for which the person is volitionally responsible. Some Christian writers have maintained that for persons with no identifiable organic brain problem there is no such thing as "psychological problems."[14] Such problems are said to be due to sin in the person's life and the solution is to repent and to choose to follow the truth. The solution for such problems must be spiritual and not psychological, the critics maintain. My problem with

14. J. MacArthur, *Our Sufficiency in Christ* (Waco, Texas: Word, 1991).

this position is not with the assertion of the importance of moral responsibility or the need for spiritual renewal. Spiritual concerns are of central importance in dealing with psychological dysfunction, and the knowledge and experience of spiritual truth is central in recovery. My disagreement with the anti-psychology position is that it virtually ignores what we know about the complexity of the functioning of our brain and the interdependence between the brain and the mind.

As we have seen to this point, there are many brain functions that occur automatically, outside of awareness. When a person experiences trauma, psychological brain dysfunctions can result which are mediated by emotional memory structures and the out-of-awareness functioning of certain brain structures. The case of the multiple personality described in the introduction is an example of psychological brain dysfunction. Various aspects of the person's experiences are split off from one another in a way that allows distinct "personalities" to exist in the same person. Psychogenic amnesia is another example of psychologically induced brain dysfunction. Extreme trauma, such as rape or physical assault, can induce various degrees of memory impairment ranging from forgetting episodes or periods of abuse in one's life to, in the more extreme and rare case, total amnesia about one's identity or past. Still another example is when a person's sensory capabilities are impaired due to psychological trauma. This is referred to as conversion disorder. Some examples would be loss of hearing, numbness in some part of the body, or loss of eye sight. While we don't know the specific mechanisms that give rise to these phenomena, it is my belief that these are all examples of brain dysfunction as a result of the interaction of programmed brain functioning (both genetic and learned) and the mind trying to cope with extreme trauma. The coping responses may help the individual psychologically "survive" the trauma experience, but the result is brain dysfunction and impairment of the self after the trauma.

The above are admittedly rare and extreme examples of psychological brain dysfunction, but I give them here because they involve impairments that we typically associate with organic brain damage. They illustrate the severe impact psychological trauma can have on brain functioning. They indicate the degree to which such dysfunction can limit the volitional functioning of the self (the mind). The earlier in the person's life and the more intense the trauma, the more impact the trauma will have on brain functioning and, hence, on the mind. If the trauma occurs in relationship with trusted adults upon whom the vulnerable child is dependent (e.g., parents), then the impairment of subsequent brain and self functioning will be more severe.

For Christians with organically caused dysfunction such as schizophrenia or a manic depressive illness, faith in Christ will not eliminate the need to have appropriate medical treatments. In fact, such treatment may significantly enhance their ability to function spiritually. Similarly, for those Christians who have experienced psychological trauma, faith in Christ doesn't eliminate the memories of the trauma. Nor does one's faith eliminate the continuing impact of these memories on self functioning through various processes of the brain. For example, Christian women who have been sexually abused will have a higher chance of sexual dysfunction in their marriage. This is not to minimize the central importance of faith in Christ for these women's recovery. It is to emphasize that understanding the psychological processes mediated by the physical brain can enhance our efforts to facilitate the emotional, interpersonal, and spiritual well-being of such persons.

## Belief Formation and Brain Functioning

One striking features of Gazzaniga's research with split-brain patients is the demonstration that emotion and action can be directed by modules in the brain outside of the awareness of the verbal self. We will look next at what happens when the verbal self has to try to understand behavior or emotion generated by these unconscious processes. In the example given below we see a unique aspect of what it means to be human, namely, the ability of humans to form beliefs about themselves and their world.

The existence of belief systems in the human mind is the basis for what we describe as free will. That is, the ability of the human mind to make inferences, to reason, leads to the formation of a symbolic system of concepts we call beliefs. Beliefs allow us to reason beyond the context of our immediate environment. Our beliefs free us from progress by trial and error and form the basis for self-direction and self-control. However, the abstract, conceptual beliefs one forms are a function of the information available to our conscious selves when the beliefs were formulated. When an individual is confronted with emotion or behavior that has been the result of mental processes of which they are not aware, then the belief formation process reflects the person's best inference to explain the event. Let's consider an example from Gazzaniga's research.

### Belief and the Left Hemisphere

A young split-brain patient named Paul sat looking at a black dot on a screen in front of him. To the left of the fixation point the researchers flashed a snow scene. To the right of the fixation point they flashed a chicken claw. Paul's task was to identify, from a set of cards on the table in front of him, which card went with what he had seen. There were eight cards with eight different objects pictured on them: a lawn mower, a rake, a shovel, an axe, an apple, a toaster, a hammer, and a chicken head. Consistent with split-brain perception, his right hand pointed to the chicken head and the left hand pointed to the shovel. Then Paul was asked why he picked the two different pictures. He responded without hesitation, "Oh that's easy. The chicken claw goes with the chicken head and you need a shovel to clean out the chicken shed."[15] Because the left half of the brain had no awareness of the snow scene, Paul constructed a rational explanation for his behavior in light of the information he had. He was able to construct a believable rationalization, a belief about his behavior. The left hemisphere mediates our conscious construction of conceptual beliefs about ourselves and the world. The process of belief formation is stimulated by events in our lives including our own actions.

### Beliefs and Action

In the New Testament Book of James we see an emphasis on the relationship between beliefs and action. We are told to show our faith by our works. Jesus also stressed the intimate connection between our internal states and our actions when he said, "If you love me you will keep my commandments." What we know about brain functioning is that experience can have a powerful influence on beliefs and vice versa. It is important that our Christian life be one of action guided by our faith as well as intellectual assent. Encouraging people to engage in activity consistent with their beliefs will strengthen their faith. Behaving in ways that are inconsistent with our faith beliefs will undermine those beliefs; it is an inevitable consequence of our brain function. We need to find constructive programs of activity in the church that will allow individuals to participate in faith-strengthening activity. A faith expressed primarily in the cerebral cortex will become weak over time. Faith and works are related in the brain.

## Ministering to the Whole Mind

Two of the most significant psychological processes of the mind mediated by our brains are emotions and thoughts. Teaching in the Christian church places a great deal of emphasis on conscious thoughts and ideas and very little on emotions and feelings. I maintain that this imbalance is due to the lack of understanding of both the implicit, rational nature of our emotional system and the principles of brain function that mediate emotions. We could say that our minds consist of two general belief systems: a conscious, conceptual system mediated by the verbally expressive left hemisphere, and a preconscious, emotional system mediated by the memory schemas and emotional systems of the brain. One consists primarily of explicit, logical rationality. The other consists primarily of implicit, intuitive rationality. The primary language of one is verbal expression; the primary language of the other is emotional expression. Advertisers, interior designers, music composers, and visual artists all understand the impact their mediums have on the emotional system through the control of sensations.

15. Gazzaniga, *The Social Brain*, 72.

What this means for those of us who work in a helping or ministry role with people is that communicating verbal concepts (propositional truth) to others is not enough. We must engage them in active relationships. We must become good observers of the "language of emotional expression" that reveals preconscious beliefs seen in the nonverbal channels of communication. Emotions are primary indicators of a person's preconscious, experientially derived beliefs. The greater the emotional reaction, the more likely it is that a core belief of the person has been implicated. Some of the most important emotional beliefs people possess are about themselves in relationship to other people.

Changing conscious beliefs is a matter of rational discourse. Changing emotional beliefs is another matter. It takes active involvement in a relationship with another person to change their emotional beliefs. It means being able to become important enough to the person that we can impact them at the emotional level. It means becoming his or her friend. It is little wonder that the most significant characteristic of believers in the early church was how they loved one another. Our brains were designed to establish and maintain significant relationships with others and with our Lord. As recovering sinners, we can learn more about ourselves and our sin in such relationships, and we can experience healing and grace as well.

## Suggested Readings

Cosgrove, M. P., and J. Malloy. *Mental Health: A Christian Approach.* Grand Rapids: Zondervan, 1977. [B]

Evans, C. S. *Preserving the Person.* Downers Grove, Ill.: InterVarsity, 1977. [A]

Gazzaniga, Michael S. *Mind Matters: How Mind and Brain Interact to Create Our Conscious Lives.* Boston: Houghton Mifflin, 1988. [I]

———. *The Social Brain: Discovering the Networks of the Mind.* New York: Basic Books, 1985. [I]

Greenberg, L. S., and J. D. Safran. *Emotion In Psychotherapy: Affect Cognition, and the Process of Change.* New York: Guilford, 1987. [A]

Myers, D. G. *The Human Puzzle.* New York: Harper and Row, 1978. [I]

Myers, D. G., and M. A. Jeeves. *Psychology Through the Eyes of Faith.* New York: Harper and Row, 1987. [B]

Penfield, Wilder. *The Mystery of the Mind: A Critical Study of Consciousness and the Human Brain.* Princeton, N. J.: Princeton University Press, 1975. [I].

Watson, D. L. *Psychology.* Belmont, Calif.: Brooks Cole, 1992, chaps. 2–8. [B]

# A Response to Keith J. Edwards

## J. P. Moreland

My response to Professor Edwards's stimulating chapter will focus on areas of agreement and an area of clarification. I am not comfortable with some of the ways he talks, for example, that memories are stored in the brain (I believe they are "stored" in the mind but have causal connections with physical states of affairs in the brain, much like the sounds of a record are not literally stored in the record's groves but are causally connected with those groves) or that emotional and conceptual systems appraise things (I would say that people, consciously or unconsciously, appraise things by means of those systems). However, these are minor compared to the vast territory we share in common.

### Areas of Agreement
*The importance of physical processes and the body for spirituality.* Edwards reminds us that "spiritual growth is a process that intimately involves changes and transformations in our material being." He also says that beliefs affect our actions, and actions change, weaken, or strengthen our beliefs. Now, while I understand the Bible to teach that we are a duality of body and soul taken as distinct entities, we are, nevertheless, a deep unity of the two. We are not disembodied souls. Current models of spiritual formation and discipleship overemphasize the importance of correct thoughts and attitudes in spiritual growth. These are surely important, but the repetitive exercise of certain bodily practices are also crucial for spiritual growth. These practices are the classic disciplines of the spirit, for example, fasting, solitude, silence, praying out loud on one's knees. Dallas Willard's *The Spirit of the Disciplines* (San

198

Francisco: Harper and Row, 1988) is a good treatment of the role of the body in spiritual formation. Edwards's observations shed further light on the importance of the body for spirituality.

*The emotions as forms of perception.* Edwards claims that emotions are not irrational or subjective, but tacit or intuitive means by which we know things. They are, he says, basic forms of perception with a rational nature. In my view, these points are not only correct but of crucial importance. Since the time of philosopher David Hume (1711–1776) it has been fashionable to treat emotions as fleeting little subjective entities that pass through consciousness and have no necessary connections with anything outside themselves. On this view, emotions are neither good nor bad, accurate nor inaccurate, nor do they have objects that they are about; they simply exist. It is only the thoughts, attitudes, or actions associated with emotions that are of importance.

By contrast, those operating in the phenomenological tradition of Franz Brentano (1838–1917) and Edmund Husserl (1859–1938) have held a richer view of emotions. On this view, emotions are modes of perception or intuition, that is, an emotion is a way of perceiving something, a way of being aware of it.

For example, to feel desire for something is to be directly aware of its desirability (or, perhaps, its goodness) or to perceive it *as* desirable. Emotions have intentionality (they are *of* or *about* things), they give us knowledge by acquaintance (i.e., through emotions we become aware of things), they can be accurate or inaccurate, and they can serve as rational grounds for certain beliefs (my feeling of desire for love can serve as rational grounds for the belief that love is an intrinsically good thing). Compared to Hume's treatment of emotions, the phenomenological view is more consistent with Edwards's position and, I believe, with the teaching of Scripture.

### An Area of Clarification

Space does not allow me to interact directly with Edwards's view of sensations and sensory perception. But it may be helpful to have one philosopher's view of these matters to use as a basis of comparison with his. Consider an act of perceiving a black dog running by. Such an act involves many things.

First, stimuli physically interact with the physical body (e.g., eyes, nervous system, brain). Stimuli are whatever physically impinges on my body and the scientist will tell a fairly standard story about them in terms of light waves, electronic impulses produced in the brain, and so forth.

Second, these stimuli cause certain physical states to obtain in the brain and other areas of the body. They also cause sensations to occur in the soul. In the case above, an awareness (or series of awarenesses) of black will occur, that is, one will be appeared to blackly. Sensations are modes of consciousness and are mental entities because (a) they do not have the properties of a material object; (b) they require consciousness before they can exist, but this is not true of any material state of affairs; (c) they have intentionality (the awareness of black is an awareness *of* the dog). Typically, sensations are passively received by subjects. Having a sensation is not an act of seeing (one can have a sensation of a bird flying over one's head that one is not consciously aware of but that can later be recalled to memory).

Third, perceiving the dog involves an active noticing of certain sensations currently in one's visual field. Perception is not passive, but active and an act of perception is something an agent intentionally does.

Fourth, through reflection upon the act of perceiving a black dog (and, perhaps, using memories to compare this act with other acts of perceiving black things), one can form the concept of "being black" and, then, one can see the dog *as* black or see *that* it is black. Seeing that or seeing as require concepts or propositions to be embedded in one's consciousness (Edwards calls them meanings or interpretations). One can see without seeing as or seeing that (e.g., one can be aware of a black dog by being appeared to blackly without having a concept of being black or having some belief in one's mind, say that this dog is black), and generally, seeing forms the grounds of justification for seeing as or seeing that. My claim to see that the dog is black is justified by the dog's appearing black to me.

Fifth, an act of perception is a whole with parts in it (e.g., the mental subject, the object of perception, the appearance of the object in the mind of the perceiving subject, the appearance of the dog in my consciousness as it is viewed from a certain angle). The physical story cited in the first point (about stimuli, brain states, etc.) are not *parts* of the act of perception, but rather necessary conditions that must be present before an act of perception can happen in an embodied person.

Thus, contrary to what Edwards claims, the brain does not mediate an act of perception—I am not spatially trapped inside my brain behind my eyeballs and the brain is not something in between me and the dog through which I see the dog. If this were so, then skepticism about the external world would be hard to avoid. Why? Because I would not really see the dog, but only the image of the dog in my mind (or my brain?). I would be solipsistically trapped behind my sensations and it would be hard to justify belief in things outside my sensations (including my belief that the brain exists!). It is better to view brain states, light waves, and other such phenomena as necessary conditions for acts of perception, not as mediating parts of those acts. And it is important to realize, as Edwards does, that acts of perception are mental events; they cannot be reduced to physical events, nor can the philosophy of perception be reduced to the psychology of perception.

# A Response to Keith J. Edwards

## Scott B. Rae

Edwards's discussion on the nature of human mental life raises some significant issues for further discussion. These relate to the motivation for ethical living and the concepts of moral responsibility and the free will of the individual moral agent.

He rightly emphasizes, as a result of brain hemisphere research applied to the spiritual life of a believer, the need for Christian teaching to do more than simply challenge the cognitive part of one's mind. It must also engage the emotions, since individuals rarely make significant changes in life unless they have been touched emotionally. One's emotions frequently reflect one's core values, and thus those values can only be changed as a person is reached in that emotional part of his life. Edwards correctly points out that teaching in most Christian traditions, particularly evangelicalism, has emphasized the cognitive, rational appeal in order to change a person's conscious thoughts and ideas. Very little emphasis has been placed on appealing to one's emotions that give access to one's preconscious beliefs. Part of the reason for this is surely the concern with emotionalism, with its potential for manipulation. But this hardly merits "throwing the baby out with the bathwater," as has been the case with a good deal of the evangelical tradition.

Edwards's emphasis on dealing with one's emotions as an integral part of maturity is strongly consistent with Scripture, which makes its neglect by the evangelical community somewhat ironic. For example, the poetic literature of the Old Testament, and the Psalms in particular, with their vivid visual images that paint pictures for the reader, are designed to recreate the emotional experiences of the authors so that the readers can share in those experiences. It

201

is quite clear that Old Testament poetry was written to touch the emotional life of the reader, so that the reader would not only read the text for information but also would feel the author's feelings in a way that would leave an indelible imprint on the reader.

Communicating truth in vivid visual images is not unique to poetry, however. Other types of biblical literature, such as prophecy, use the same high, rich poetry as the traditional poetic literature, with the same intent, namely, to touch the reader emotionally as a precursor to substantial and difficult change. Narratives and parables paint extended visual pictures for the reader, enabling them to identify with the material in a way that goes beyond simply cognitive understanding of truth. One striking example of this occurs in 2 Samuel 11–12, when the prophet Nathan confronts David with his adultery and murder. Using a parable, Nathan accesses David's emotional life as well as his cognitive understanding. Once he is touched emotionally, Nathan's point is made and repentance results shortly thereafter. Taken together, these types of literature contained in Scripture constitute a majority of the biblical revelation. Even the epistles, which appear on the surface to be the more cognitively oriented literature, contain numerous examples of figurative language, and consistently appeal to the believer living out life *in community*, that is, within relationships that embody the truths being taught in the epistles. Perhaps this biblical emphasis is one reason, though certainly not the only one, why precursors to the ancient heresy of gnosticism (which established an elitism based on possession of mysterious spiritual knowledge) were so resisted by the New Testament authors.

Split brain research also raises issues of moral responsibility and free will. As Edwards has shown, psychological brain dysfunction occurs in response to extreme trauma. Though clearly not the same thing as organic brain syndrome or other psychological problems that have a clear organic source, nevertheless there seems to be a connection between trauma suffered by an individual and the production of brain dysfunction. Without a clear organic cause, there has been hesitancy to exempt a person from moral, and criminal, when appropriate, responsibility for their actions. But this research raises new issues of free will, and thus moral responsibility, in that in cases of psychological trauma there does appear to be a connection between brain dysfunction and a response to extreme trauma. Edwards cites the multiple personality disorder, psychogenic amnesia, and the psychogenic fuge state as examples of this link. Whether this should exempt one from moral and even criminal responsibility is a new question presented by such research. At the least, it should make Christian leaders more realistic about the effects of a person coming to Christ and becoming a new creation, without, of course, minimizing the place of one becoming a new person spiritually speaking before God. The process of living out one's new relationship to God may be much more difficult if such trauma induced dysfunction is part of an individual's background. Further, it should make all believers much more compassionate with fellow brothers and sisters who are struggling with addictions of various kinds and other similarly difficult issues of life. Part of the pastoral task in encouraging the moral life is helping individuals understand why they are stuck in particular areas of life. Though people certainly reap what is sown in consequence of sin, it may be that they are suffering not because of a sin they committed, but because of a sin committed *against them*. People who have suffered sexual or physical abuse, who then turn around and become abusers themselves, or compensate for that trauma in some other way, deserve understanding and compassion since they began the moral life with some significant strikes against them. Whether this alleviates moral responsibility is another issue, though in cases of extreme trauma, at least it makes the coping mechanism easier to understand without perhaps justifying it.

# Part 4

# Understanding the Moral/Spiritual Dimension of Being Human

*Christian Perspectives
from New Testament Studies,
Medical Ethics, and Education*

# 7

# The Apostle Paul's View of the "Sin Nature"/"New Nature" Struggle

*Walt Russell*

## Introduction

Building a Christian theology of being human traditionally has been the construction project of our systematic theologians. The history of the Christian church testifies to their fine workmanship. However, the quality of their work is only as good as the materials with which they are given to work. As a New Testament exegete, my task is to be one of the key suppliers of contextually-accurate and exegetically-sound biblical insights for our theologians. This chapter is an attempt to supply some fresh exegetical building materials to the theologically-minded for improving our Christian perspective on being human. In this sense, it is foundational to developing both our systematic theology and Christian world view.

Throughout most of the history of the Christian church, theologians have not spoken of human beings possessing a "sin nature" or a "new nature," but only of possessing *human* nature. However, within the last century or so the behavior of humans has been attributed by Christian writers to the possession

of either a "sin nature" or a "new nature." All human beings are posited as
having sin natures, but Christians are said to have the additional distinction
of possessing a new, regenerated nature. Moreover, it is commonly asserted
that these two antithetical natures within Christians lead to a serious clash of
purposes. Within this clash Christians have been graphically portrayed as
cages that contain both the black dog of the old nature and the white dog of
the new nature.[1] Allegedly, these dogs are at each others' throats fighting for
control of these cages! The result is that Christians are described by scholars
across a broad theological spectrum in terms like "a battlefield of the opposing forces of flesh and Spirit."[2] Or continuing the warfare metaphor, "the
flesh" is the "traitor within the gates" of Christians who insidiously wars
against their regenerated being.[3]

While this two natures view has serious metaphysical problems, these are
not the focus of this chapter.[4] Rather, the focus is upon the fact that the New
Testament *never* speaks of a person possessing a sin nature nor of a Christian
possessing a new nature. In other words, the writers of the New Testament
never use the most common and obvious term for a "nature" (*phusis*) to refer
to a sin nature or a new nature.

Perhaps at this point you are asking yourself the timely question, "Well
then, what is the basis of this widely held doctrine?" Excellent query! The
doctrine of sin natures and new natures seems to have its basis in a certain interpretation of Paul's use of the flesh/Spirit antithesis in several of his epistles.
According to that interpretation, "the flesh" is viewed as corresponding to the
sin nature and "the Spirit" is viewed as corresponding to the new nature. It is
the thesis of this chapter that such an understanding of the duality or antithesis of the flesh and the Spirit has nothing to do with having a sin nature or a
new nature. Our goal is to dismantle such a connection and to understand
correctly Paul's use of the flesh/Spirit antithesis and thereby gain better insight into the sinful dimension of Christians. To accomplish this goal, we will
briefly survey the present view of the flesh/Spirit antithesis, examine a new

1. Charles R. Smith, "Two Natures—or One? An Attempt at Theological Clarification," *The
Voice* (July-August 1983), 19–21.

2. Hans D. Betz, *Galatians: A Commentary on Paul's Letter to the Churches in Galatia*, Her-
menia—A Critical and Historical Commentary on the Bible (Philadelphia: Fortress, 1979), 272.

3. William D. Lawrence, "The Traitor in the Gates: The Christian's Conflict with the Flesh,"
in *Essays in Honor of J. Dwight Pentecost*, ed. Stanley D. Toussaint and Charles H. Dyer (Chicago:
Moody, 1986), 115–31.

4. The fundamental flaw of the present two natures view is that it treats a nature as, roughly,
an Aristotelian substance (which is a particular individual entity), rather than as a complex of essential properties or attributes possessed by a substance (which, if lost, cause the substance to
cease to be). For more discussion of this, see Smith, "Two Natures—or One?" 19–21. See also
J. Oliver Buswell, *A Systematic Theology of the Christian Religion*, 2 vols. in 1 (Grand Rapids:
Zondervan, 1962–63), 2:52.

lens for viewing the flesh/Spirit duality, and then test our lens on the key passages in Paul's epistles that contain the flesh/Spirit antithesis.

## The View Through Our Present Interpretive Glasses

Probably since Augustine we have used a set of interpretive glasses to read Paul's writings that some have argued does not correspond to Paul's set of glasses.[5] Specifically, in passages where one encounters the flesh/Spirit antithesis (e.g., Rom. 7–8; Gal. 5–6), we have read Paul's descriptions of human behavior metaphysically, rather than historically. We have taken his ethical statements primarily as abstract anthropological descriptions of "parts" of the Christian, rather than as historical descriptions of the whole identity of persons. While the Bible's teaching in general, and Paul's theology in particular, does indeed speak of "parts" of persons with metaphysical implications, we will see that these are not the focus of the flesh/Spirit passages in Paul.

In extended passages where "flesh" (*sarx*) and "Spirit" (*pneuma*) are prominent, they are facilely viewed as a description of the internal duality of the sin nature and the new nature. Within this understanding, *the flesh* is defined as "that element in man's nature which is opposed to goodness, that in him which makes for evil; sometimes thought of as an element of himself, sometimes objectified as a force distinct from him, this latter usage being, however, rather rhetorical."[6] Lexical works like Louw and Nida's *Greek-English Lexicon of the New Testament Based on Semantic Domains* echo this view of *sarx* in contexts like Romans 7–8 and Galatians 5–6. Louw and Nida, in particular, place *sarx* within the semantic domain of "psychological faculties" with similar terms like "the inner man," "the hidden person," "heart," "the inner self." They define *sarx* as "*the psychological aspect of human nature which contrasts with the spiritual nature;* in other words, that aspect of human nature which is characterized by or reflects typical human reasoning and desires in contrast with aspects of human thought and behavior which relate to God and spiritual life . . . 1 Cor. 1:26; Gal. 5:19; Gal. 6:8."[7]

Recent English translations also reflect this internal, non-physical interpretation of *sarx* by rendering it with the extended, less body-oriented term *nature*. Note, for example, three contemporary translations of Galations 5:16.

5. For example, Krister Stendahl, "The Apostle Paul and the Introspective Conscience of the West," in *Paul Among Jews and Gentiles* (Philadelphia: Fortress, 1976), 78–96.

6. Ernest DeWitt Burton, *A Critical and Exegetical Commentary on the Epistle to the Galatians,* The International Critical Commentary (Edinburgh: T. and T. Clark, 1921), 493. This is the seventh and final meaning of (σάρξ) in its New Testament usage according to Burton.

7. Johannes P. Louw and Eugene A. Nida, eds., *Greek–English Lexicon of the New Testament Based on Semantic Domains,* 2 vols. (New York: United Bible Societies, 1988), 1:322 (emphasis mine).

New International Version: "So I say, live by the Spirit, and you will not gratify the desires of *the sinful nature.*"

Revised English Bible: "What I mean is this: be guided by the Spirit and you will not gratify the desires of your *unspiritual nature.*"

Today's English Version: "This is what I say: let the Spirit direct your lives, and do not satisfy the desires of *the human nature.*

Amazingly, in these respective translations, when the reader gets to Galatians 5:24 with its talk of the crucifixion of the flesh, he finds that Christians have already put to death the *sinful nature* or *unspiritual nature* or *human nature.* With the death of this alleged nature or capacity in the Christian, one is hard-pressed to explain why the Christian still sins apart from what appears to me to be confusing identity talk.[8] My dissatisfaction with these explanations, among other factors, has driven me to rethink Paul's use of the flesh/Spirit antithesis as it relates to the sinful dimension of Christian experience. In short, I have come to believe that we need a new set of interpretive glasses for understanding Paul's application of the flesh/Spirit terminology to Christians.

## A Suggested New Set of Interpretive Glasses

I believe we have misunderstood the main aspect of Paul's usage of *flesh* and *Spirit.* I would suggest that he does *not* use these terms primarily to describe an internal duality. Rather, as Herman Ridderbos has argued in other contexts,[9] these two terms are primarily used in a redemptive-historical manner and represent two successive historical eras or modes of existence, separated by Jesus Christ's death, burial, and resurrection. The Christian does not *have* "flesh" (in the ethical sense) *in him/her,* but rather was "in the flesh" (*en sarki*) apart from Jesus Christ. "Flesh" or *sarx* is the merely human, frail and transitory body that stands in stark contrast to God as Spirit. To be "in the flesh" is to be in a mode of existence of "what is merely human."[10] "In the flesh" stands in contrast to being "in the Spirit," that is, indwelt and empowered by God's *pneuma. Everyone* was "in the flesh" *before* Christ's death, burial, and resurrection. The Christian enters a new mode of existence in Christ and is now "in the Spirit" (*en pneumati*), rather than "in the flesh." As Paul flatly states: "However, you are not in the flesh but in the Spirit, if indeed

8. E.g., David C. Needham, *Birthright: Christian Do You Know Who You Are?* (Portland: Multnomah, 1979).

9. Herman Ridderbos, *Paul: An Outline of His Theology,* trans. John R. DeWitt (Grand Rapids: Eerdmans, 1975), 57–68; idem, *When the Time Had Fully Come: Studies in New Testament Theology* (1957; reprint, Jordan Station, Ontario: Paideia, 1982), 44–60, esp. 51–52.

10. John M. G. Barclay, *Obeying the Truth: A Study of Paul's Ethics in Galatians.* Studies of the New Testament and Its World, ed. John Riches (Edinburgh: T. and T. Clark, 1988), 206.

the Spirit of God dwells in you. But if anyone does not have the Spirit of Christ, he does not belong to Him" (Rom. 8:9 NASB).

Particularly, Paul uses *flesh* and *Spirit* in antithesis in his extended discussions of the relationship between Jews and Gentiles in the church in Galatians 3–6, Romans 7–8, and Philippians 3. In these contexts, *flesh* is in tandem with *nomos* ("law") and is associated with the era of Israel under the Mosaic Law. Paul connects *flesh* and *law* in passages like Galatians 5:17–18, Romans 6:12–14, and Romans 8:1–4 in a manner that is very disconcerting to many commentators. He is arguing against the Jewish Christians' advocacy of the proselyte model of Gentile incorporation and against their advocacy of the use of the Mosaic law as the primary means for constraining the Christians' behavior. These Jewish Christians were advocating an anachronistic redemptive-historical model and Paul's response is appropriately redemptive-historical in its logic. In other words, the Jewish Christians were continuing to emphasize the necessity of Gentile Christians entering the community of belief via circumcision. Membership in this community of God's people was to be distinguished by two things: "flesh" (physical kinship or symbolic representation through circumcision) and observance of Torah (the Mosaic law). Paul counters such reasoning by emphasizing the entrance of all peoples into God's people through justification by faith and by underscoring the distinguishing mark of God's people is not "flesh," but possession of the Holy Spirit.

If this new set of interpretive glasses is accurate, then it should clarify the usages of *sarx* in Paul's epistles when they have a moral or ethical sense (Rom. 6:19; 7:5, 18, 25; 8:3, 4, 5, 6, 7, 8, 9, 12, 13; 1 Cor. 5:5; 2 Cor. 1:17; 11:18; Gal. 3:3; 5:13, 16, 17, 19, 24; 6:8; Eph. 2:3; Col. 2:11, 13, 18, 23).[11] Most commentators, operating within the traditional perspective, posit a shift from the bodily sense that *sarx* has in most of its New Testament occurrences to a more extended sense in these "ethical" usages. Some argue that this extended sense is achieved by a figure of speech (a metonymy of container) where the container is used in place of its contents. In other words, the evil impulse is focused upon by referring to the bodily tissues that contain it.[12] E. D. Burton is representative of most commentators when he writes on Galatians 5:13:

The word σάρξ [*flesh*], previously in this epistle a purely physical term, is used here and throughout this chapter (see vv. 16, 17, 20, 24) in a definitely ethical

11. This list is from George E. Ladd, *A Theology of the New Testament* (Grand Rapids: Eerdmans, 1974), 469 n. 44. I would delete 1 Cor. 5:5 from his list because of its synonymous use with *body* (*soma*), and I would add Romans 13:11–14; 1 Corinthians 3:1–3; 2 Corinthians 5:16; 10:2–4; and especially Philippians 3:3–4.

12. E.g., Ernest DeWitt Burton, *Spirit, Soul, and Flesh: The Usages of Πνεῦμα, Ψυχή, and Σάρξ in Greek Writings and Translated Works from the Earliest Period to 180 A.D.; and of their Equivalents* רוּחַ, *and* נֶפֶשׁ, *and* בָּשָׂר *in the Hebrew Old Testament,* Historical and Linguistic Studies, Second Series, Vol. 3 (Chicago: University of Chicago Press, 1918), 191–98.

sense, "that element of man's nature which is opposed to goodness, and makes for evil," in which it appears also in Rom., chap. 8; . . . Of any physical association with this ethical sense of the term there is no trace in this passage.[13]

The heart of my thesis is that *sarx* does not change its basic sense by metonymy in any of the passages where Paul uses it in an ethical or moral sense. Rather, the term's basic bodily sense is simply enriched by Paul's use of redemptive-historical reasoning. This means that the basic proof-texts for the two-natures view would be invalid. The ideal way to validate this bodily sense of *flesh* would be by the careful exegesis of all the relevant passages. I have done this elsewhere for Galatians 5–6.[14] However, the best we can do at this point is to survey Paul's use of the flesh/Spirit antithesis in the most important passages in which it occurs and to seek to validate the new interpretative perspective. Clearly the most important passage is Galatians 5–6, and therefore, the majority of time will be devoted to this passage. Of secondary significance is Romans 7–8 and it will also receive some extended attention. Of lesser importance still are 1 Corinthians 3:1–3, Ephesians 2:1–3, and Colossians 2:6–23 and these passages will receive a more cursory treatment. Of course, the goal is to seek to overturn the use of these passages to support the existence of a sin nature and a new nature and to understand them as Paul apparently intended.

## The Key Passages Containing the Flesh/Spirit Antithesis

### Galatians 5–6

The traditional understanding of the central issue of Galatians is that of an ideological clash between Paul's justification by faith and the Judaizers' legalism (see, e.g., Luther's 1535 commentary on Galatians). This understanding has been modified within the last few years through better literary analysis of Galatians and through better sociological/anthropological analysis of first-century Mediterranean peoples like the Galatians. The newer understanding of the central issue of Galatians is represented by scholars like T. David Gordon and John Barclay.[15] In his excellent monograph on Galatians, Barclay specifically concludes that the central issue of the Galatian crisis is twofold:

13. Burton, *Galatians*, 292.
14. Walter Bo Russell, III, *Paul's Use of Σαϛρξ and Πνεῦμα in Galatians 5–6 in Light of the Argument of Galatians* (Ph.D. diss., Westminster Theological Seminary, 1991).
15. David T. Gordon, "The Problem at Galatia," *Interpretation* 41 (1987): 32–43; John M. G. Barclay, "Mirror–Reading a Polemical Letter: Galatians as a Test Case, *Journal for the Study of the New Testament* 31 (1987): 73–93; idem, *Obeying the Truth*.

The issues at stake in the Galatian crisis were *the identity* of these Galatian Christians and their *appropriate patterns of behavior*: should they regularize and confirm their place among God's people by getting circumcised and becoming proselytes? And should they adopt the ritual and ethical norms of the Jewish people? Our investigation has demonstrated how attractive and reasonable the agitators' proposal in these matters appeared.[16]

Recent rhetorical analyses of Galatians by Fletcher, Kraftchick, and Matera,[17] to name a few, confirm that Paul develops his argument about the Galatians' identity as the sons of God/sons of Abraham and about their appropriate pattern of behavior through three main rhetorical headings or proofs in the epistle:

1:11–2:21: The universal nature of his gospel and its resulting identity was legitimately confirmed by Jerusalem, while the ethnocentric nature of the Judaizers' non-gospel was rejected.

3:1–4:31: Only Paul's universal gospel gave them their identity as the true people of God through their faith in Christ.

5:1–6:10: His gospel alone also provided them with true deliverance from sin's power and with the true pattern of behavior for God's people through the receiving of the Holy Spirit.

Understanding that Galatians 5–6 actually continues and climaxes Paul's previous argumentation against the Judaizers' non-gospel has helped clarify the lingering discussion of the beginning point of the moral exhortation portion of Galatians. Using rhetorical analysis has helped us trace the flow of Paul's argument in Galatians better than previous analyses have done.

One reason why we can posit that Galatians 5–6 is the climax of Paul's persuasive argument toward the Galatians is because it is not until 5:1–12 that he finally mentions circumcision. This recognition caused Matera to conclude:

> Gal. 5.1–6.17 forms the culmination of Paul's argument to the Galatians, the point he has intended to make from the beginning of the letter: the Galatians must not submit to circumcision. Thus, although these chapters contain a great deal of moral exhortation, they should not be viewed exclusively as paraenesis.

16. Barclay, *Obeying the Truth*, 73 (emphasis his).
17. Douglas K. Fletcher, *The Singular Argument of Paul's Letter to the Galatians* (Ph.D. diss., Princeton Theological Seminary, 1982); Steven J. Kraftchick, *Ethos and Pathos Appeals in Galatians Five and Six: A Rhetorical Analysis* (Ph.D. diss., Emory University, 1985); and Frank J. Matera, "The Culmination of Paul's Argument to the Galatians: Gal. 5:1–17," *Journal for the Study of the New Testament* 32 (1988): 79–91.

They are the climax of Paul's deliberative argument aimed at persuading the Galatians not to be circumcised.[18]

George A. Kennedy echoes Matera's conclusion when he says, "What Paul is leading to in chapters 1–4 is the exhortation of chapters 5–6. This is the point of the letter."[19]

Galatians 5:1 signals the beginning of the discussion of the epistle's second issue of the appropriate pattern of behavior and moves beyond the first issue of the identity of the true people of God that was discussed from 1:11–4:31. The argument flows smoothly from the subject of the identity of God's true children as those who are free (4:21–31) to the topic of their experience and use of that freedom in 5:1ff. The question Paul is answering in 5:1–6:10 is "Which pattern of behavior manifests true freedom from sin's power?" This issue of freedom from the power of transgressions was apparently the primary felt need to which the Judaizers appealed.[20] Of course, their answer was to exhort the Galatians to take up the yoke of Torah and to receive the mark of circumcision so that they could be included within the safety of God's covenant community, ethnic Israel.

Paul's answer to the burning issue in 5:1–6:10 is found in a comparison of the behavior patterns of these two competing identities of God's people. While the content of this section is ethical and exhortative in nature, its function is argumentative and not purely exhortative within the larger context of Paul's epistle. The following observations bear out my point. First, Paul continues his antithetical or contrastive argumentation against the Judaizers, insisting on the superiority of his position to theirs. Second, he is now proving the superiority of his true gospel to their non-gospel in the third area of concern that he addresses in Galatians. The first area concerned the antithetical nature of his message and that of the Judaizers ("according to man" versus "according to God") and the confirmation of his gospel by Jerusalem (1:11–2:21). The second area of concern involved the respective authority of the two "gospels" in the matter of true Abrahamic sonship (3:1–4:31). Now in the third major area, Paul is proving the superiority of his gospel within the ethical realm. He contends that his gospel provides the only adequate and appropriate constraint for their behavior: the Holy Spirit (versus the constraint of circumcision and Torah-observance). There is nothing new about Paul's exhortation to choose between these alternatives in 5:1–6:10. What *is* new is the realm of choice—the ethical or behavioral. Therefore, this exhortative ma-

18. Matera, "The Culmination of Paul's Argument to the Galatians," 79–80.

19. George A. Kennedy, *New Testament Interpretation Through Rhetorical Criticism* (Chapel Hill: University of North Carolina Press, 1984), 146.

20. Hans Dieter Betz, "Spirit, Freedom, and Law: Paul's Message to the Galatian Churches," *Svensk exegetisk årsbok* 39 (1974): 153–55.

terial serves a vital, perhaps climactic function, within the whole rhetoric of Galatians.[21]

The conclusion that I am pointing toward about the climactic role of Galatians 5–6 is also true of Paul's climactic usage of the flesh/Spirit antithesis in these chapters. This antithetical usage of flesh and Spirit began in Galatians 3:3. Paul initiated the first stage of the antithesis in 3:3 when he contrasted his means for spiritual growth ("by the Spirit") with the Judaizers' means ("by the flesh"). The Judaizers were emphasizing the means of the circumcision of the Galatians' bodies. However, this is not the end of the antithesis. Paul enriched it in a second stage of discussion with his consideration of Ishmael and Isaac in 4:21–31. In a powerful use of irony against what appears to be a key Judaizer proof-text, Paul notes that the true son of Abraham is the one born "according to the Spirit," not "according to the flesh" (4:23, 29). This builds upon his earlier point in 3:1–14 that the undeniable proof of Abrahamic blessing is the possession of the Holy Spirit. Therefore, the distinctive of the true Isaacites is that they are born like Isaac, according to the Spirit. To emphasize being born according to the flesh is to emphasize that you are really an Ishamelite! We now see that Paul has brought flesh and Spirit into full dialectic: "He correlates flesh with the old aeon, the law, slavery, the present Jerusalem and the agitating Judaizers, while opposing flesh with spirit, which in turn was correlated with the new aeon, the promise given to Abraham, freedom, and the church."[22]

The rhetorical stage is now set for the third and climactic phase in Paul's usage of *flesh* and *Spirit* in Galatians. If the Judaizers are characterized as those who are born according to the norm or standard of the flesh in 4:21–31, it logically follows that they will also live or walk according to the norm or standard of the flesh. This is Paul's point in Galatians 5–6. He now rips back the curtain to reveal how the community of the flesh will really function in the absence of the empowering work of the Spirit. Such a community stands in stark contrast to the functioning of the community of the Spirit.

In Galatians 5:1 Paul begins the third and climactic argument within the lengthy proof section (1:11–6:10) where he would show the superiority of his gospel over the Judaizers' non-gospel. In the first section, 5:1–12, Paul exhorts and warns about the consequences of the Galatians' identity choice as it relates to their continued deliverance from sin's power. Then, in 5:13–26 Paul develops the theme of deliverance from sin's power by contrasting relational dynamics within his community and the Judaizer's community.

<hr />

21. See Kraftchick, *Ethos and Pathos Appeals in Galatians Five and Six,* 3–61 and Barclay, *Obeying the Truth,* 1–35, for recent surveys of the role of Galatians 5–6 within the whole epistle.

22. Robert Jewett, *Paul's Anthropological Terms: A Study of Their Use in Conflict Settings,* Arbeiten zur Geschichte des antiken Judentums und des Urchristentums, vol. 10 (Leiden: E. J. Brill, 1971), 113.

5:13–26 *The Fundamental Manifestation of Deliverance from Sin's Power* in the Community of God's people is not competitive striving with one another, but rather the serving of one another through love.[23]

5:13–15 *The Initial Expression of the Antithetical Choices:* The manifestation of freedom from the constraints of the Mosaic law within the community of God's people should not be used as an opportunity for continued fleshly failure, which is vitriolic and self-consuming, but rather as an opportunity through love to serve one another, which is the summarizing principle of the whole Mosaic law.[24]

5:16–24 *The Antithetical Manifestations of the Two Choices:* Those who insist on living according to the past standard of fleshly behavior within the community under the Mosaic law will share in the sins of a community composed of those who will not inherit the kingdom of God; but those who identify with the community of the Spirit will be enabled by God's Spirit to manifest the fruit of loving unity apart from the daily constraints of the Mosaic law.

5:16–18 The standards of the Holy Spirit and the community of the Spirit are diametrically opposed to the fulfillment of fleshly behavior that takes place within the community of the flesh which is "un-

---

23. The basic argument of Galatians 5:1–6:10 is one that argues from obvious effects to the causes that created them. In 5:1–12 Paul would persuade the Galatians to question the cause behind the Judaizers if the negative effects of 5:7–9 were present among them. In 5:13–26 Paul continues his argument by again arguing from the effects to the cause that produced them. Here he invites the comparison of the two communities—the Judaizers and his—in the area of community unity and coherence. If, in fact, Christ is delivering them from sin's power, then that deliverance should manifest itself in a unified and loving community of believers. This is the only appropriate community manifestation for those born according to the Spirit. To paraphrase Scripture, by *their* fruits you will know *him*! Conversely, those born according to the flesh will aproach community as an opportunity for the flesh (5:13) and will manifest community phenomena or effects that are readily observable as a fulfillment of the desire fo the flesh (5:16). Therefore, structurally, Paul brackets the listing of these two antithetical *effects* or manifestations of community life in 5:16–24 with the corresponding antithetical *causes* of those effects in 5:13–15 and 5:25–26. He is persuading the Galatians that the people of God, who are born according to the Spirit, should manifest a life in community that is directly traceable to God's Spirit. An objective comparison of the community lives of the two groups will clearly reveal both the standards and causes of such a life.

24. These verses introduce the theme of this section (5:13–26). Paul is showing the contrary ends of the two gospels that the Galatians have heard. The "gospel" preached by the community of the flesh ends up in providing more opportunity for fleshly expression. The end of this Judaizing emphasis is mutually destructive relationships. Ironically, the end of the true gospel and its manifestation is the fulfillment of the basic purpose of the whole Mosaic law: loving edification of your neighbor. In other words, the law's fulfillment ultimately can be distilled into relational terms. Therefore, in another manifestation of the argument of this whole section (5:1–6:10), Paul is arguing that observing the *effects* of community relationships and unity should reveal the true *cause* of those effects. This is why mutual destruction is powerfully tied to flesh and mutual edification to Spirit. Observing the community *effects* reveals the root community *cause*.

der law," so that those who possess the Spirit but live within the flesh community will not be able to do what they wish.

5:19–21 The community of the flesh manifests the relationally destructive effects of fleshly behavior, confirming that this community is not composed of the true sons of Abraham, who will inherit the kingdom of God.

5:22–24 In contrast, the community of the Spirit manifests the relationally edifying effects of spiritual behavior which are not legally prohibited and which evidence that those in the community of the Spirit have seen their flesh and its manifestations crucified.

5:25–26 *The Closing Expression of the Antithetical Choices:* Being a part of the community of the Spirit means that one should choose to live according to the rule or standard of the Spirit and not according to the competitive striving that characterizes the community of the flesh.[25]

This brief overview of Paul's argumentation in Galatians 5:13–26 was an attempt to highlight the viability of the continued bodily sense of *flesh*. Paul has enriched *flesh* with a redemptive-historical depth, thus appropriating a central Judaistic term and turning it on its head. In Paul's framework *flesh* now represents not only the Judaizers' emphasis on their covenant in the flesh with Abraham (Gen. 17:13 LXX), but tragically also all the moral frailty and weakness that characterizes persons on their own, unaided by God's Spirit.

In this sense, I believe that *flesh* and *Spirit* have become abbreviations in Paul's argument, representing the two competing identities for the people of God at Galatia. The "flesh community" (Judaizers) is a community identified with the Mosaic law era, and therefore is a community identified and characterized by the frailty and transitoriness of bodily existence and the absence of God's Spirit. This community is representative of human beings *before* or *apart from* Christ's liberating death and resurrection. By contrast, the "Spirit community" is a community identified and characterized by the presence of God's Spirit and liberation from sin's dominion in the midst of bodily existence. Such is a group experiencing the liberation of Christ's death and resurrection. They are experiencing the freedom that Jesus Christ set them free to experience (5:1).

The responsibility before the Galatians was to continue to follow the true gospel that Paul had preached to them and not to desert to a non-gospel

---

25. In Galatians 5:13–26 Paul ues several synonyms to describe the Christian life in relationship to the Holy Spirit: *walk* (5:16), *be led* (5:18), *live* (5:25), and *walk* (corporately) (5:25). George S. Duncan (*The Epistle of Paul to the Galatians* [London: Hodder and Stoughton, 1934], 178) paraphrases 5:25 to bring out the corporate nature of Christians' relationship with the Holy Spirit that "walk corporately" seems to indicate: "If our individual lives are lived 'by the Spirit,' let us allow the Spirit to marshal us in our corporate relationships."

(1:6–7). They must reject becoming proselytes to Judaism and being circumcised (5:1–12). Ethically, this meant they must "walk according to the rule of the Spirit" that they might not fulfill the desires connected with those who still live according to the rule of the flesh (5:16). To be "led according to the rule of the Spirit" is not to be "under the law" (5:18 NASB). The choice to live in the Judaizers' "law/flesh community" will manifest itself in the behavior of that community: the deeds of the flesh (5:19–21). Conversely, the choice to continue to live in the "Spirit community" will manifest itself in the fruit of the Spirit (5:22–23). This is true because Christians have crucified the flesh, that is, that mode of existence in which their body was under sin's mastery and not indwelt by God's Spirit has ended (5:24). Since they live according to the rule of the Spirit, they should also corporately walk according to the rule of the Spirit (5:25).

Essentially, what Paul is saying in Galatians 5–6 is that the Galatians who have been born "according to the Spirit" (4:29) should continue to live "according to the rule of the Spirit." This is the greatest antidote to Judaistic (i.e., fleshly) behavior. Therefore, "the flesh," for which the Galatians are not to make opportunity (5:13) nor to walk according to its rule and thereby fulfill its desire (5:16), refers to the bodily emphasis of the Judaizers. In other words, *flesh* in this context is "that which is merely human and distinctively Jewish." It would be an anachronistic historical mode of existence and redemptively-historical inferior way of life for the Galatian Christians to turn back to in light of their crucifixion of this bodily state in Christ Jesus (5:24)! Therefore, the Christian does *not* have "flesh" in Galatians 5:13–26. Instead, the Christian has the true identity mark of the children of Abraham (3:6–14) and the antithetical bodily condition to the flesh (3:1–5). The Christian has the Holy Spirit, not the flesh. Certainly no internal duality exists between these antithetical modes of existence.

### Romans 7–8

Paul's use of the flesh/Spirit antithesis in this passage makes it an important one to consider because of its widespread use as a proof-text for the existence of two natures within the Christian. Interestingly enough, this passage also has a Jewish Christian context that is established by three major indicators at the beginning of the section:

> The opening address to "brethren" in 7:1 is clarified by the explanatory phrase *for I am speaking to those who know the law*. These "brothers" are described apart from the rest of the Roman church by their knowledge of Torah. They are the Jewish Christians (and proselytes) within the Roman church.

The topic is Torah, not Roman law or law in general, because the specific example of 7:2–3 was a debated point of Torah, because the Jewish law had this immediate death provision and Roman law did not, and because almost all of the previous forty uses of *law* in Romans refer to Torah, not law in general.

The newness/oldness and Spirit/letter contrasts of 7:6 clarify the intent of the marriage illustration of 7:1–5 because these contrasts are clear Pauline references to the new and Mosaic covenants, respectively (cf. 2 Cor. 3:1–11). Therefore, the contrast introduced in 7:1–6 is the redemptive-historical movement from the Mosaic covenant to the new covenant and the ramifications of this movement for the role of Torah in the lives of these Jewish Christians (e.g., 7:4).

Romans 8:1–17 continues this same contrast between the law and the Spirit, only expanding the law-side of the contrast with its familiar tandem member, the flesh, which had already been added in 7:5. Therefore, 7:1–6 and 8:1–17 both speak of the redemptive-historical progression from the flesh/law era to the Spirit/Christ era, with special reference to the ramifications of this progression to the present role of Torah. The two passages, 7:1–6 and 8:1–17, act as brackets or enclosures for the material in 7:7–25. This leads to an important structural observation about 7:7–25 and the discussion about Torah and flesh contained in it: the discussion must be read within a redemptive-historical light and the redemptive-historical significance with which Paul enriches *flesh* in these types of Judaistic contexts must be heavily weighted.

Additionally, Paul's clear and overt temporal statements in these bracketing passages about the former era of flesh must be adequately weighted:

7:5a: "For while we *were* (imperfect tense) in the flesh . . . "
7:6a: "But *now* we were released from the Law because we died [to that] by which we were being confined . . . "[26]

To be "in the flesh" in 7:5a is the same as being "under law" in 7:6a. Again, we encounter Paul's familiar tandem of flesh and law as a two fold reference to the past redemptive-historical era of the Mosaic law. This era for God's people has been historically succeeded by the era of the Spirit, as Paul declares in 8:9 (NASB): "But you are *not in the flesh,* but *in the Spirit,* since the Spirit of God dwells in you. And if anyone does not have the Spirit of Christ, this person does not belong to Him."

26. This translation and emphasis and the following ones are mine.

Therefore, the two references to "flesh" in 7:18 and 7:25 and the one reference to "of flesh" in 7:14 must be viewed within the very clear redemptive-historical argumentation that Paul initiates in 7:1. Within this type of antithetical argumentation, the absence of any mention of Spirit in 7:7–8:1 is also significant. The occurrence of *Spirit* in 8:2 is significant because it follows the logical and temporal contrast of 8:1: "There is therefore *now* no condemnation for those in Christ Jesus." This absence of condemnation "in Christ Jesus" is explained by Paul in 8:2–17 in contrast to being "under the law" (8:2–4) and "in the flesh" (8:3–9, 12–13). The clear thrust of Paul's argument is that the redemptive-historical era of law/flesh has been superseded by the redemptive-historical era of Christ/Spirit. The sense of condemnation described in 7:15–24 is therefore that which *previously occurred during the era of the Mosaic law.* In other words, there was in the past a sense of the condemnation of sin for those *in Moses* that is in the present now absent for those *in Christ.*

Thus, when Paul begins his discussion of the possible sinfulness of the Mosaic law with the rhetorical question of 7:7 ("Is the Law sin?"), he is initiating a very sensitive and lengthy explanation (7:7–25) of life under the "oldness of the letter" (7:6c). Such a discussion might reinforce the already negative conclusion that the Jewish Christians in Rome might have reached about his view of Torah. In favor of this conclusion, they might cite his previous argumentation about God's people no longer being "under law" (e.g., 6:14), coupled with a slanderous report that had preceded his epistle (3:8). In response to these misunderstandings Paul argues in 7:7–25 that the law is holy, righteous, and good (7:12). However, he also argues that Torah is inadequate as a means of totally constraining body behavior because of the pervasive dominion of sin over its subjects. This very fervent exposition of the Mosaic law's inadequacy in 7:7–25 comes on the heels of Paul's point about the inappropriateness of living as if the deceased husband, Torah, is still alive (7:1–6). Both of these points are directed toward "those who know Torah" within the Roman church (7:1). All of this is to say that Romans 7 is Paul's rejection of the Mosaic law as the means of moral restraint for Christians because it is both inappropriate in the era of the Spirit, and inadequate as such a restraint.

In view of the preceding considerations, I propose that in 7:7–13 we see Paul's first person narrative of the coming of the law to Israel at Mount Sinai,[27] is followed in 7:14–25 by his first person narrative of the convicting and condemning function of the law throughout Israel's post-Sinai history. For over sixty years, Paul's use of first person narration in these verses has been recognized as a rhetorical or literary device most appropriate in such an inflammatory context. However, the redemptive-historical argumentation of

---

27. Among several who take this view, see Douglas J. Moo, "Israel and Paul in Romans 7:7–12," *New Testament Studies* 32 (1986): 122–35.

Romans 7 has been recognized only sporadically.[28] This may be due in part to the main hermeneutical question used to interpret Romans 7: "Is Paul describing a Christian or a non-Christian?" Such a question has tended to frame the discussion of this passage in a manner that is not particularly conducive to a redemptive-historical understanding. If, however, Paul's argumentation is viewed apart from this main hermeneutical question and through a redemptive-historical lens, then he is probably describing neither a Christian or non-Christian. Rather, he is describing the pious Israelite during the Mosaic law era who struggled with the convicting and condemning work of Torah because he or she was still in the flesh, that is, in a body distinguished by circumcision and restrained by Torah, yet still under sin's dominion and not indwelt by God's Spirit (7:14). This condition led to a unique state of wretchedness for the believing Israelite (7:24a): Paul's plaintive cry for a deliverer from such a state in 7:24b elicits the spontaneous answer of 7:25a: "Thanks be to God— through Jesus Christ our Lord!" However, this jubilant shout is premature in Paul's argument. It necessitates that he return to his description of the dividedness between law and flesh that he and his fellow believing Israelites had experienced. Paul does this by summarizing 7:14–24 in 7:25b. He is now ready for his climactic point: this wretchedness is now removed only in Christ Jesus (8:1) through his death, burial, and resurrection (6:3–11; 8:2–11).

From his exposition of Israelite history under Moses, Paul would have the Jewish Christians in Rome learn the proper and limited function of Torah during the era of the flesh. That era, now past, had Torah as a necessary corollary (7:5). In the new era of the Spirit, however, Paul would not have Torah imposed upon the Gentile Christians in Rome as a proper restraint for their behavior (7:6). Clearly, within this specific historical and polemical context, *flesh* takes on the more specified sense of "what is merely human *and* distinctively Jewish." Such an insight adds great significance to Paul's statements about being "of flesh" in 7:14, about nothing good dwelling "in my flesh" in 7:18, and about serving the law of sin "with the flesh" in 7:25. Rather than being anthropological statements, these are more likely polemical statements against the efficacy of circumcision and Torah-keeping in constraining bodily behavior. This is why Paul clearly explains the appropriate and adequate means of constraining bodily behavior through the person of the Spirit in terms of fulfilling Torah and in contrast to attempting to do so in a Judaistic manner in 8:2–4. In an echo of Galatians 5:13–14, Paul culminates his explanation in 8:4: "that the righteousness of the law might be fulfilled in us who do not walk according to the standard of the flesh, but according to the standard of the Spirit" (my translation).

28. See Moo, "Israel and Paul in Romans 7:7–12," 130, n. 4 for a list of nine advocates. See also Mark W. Karlberg, "Israel's History Personified: Romans 7:7–13 in Relation to Paul's Teaching on the 'Old Man,'" *Trinity Journal,* new series, 7 (1986): 64–74.

The contrast between those who walk according to the flesh and those who walk according to the Spirit is expanded in 8:5–8 in language reminiscent of Galatians 5:16–25. This contrast is not simply a contrast between non-Christians and Christians. Rather, the issue is what one would suspect within a Judaistic context: "How do you please God, keep his law, and have life and peace?" Paul's answer to each aspect is, "Walk according to the Spirit, not according to the flesh" (cf. 8:12). He then clarifies in various ways in 8:9–17 the distinctiveness of life according to the Spirit. Particularly noteworthy is his clarification of the Roman Christians' life in the Spirit in 8:9 and his definition of "sons of God" in 8:14 (NASB): "For all who are being led by the Spirit of God, these are sons of God." Such a clarification has meaning only within a context where the definition of "sons of God" is being debated. Paul goes on to elaborate the clarification of 8:14 in 8:15–17 with reasoning that parallels his argumentation in Galatians 3:1–14 where the possession of the Spirit confirms the Christians' true sonship as children of God.

If the above explanation of Paul's argument in Romans 7:1–8:17 is accurate, then it follows his reasoning in Galatians 5–6 very closely, as one would expect. Again, an internal duality within the Christian of flesh and Spirit, a sinful nature and a new nature, is totally absent. In fact, such theologizing completely misses Paul's theological argument and creates an artificial construct in its place. The flesh/Spirit antitheses used by Paul does not draw the flesh and the Spirit together as parts of an internal duality within the Christian; rather it separates them as totally antithetical lifestyles delimited by the death, burial, and resurrection of Jesus Christ. To miss this argument by Paul is to dilute the uniqueness of the Christian life.

### 1 Corinthians 3:1–3

Paul rebukes the Corinthian Christians for being "fleshly" rather than "spiritual" in 1 Corinthians 3:1–3. To be "spiritual" would be to live in a manner of appraising all things (2:15) according to the "mind of Christ" (2:16). However, the Corinthians are living as babies in Christ (3:1). They are still milk-drinkers, not solid-food eaters in their spiritual diet after the several years they have known Christ. They are, therefore, still "fleshly" (3:2–3a). Paul validates this fleshliness in 3:3b by referring to the continued existence of jealousy and strife among them (cf. Gal. 5:20; Rom. 13:13; James 3:14, 16).

Particularly significant for our understanding of *flesh* in these kinds of passages is the final part of Paul's validation in 3:3c: "Are you not fleshly, are you not walking according to the standard of man?" (my translation). To be "fleshly" is to be walking (living) only "according to man." In other words, it is to live as if you are on your own as a human being and unaffected and unaided by God. This is, of course, to be living like a non-Christian (e.g., 1 Cor. 2:14). Therefore, to be "fleshly" is to be "non-Christianly." It is to be living as if your only standards and resources were what you could muster. It is to live as if, in this bodily existence, you were on your own and unaided by God's Spirit. Such a life stands in stark contrast to the Christian who is spiritual (1 Cor. 2:15) and whose pattern of behavior should reflect such an identity. This contrast explains why the Corinthians' non-Christian pattern of behavior regarding jealousy and strife was unthinkable to Paul and contrary to the Spirit-like pattern of behavior that they should have been manifesting. They were reverting back to the behavior of their previous identity and mode of existence as non-Christians, that is, as "persons of flesh."

This passage clearly manifests the same basic flesh/Spirit antithesis that Paul used in Galatians 5–6 and Romans 7–8, apart from the additional Judaistic aspects in the former passages. Again, however, flesh and Spirit are not in an internal duality within the Christian, but rather represent antithetical modes of living separated by faith in Christ.

### Ephesians 2:1–3

This passage is one of Paul's descriptions of the depth of human sinfulness that precedes one of his descriptions of the depth of God's mercy and grace (2:4–10). In particular in 2:1–2 he speaks in the second person plural of "you" (the Gentiles) being morally dead in "your" sins and walking according to the satanic rule of this world. Some anti-Judaistic sentiment comes to bear in an indirect way in 2:3 when Paul switches to the first person plural and includes himself and the Jewish people in this universal sinfulness ("we too all"): "Among them we too all formerly walked in the lusts of our flesh, indulging the desires of the flesh and of the mind, and were by nature children of wrath, even as the rest" (NASB). Long ago Calvin noted this inclusion:

> Lest he should seem to slander the former character of the Ephesians, or as a Jew to despise the Gentiles, he associates himself and his race with them. This is not said in hypocrisy, but in a sincere confession of glory to God. Yet it may seem strange that he should admit that he had walked in the lusts of the flesh, when on other occasions he claims that his life had been throughout irreproachable. I reply, this applies to all who have not yet been regenerated by the Spirit of Christ. However praiseworthy in appearance the life of some may be because their lusts do not break out in the sight of men, there is nothing pure or incorrupt save from the mountain of all purity.[29]

This specific usage of *flesh* to refer to the Jewish people parallels the interpretation of Galatians 5:19–21 above, namely, that the "deeds of the flesh" is a description of life within the community of Israel. Paul's stark description in

---

29. John Calvin, *The Epistles of Paul The Apostle to the Galatians, Ephesians, Philippians, and Colossians,* Calvin's New Testament Commentaries, vol. 11, ed. David W. Torrance and Thomas F. Torrance, trans. T. H. L. Parker (Grand Rapids: Eerdmans, 1965), 141.

Ephesians 2 would make this understanding of Galatians 5:19–21 quite reasonable. However, given the very subtle confrontation with Judaistic sentiments that 2:3 represents and the non-Judaistic context of Ephesians in general, the two references to *flesh* in this verse should probably be understood in the more general sense of human frailty and transitoriness without the additional sense of the bodily distinction of circumcision and the constraint of Torah. This would follow the pattern that has been emerging in Paul's use of *flesh* in non-Judaistic contexts. It simply refers to the former mode of existence of Christians ("formerly," 2:3a), whether they were Gentiles or Jews ("even as the rest," 2:3c).

Paul goes on to say in 2:11–22 that the fleshly distinction between Gentiles and Jews due to circumcision (2:11–12) has been abolished in Christ Jesus' "flesh" (2:13–17). This abolition has resulted in access "in one Spirit" through him (2:18) and has included Gentiles ("you") in the habitation of God "in the Spirit" (2:22). While his use of the flesh/Spirit antithesis is more subtle than in Galatians, it is clear, nevertheless, that Paul also uses the terms in a redemptive-historical sense in Ephesians 2.[30]

### Colossians 2:6–23

This final passage is similar to Ephesians 2:3 in that it also has some Jewish elements within it, although it is not an anti-Judaistic passage like Galatians 5–6. The generally accepted view of Colossians is that the threat addressed in the letter is an incipient, primitive form of what later became the heresy of Gnosticism. Although there were some syncretized Jewish practices within this threat, this was not a specific Judaistic threat that emphasized "the covenant in the flesh."[31] Therefore, the four occurrences of *flesh* in 2:11, 13, 18, and 23 should be understood in the more general sense of the body that is frail and transitory and that is not indwelt by God's Spirit. Also, *flesh* is not used in explicit antithesis with *Spirit*. These four uses conform to the usage of *flesh* in 1 Corinthians 3 and Ephesians 2 as references to the bodily state of non-Christians before coming to know Christ:

30. When translations like the NIV translate *sarx* in Ephesians 2:3 as "sinful nature," they destroy any hope of grasping Paul's redemptive-historical point in Ephesians 2 about the ending of the era of the flesh and the beginning of the era of the Spirit for God's people.

31. A few scholars believe that the threat addressed in Colossians can be explained within a Judaistic context (e.g., Morna D. Hooker, "Were there false teachers in Colossae?" in *Christ and Spirit in the New Testament: Essays in honour of Charles Francis Digby Moule,* ed. Barnabas Lindars and Stephen S. Smalley [Cambridge: Cambridge University Press, 1973], 315–31. However, the majority of New Testament scholars believe that a heresy that combines some elements of Judaism with some form of Hellenistic teachings in a syncretistic manner is a more likely description (e.g., Roy Yates, "Colossians and Gnosis," *Journal for the Study of the New Testament* 27 [1986]: 49–60). For the view that the heresy was from a Jewish nonconformist *merkabah* mysticism, see F. F. Bruce, "Colossian Problems. Part 3: The Colossian Heresy," *Bibliotheca Sacre* 141 (1984): 195–208.

Colossians 2:11 emphasizes the true circumcision of "the body of the flesh," which is without hands in Christ.

Colossians 2:13 contrasts the former state of death in "transgressions" and in uncircumcision "of the flesh" with the present state of life with Christ.

Colossians 2:18 warns that those deceiving the Colossians are vainly puffed up by the alleged authority of the working of their "fleshly mind," rather than by submitting to Christ.

Colossians 2:23 ironically concludes that all of the anachronistic, overly-harsh ascetic practices that are the work of men (2:22) never adequately restrained the sinful satisfaction of "the flesh"; such restraint comes only from being in Christ (3:1–11).

The combined effect of these four uses of *flesh* is to emphasize the helplessness (2:11, 13) and wrong-headedness (2:18, 23) of human life apart from the redeeming work of Christ. If this state of helplessness is not adequately acknowledged, then the resulting state of wrong-headedness is greatly heightened.

In light of this general effect, one more specific point can be made. In the Greek text of 2:11 Paul uses the seemingly redundant expression *in the putting off of the body of the flesh* in parallelism with *in the circumcision of Christ.* Following many commentators, translations like the NIV render the first phrase as "in the putting off of the sinful nature." Such renderings involve many problems, but the most obvious is that it ignores the presence of *the body* in the original text. A far better contextual solution would be to recognize that Paul is making a play on words with flesh and its role in circumcision. Apparently the troublers in Colossae were advocating the use of circumcision to provide some kind of cleansing from the alleged innate bodily defilement. This obviously involved the putting off or removal of part of the flesh—the frail, temporary, sin-dominated human body. Paul ironically overwhelms such a theology with the truth that, in Christ, the entire "body of the flesh" has been put off in the spiritual circumcision of Christ. He then proceeds in verse 12 to link the removal of the sin-dominated body to burial with Christ in baptism and resurrection with Christ to new life (e.g., 2:12b–15; cf. Rom. 6:1–11). Therefore, Paul can speak of mortifying the members of the earthly body in relation to various sins in 3:5–11 because the Colossians' former bodily condition of frailty and sin-dominance has ended (2:20) and their lives are now raised up to newness of life with Christ (3:1–4). It seems that, as we saw above, Paul has simply used the rhetoric and terminology of the threatening group and has turned it on its head to refute it. However, he is consistent in his view of flesh, using it to designate the pre-Christ era of redemptive history, not a part of the inward make-up of a Christian. In other words, there are no sin natures or new natures in this passage.

## Conclusion

After surveying the two major and three minor passages that are used as proof of a flesh/Spirit, sinful nature/new nature duality within Christians, we must conclude that this view is not in those passages. In fact, it is not anywhere else in the New Testament either. Rather, it is a recent aberration in our view of persons that now has been widely disseminated through recent translations. This is very unfortunate because the two natures view obscures the beauty and uniqueness of the Christian life in its contrast to life apart from Christ. Without the vivid contrast of our new life in the Spirit with our former life in the flesh, the Christian life that emerges is a *tertium quid* or a "third thing" that drably partakes of the characteristics of both the life of the flesh and Spirit. Perhaps no truer description of the present state of the Church in the West could be made than this.

However, there is hope of recapturing a loftier view—a more biblical view—of the Christian life and it may rest in part in rightly understanding Paul's use of the flesh/Spirit antithesis in his epistles. It appears that Paul's intent was to elevate the distinction of the Christian life by focusing on the new freedom from sin's mastery that the new covenant life in the Holy Spirit has brought. Rather than a divided self, distraught over an internal battle between flesh and Spirit, Paul pictures a new self, emboldened by the liberating work of the Holy Spirit and in vibrant community with others of like identity.

While it is beyond the scope of this chapter to draw out and develop all of the important ramifications of this view, nevertheless three important implications should be noted. First, good exegesis is of immeasurable importance for the work of systematic theology. Hopefully, we have demonstrated how new exegetical insights can help reshape our theology in its perspective on being human. Such dynamic interaction is needed in all areas of Christian theology.

Secondly, while the individual self is important biblically, its importance has been overestimated significantly in Western culture and theology. Our pervasive individualism is so fundamental to our world view that it has distorted our view of biblical discussions of the communal self. This is probably the fundamental distortion that has been at work in the interpretation of the flesh/Spirit antithesis in Paul's epistles. While Paul appears to be appealing to our identity within the new communal self of the church, we persist in individualizing that identity and inappropriately psychologizing it into "parts." While there are parts of us, they do not seem to be Paul's focus in the flesh/Spirit passages. Rather, Paul is appealing to the historical reality of our new corporate identity as the people of God and the corresponding set of behaviors or ethics that flow out of such an identity. Essentially, Paul's general appeal in all of these passages is "to live a life worthy of the calling you have received" (Eph. 4:1).

Lastly, the individual and abstract focus upon combating our "sin nature" or "flesh" has deterred us from focusing upon the true means of transformation in the Christian life. Paul's command is to put to death the deeds of our body according to the working of the Holy Spirit, not to mortify our sin nature or "flesh" (Rom. 8:12–14; 6:12–14). We have wrongly abstracted his very concrete, bodily focus. This has led to the lack of emphasis on the classic means of Christian transformation: practicing the spiritual disciplines (e.g., fasting, solitude, silence) in Christian community. Our stumbling block is not "our flesh" (in the ethical sense), but "our fleshliness" (the characteristics of having been in the flesh). Sin has pervasively marked every part of our being and we must now, in the power of the Holy Spirit, retrain all of our members (parts) so that God can use them for his service (Rom. 6:12–14; cf. 1 Cor. 3:1–3). One of the joys of the Christian life is that we have the privilege of doing this in community with other believers in Jesus Christ. One of our tasks in this community of the Spirit is to be a community of believers genuinely in the process of becoming like Christ.

## Suggested Readings

Most of the works recommended will be only partially helpful and none will fully represent the view advocated in this chapter.

### General Works

Ridderbos, Herman. *Paul: An Outline of His Theology.* Translated by John R. DeWitt. Grand Rapids: Eerdmans, 1975, chap. 2. [I]

Smith, Charles R. "Two Natures—or One? An Attempt at Theological Clarification." *The Voice* (July-August 1983): 19–21. [B/I]

### Galatians

Barclay, John M. G. "Mirror-Reading a Polemical Letter: Galatians as a Test Case." *Journal for the Study of the New Testament* 31 (1987): 73–93. [A]

_____. *Obeying the Truth: A Study of Paul's Ethics in Galatians.* Studies of the New Testament and Its World. Edited by John Riches. Edinburgh: T. and T. Clark, 1988. [A]

Gordon, David T. "The Problem at Galatia." *Interpretation* 41 (1987): 32–43. [I]

Russell, III, Walter B. "Paul's Use of Σάρξ and Πνευμα in Galatians 5–6 in Light of the Argument of Galatians. Ph.D. diss., Westminster Theological Seminary, 1991. [A]

*Romans*

Moo, Douglas J. "Israel and Paul in Romans 7:7–12." *New Testament Studies* 32 (1986): 122–35. [A]

Karlberg, Mark W. "Israel's History Personified: Romans 7:7–13 in Relation to Paul's Teaching on the 'Old Man.'" *Trinity Journal*, new series, 7 (1986): 64–74. [I/A]

# A Response to Walt Russell

## David M. Ciocchi

Walt Russell writes not only as a New Testament scholar, but also as a Christian thinker concerned with the integration of faith and learning. He puts his scholarly specialty to work in the service of developing a biblically informed theological anthropology, making it clear that he sees himself as a supplier of the deeper biblical understanding that the systematic theologian needs in order to construct an authentically Christian theology. Russell also makes it clear that he sees his own contribution to theology as depending in part on the work of disciplines such as literary theory, sociology, and anthropology—studies that have increased our understanding of, for instance, the letter to the Galatians. In sum, Russell writes as a scholarly specialist who wants to participate in the interdisciplinary integration of faith and learning which is essential to a fully developed Christian view of what it is to be human.

Russell contends that neither Paul's flesh/Spirit antithesis nor anything else in the New Testament supports the view that the Christian believer has two natures, one antedating conversion ("the sin nature") and one gained at conversion ("the new nature"). Since he is writing primarily as an exegete, he chooses to say little about the *philosophical* problems generated by the "two-natures" view, although he does direct his readers in a note to some related literature. I think, though, that a couple of comments on this topic are important for appreciating the value of Russell's work. First of all, to say that the redeemed human being has two natures in the sense of *nature* as "substance" or "entity" is an exegetically unnecessary complication of Paul's thought. It generates problems about the personal identity of the believer which are analogous to the difficulties we have in understanding how Christ can be *one per-*

*son* and yet have *two natures*. The New Testament gives us good grounds for talking of Christ's having two natures. What Russell is trying to show us is that it does not give us good grounds for using this language to describe the believer in Christ. Second, even if *nature* is taken alternatively to mean a complex of properties or attributes possessed by a *single* substance, this does not eliminate all possible philosophical problems about the personal identity of the believer. There would remain serious questions about the coherence of the idea of a single person with two radically opposed sets of character traits, that is, the "fleshly" and the "spiritual." Is this, we might ask, one person or two? Russell's exegetical work goes a long way towards giving us biblical relief from such philosophical worries.

In the course of his argument, Russell shows us that Paul's talk of flesh and Spirit are best taken not in the philosophical sense of denoting parts or functions of persons, but in the redemptive-historical sense of denoting antithetical modes of existence, namely, the Judaic and the Christian. These are two "lifestyles" which are separated by the death, burial, and resurrection of Jesus. It is, then, not a matter of having to struggle with an internal duality of flesh and Spirit, but rather of choosing either to live in the spiritually powerless, "merely human" flesh, or to live in the liberating power of the Holy Spirit.

As Russell sees it, then, those who talk in terms of two natures seriously misrepresent the life of the redeemed human being. They present it as a divided self—that problem of personal identity again—"distraught over an internal battle between flesh and Spirit," while Paul "pictures a new self, emboldened by the liberating work of the Holy Spirit and in vibrant community with others of like identity." Russell's exegesis is convincing, and his conclusions come down firmly on the side of viewing the believer's life as a positive, hopeful, spiritually productive one. In spite of the high quality of Russell's work, some troubling questions remain. I have space to address only one of them.

One of the Pauline passages Russell discusses is Romans 7–8, with particular attention paid to the spiritual struggle described in 7:14–25. Russell's understanding of these verses differs significantly from much traditional exegesis. He sees Paul's references to being "of flesh" (7:14) and to serving the law of sin "with the flesh" (7:25 NASB) as most likely polemical statements about the inadequacy of circumcision and Torah-keeping as means for constraining bodily behavior. The person described in this passage is a pious Jew living under the Mosaic economy, someone doomed to spiritual frustration because he has not experienced the power of the Holy Spirit which is the appropriate and adequate means for constraining bodily behavior. Some other exegetes have seen the person in this passage as being not only a Christian believer, but even a spiritually mature one, and they have understood the struggle Paul describes as characteristic of those who are engaged in serious spiritual growth. Although I am inclined to agree with Russell's exegesis, it does raise a troubling question.

Taken as a description of the believer's *experience*—that is, taken in a *psychological* or *phenomenological* sense—the struggle described in Romans 7 fits the experiences of many serious Christians. They recognize in it their own inner conflict between their passionate desire to serve God fully and their simultaneous experience of sinful desires which at times seem almost like the intrusion of an alien power in their lives. If Russell is correct in his exegesis, then why does a passage that describes a frustrating, pre-Christian spiritual experience seem to fit the experience of mature Christian believers? The easy answer is what Russell says, that we conceive of the Christian life as something that "drably partakes of the characteristics of both the life of the flesh and Spirit." In other words, we have set ourselves up for spiritual frustration by failing to see what a life empowered by the Holy Spirit can really be like. This answer to the question seems to lead to an optimistic theology of "victorious living," even to some sort of perfectionism. For those who find that sort of theology unconvincing on both biblical and experiential grounds, another answer will be needed.

The options we have here are not limited to the internal duality of the two natures view and the internal cohesion and perfection of a "victorious living" theology. There is a third possibility, and that is to understand the personal identity of the believer in Christ as *cohesive* and yet *incomplete*. The believer is a new creation in Christ, and he does have the liberating power of the Holy Spirit. As Russell shows us, the believer is no longer "in the flesh." Now living "in the Spirit," the believer has what he needs for successful, but not perfect, obedience to God. The coherence of his personal identity is secured by his status as a new creation in Christ, but he still has a need for spiritual growth. Coming to love God more and the world less takes time, even a lifetime. The believer retains tendencies towards sin with which he must struggle, and it is this (long-term) struggle that some interpreters have improperly read into certain biblical passages, such as Romans 7.

# A Response to Walt Russell

*Sherwood G. Lingenfelter*

From the perspective of a social anthropologist, Walt Russell's paper is particularly instructive in illustrating how cultural biases can lead biblical scholars to faulty exegesis and erroneous theological interpretation. The preoccupation of Americans with understanding of self and their commitment to an individualist value system to the exclusion of others certainly biases their reading of Scripture. While scholars bring the skills of their discipline and research to exegesis and interpretation, these hidden personal and socio-cultural needs create subtle biases which are nearly impossible to hold in abeyance. The subtle misunderstandings and misinterpretation of the texts that Walt Russell challenges in this paper are rooted in the pastoral concerns of Bible scholars and teachers working in American churches and communities.

One wonders how we can protect ourselves from reading into the Scripture those meanings which are either comforting to us, or fit logically within our frames for the interpretation of our worlds? Russell's point that the "sin nature"/"new nature" struggle is relatively recent in the history of theology should be instructive. If in fact the early church fathers did not speak of human beings in these terms, then our present theological insight is probably culturally biased. We would do well to re-examine our current thinking in the light of the theological thinking of the Christian community much closer to the life and times of New Testament writers. Much of the heresy that has entered the Christian church over the centuries has arisen because of "new interpretations" of the gospel.

Russell also does great service by clarifying Paul's argument in terms of "the community of the flesh" and "the community of the Spirit." By equating the Judaizers with Ishmaelites, and those who followed the gospel of Christ with Isaac, the son of the promise, Paul distinguishes these separate communities of relationship in terms of contrasts between "in the flesh, under the law" and "in the Spirit, subject to Christ." The point of Russell's discussion is that the "modes of living" that characterize human beings grow out of the community and the relationships to which they have committed themselves. Those who have committed themselves to Christ and to living within the Christian community do not live according to the flesh but rather according to the Spirit.

I have argued elsewhere that our social environments and our world views constitute "prisons of disobedience," keying upon Paul's statements in Galatians 3:22 and Romans 11:32: "God has bound all men over to disobedience so that he may have mercy on them all." Russell's notion of "community of the flesh" sustains that argument and provides much substantive exegetical evidence for its truth. The key point we both make is that it is impossible to separate Christian or non-Christian living from community. The equation of law=flesh and Christ=Spirit is further evidence of the centrality of community relationships to human life. Law by very definition governs relationships within community. Those who live according to the law of their society will die by that law, while those who live in Christ are governed by their relationship to Christ and Spirit-directed relationships with others. The centrality of community for vital Christian living is a key contribution of Russell's paper.

# 8

# Views of Human Nature at the Edges of Life

## Personhood and Medical Ethics

### Scott B. Rae

Professor Saucy has rightly reminded the Christian community of the critical link between personhood and the image of God. This is what gives man his unique position among all the creatures in God's creation, giving him his dignity and separating him from the animals. Though the *imago dei* is never explicitly defined, one can surely grasp the meaning of the term from the whole scope of the biblical revelation. Dr. Saucy has helped us see that clearly in his theological anthropology.

Essentially, the image of God is what gives man his ability to form significant relationships with those in the human community. But more importantly, it gives him his ability to relate intimately with God himself. This is what gives man his dignity and places him at the pinnacle of creation. Personhood is intricately intertwined with the image of God, setting man apart from the animals. Some higher forms of animal life may very well possess qualities that characterize personhood, such as self-awareness and an ability to communicate. However, membership in the species *homo sapiens* is what gives a person the image of God and the unique ability to relate to him. It is this, not the other indicators of personhood,[1] that sets man entirely apart from the animal world.

However, as medical technology continues to advance, distinctions surrounding personhood are being increasingly blurred. New distinctions between being a *human being* and being a *person* are emerging out of bioethics discussions about life at both its beginning and ending edges. It is no longer assumed that a living, breathing human being is also a person, with all the attendant rights that accompany personhood. It is possible for a patient to be a human non-person if he fails to satisfy the conditions thought necessary to count as a person. For example, since medicine now can keep people in a permanent vegetative state alive for decades, medical professionals are faced with a patient who has lost all of the functions that are unique to human beings as persons. They are faced with the prospect of keeping alive a "body," that is, corporeal existence without any brain activity other than the involuntary functions, such as breathing and heartbeat, controlled by the brain stem. Many see the use of scarce medical resources on such patients as wasteful, particularly when the money spent on such critical care situations could be spent to prevent more of the same in the future. To justify withholding/withdrawing life-sustaining treatment and even active euthanasia (commonly called "mercy killing," i.e., enlisting a physician to administer a lethal injection of pain-killing drugs), some bioethicists are making critical distinctions between a human being and a person. The result is that when euthanasia is contemplated for such a patient, the one who makes the decision to administer it cannot be accused of killing a person, since the elements of personhood are said to have been lost, or in the case of newborns, were never possessed. In short, the patient has become a human non-person.

Some make a distinction between *biological and biographical life*.[2] They argue that at a certain point at the end of one's life, a terminal illness has taken so much of a toll on a person that all the elements that make life meaningful (biographical life) have been lost. Virtually all that is left is a shell of a person or, for all practical purposes, simply a body. For the elderly who have been ravaged by terminal illness, face imminent death, and suffer substantially while waiting for the merciful prospect of death, active euthanasia is not only re-

1. This term is taken from Joseph Fletcher's discussion of personhood in the midst of emerging new medical technologies. His indicators of humanhood include things such as self-awareness, self-control, a sense of the future, a sense of the past, the capacity to relate to others, concern for others, communication, and curiosity. See Joseph Fletcher, *Humanhood: Essays in Biomedical Ethics* (New York: Prometheus, 1979); idem, "Four Indicators of Humanhood—The Enquiry Matures," *Hastings Center Report* 4 (December 1974): 4–7.

2. See, for instance, James Rachels, *The End of Life* (New York: Oxford University Press, 1986) for further development of this. Rachels's work will be addressed later in this chapter.

garded as merciful, but is not regarded as killing a person. Since personhood had been lost at some point during the terminal illness, the charge that the physician had actively killed a person cannot be made.

Others make this distinction between biological and biographical life not to justify active euthanasia, but to remove medically provided food and water from the patient in a permanent vegetative state (PVS).[3] The person in a PVS has only the lower brain (that is, the brain stem) still functioning. This portion of the brain controls the involuntary functions such as breathing, heartbeat, and digestion. The person in a PVS is not technically dead nor in a coma, but usually, as a result of a stroke or massive head injury, the part of the brain that controls functions normally associated with personhood (e.g., self-awareness) no longer functions. Therefore there is no point in sustaining such a patient with medically provided food and water, since all the physician is accomplishing is keeping a body alive. When such nutrition and hydration is withdrawn, it again is not killing a person, since the elements of personhood no longer exist. On this view, the patient still has biological life (he or she is still a human being), but fails to have biographical life, and the latter is what gives the patient moral value.

Still others apply this distinction between a human being and a person to the beginning of life. For example, many pro-choice advocates admit that the fetus is a human being but deny its personhood, and thus deny it the right to life, at least until the point of viability (around twenty-four weeks gestation). The personhood of the fetus is a significant debate but beyond the scope of this chapter.

The debate over personhood is most acute when the seriously ill newborn is in view.[4] Some would not recognize personhood in any newborn baby,[5] but this is a more extreme view and most in the bioethics community would recognize full personhood with all its attendant rights at least from the moment of birth. However, many would deny such personhood to newborns with severe abnormalities at birth, such as anencephaly (a genetic defect in which the child is born with only a brain stem and no functioning higher brain), severe Down's syndrome, or spina bifida (an opening in the sac that protects the spinal column, usually resulting in severe neurological damage prior to birth). Such newborns will never possess the ability to exercise the principal functions that characterize personhood. Thus, some suggest that it is morally appropriate to deny them life sustaining treatment since to do so would not be killing a person. In addition, some advocate active euthanasia for these newborns as

3. See Robert N. Wennberg, *Terminal Choices: Euthanasia, Suicide and the Right to Die* (Grand Rapids: Eerdmans, 1989).

4. See, for example, Helga Kuhse and Peter Singer, *Should the Baby Live?: The Problem of Handicapped Infants* (New York: Oxford University Press, 1985).

5. See, for example, Michael Tooley, *Abortion and Infanticide* (Oxford: Clarendon, 1983).

morally superior to allowing them to die over a period of days or weeks. Again, it is not technically killing a *person*, only something *less than a person*.

This chapter will defend the view that the distinction between being a human being and being a person is philosophically untenable and inconsistent with the biblical teaching on the image of God. Three specific areas in which this distinction is made in medical ethics will be examined. The concept of personhood will first be related to the treatment of seriously ill newborns, those at the beginning of life. At the end of life, the concept of personhood will be related, secondly, to the morality of active euthanasia, and, finally, to the morality of withdrawing medically provided nutrition and hydration (food and water). These three areas are the ones in which the human being-person distinction are most commonly made.

## Personhood and the Seriously Ill Newborn

In 1963 at Johns Hopkins Medical Center, in the first well-publicized case of infanticide, a child was born with a moderate case of Down's syndrome. In this case, the child born with Down's syndrome also suffered from an intestinal blockage that kept digestion from occurring. Though the necessary surgery to correct the blockage was relatively simple, the parents refused to authorize it and the child was allowed to die, essentially of starvation, over a period of close to two weeks. The pain and anguish experienced by all the parties involved—the child, the parents and the hospital staff—were not difficult to imagine. Three options were available to the parents: (1) *aggressive treatment* to correct the blockage, (2) *passive euthanasia,* that is, allowing the child to die naturally, of starvation, by refusing to authorize the surgery, and (3) *active euthanasia,* that is, intentionally administering "mercy killing" to end the suffering of the child. The parents chose the second of these options, since active euthanasia was against the law and since they did not want to raise a child with Down's syndrome. Many who have commented on this case suggest here that the parents chose the least moral option. In this case, aggressive treatment is the only moral option since the child had a reasonable prospect for a relatively normal and functional life, as is true with many children born with Down's syndrome. From a biblical perspective, which holds human life to have immeasurable value and values people irrespective of birth defects, both passive and active euthanasia would be immoral options in this case, because the child's handicap can be considered the ultimate reason for his death. Had the child not been born with Down's syndrome, there is little doubt that the parents would have consented to the necessary surgery.

A second and virtually identical landmark case in 1982 in Bloomington, Indiana prompted the federal government to intervene. Routine treatment was being denied to newborns due to the presence of non-life-threatening handicaps, and in response the U.S. Department of Health and Human Services issued what came to be known as the "Baby Doe Regulations." These guidelines prohibited physicians and medical facilities from withholding treatment on the basis of mental or physical deformity.

Most commentators on these two cases believed that withholding treatment from these two infants involved immoral discrimination and a grave violation of their right to life. There can be little doubt about the full, or at least potential, personhood of these infants, by virtually anyone's definition of personhood, and in any case, the infants were certainly human beings. But not every case in the neonatal intensive care unit is this clear. Other cases involve infants who suffer from anencephaly, more severe Down's syndrome, or spina bifida. These are much more difficult to resolve because there is more room for debate concerning the child's ability to develop his potential for exercising the many qualities that characterize persons. Some have even suggested that since newborns suffering from anencephaly usually live only a few weeks, that they be allowed to be organ donors before they are declared clinically dead, so that their short and tragic lives have some redeeming value.

Some ethicists and philosophers have suggested that there is a difference between physical life and personhood in some newborns who suffer from severe handicaps.[6] That is, these newborns possess neither actually nor potentially the necessary capacities to exercise the key functions that are characteristic of persons. Ethicist Joseph Fletcher has set out his indicators of humanhood as including self-awareness, self-control, a sense of the future, a sense of the past, the capacity to relate to others, concern for others, communication, and curiosity.[7] Others have included aspects such as rationality, ability to communicate with language, the ability to make rational decisions for oneself, the ability to form meaningful personal relationships, possession of a minimal I.Q., and ability to carry on minimal independent existence. Australian philosopher Peter Singer summarizes these aspects of personhood as the ability to experience a *continuing self* with an interest in a continued life.[8]

These philosophers object to emphasizing the inherent value of human life without considering the functional aspects of personhood. They insist that personhood involves the ability to see oneself as existing over time, with a continuity about one's life. Singer and Kuhse state it this way:

6. See, for example, H. Tristam Englehardt, *The Foundations of Bioethics* (New York: Oxford University Press, 1986); and Mary Ann Warren, "On the Moral and Legal Status of Abortion," *Monist* 57 (1973): 43–61. See also the expanded version of this latter paper with a discussion of infanticide in Richard Wasserstrom, ed., *Today's Moral Problems* (New York: Macmillan, 1975): 120–36.

7. See Joseph Fletcher, "Indicators of Humanhood: A Tentative Profile of Man," *Hastings Center Report* 2 (1972): 1–4; idem, "Four Indicators of Humanhood."

8. Singer and Kuhse, *Should the Baby Live?* 131–32.

> We must recall, however, that when we kill a newborn infant (particularly one that is severely deformed) there is no person whose life has begun (or will ever begin) . . . It is the beginning of the life of the person, rather than the physical organism, that is crucial so far as the right to life is concerned.[9]

Though they end up concluding that all newborns fit into this category of non-person human being, this is more of a tension for those newborns who will never experience the full life that persons, according to their definition, will. Thus personhood is separated from physical existence, and there is a distinction made between a human being and a person, between corporeal existence and personhood.

Those who hold that all human beings possess personhood because of their membership in the species *homo sapiens* are said to be guilty of "speciesism," a belief in the superiority of one's own species to the discriminatory disregard for other species. The relevant factor is not membership in the species, but whether one meets the specific criteria that determine personhood.

This distinction between a human being and a person has been the subject of much criticism. Those who uphold the sanctity of life and generally favor aggressive medical treatment for seriously ill newborns suggest that the criteria for personhood are both highly subjective and quite vague. Given the wide variety and number of criteria used to determine personhood under these models, one should be cautious in basing something so fundamental on something about which we know so little and have such sharp disagreement. In addition, the time at which one actually becomes a person is at best unclear, and at worst, highly arbitrary. It is very difficult, if not impossible, to determine accurately when an individual has crossed the line from simply being a human being to being a person (e.g., many of these qualities are not present when one is asleep, yet no one would consider denying personhood to someone during the nighttime hours; clearly a person can have a capacity and not be exercising it). These qualities further appear to be quantifiable during the time when they are being exercised. The implication that follows from this is that the more of these qualities an individual possesses, the more of a sense of personhood, and thus the attendant moral rights that one possesses. Yet very few would accord a higher degree of personhood to, for example, well-adjusted working professionals than to dysfunctional janitorial workers. As philosopher J. P. Moreland states, "It is difficult to apply these criteria so as to avoid denying equal moral rights to all persons and avoid ruling out certain classes of persons who most would agree are persons but who fail to have a specific property for personhood."[10]

9. Ibid., 133.
10. J. P. Moreland and Norman L. Geisler, *The Life and Death Debate: Moral Issues of Our Time* (New York: Praeger, 1990): 56–57.

Personhood has three important aspects to it: the *inherent,* the *functional,* and the *social.*[11] *Inherent personhood* refers to the possession of personhood that comes innately from membership in the human community. *Functional personhood* refers to the ability to perform the functions that characterize a person, and *social personhood* refers to recognizing one's rights based on an individual's social utility. *The functional and social aspects of personhood are grounded in the inherent.* The basic definition of personhood is the inherent one, as distinct from one's functions or utility. From the perspective of Scripture, and with centuries of theological precedent, each member of the human species is a creature of incredible intrinsic worth. The weakness of those who hold the distinction between human and person is that "to do," or "to function," has become synonymous with "to be." Yet clearly the testimony of Scripture is that, as Catholic ethicist Richard Sparks puts it, "one's value is not wholly or even primarily ability-related . . . [o]ne's basic significance does not depend on the amount of functional abilities one has been endowed with nor on how well one exercises those talents."[12] One can see from Jesus' emphasis on caring for the poor, crippled, lame, and demon-possessed that he cared the most for the least functional and least useful in his time. Rather than seeing seriously ill newborns as having lesser value, if any at all, one senses the high value placed on them by Jesus and the resulting responsibility of stewardship for them emphasized in the Gospels. Sparks summarizes this emphasis in this way:

> In short, it is not so much a question of denying the significance of mental functions or social value in ethical decision making (about treatment decisions) as it is to acknowledge that there is another, more basic, rights-imputing reality . . . which makes each human patient, however functional, defective or socially unwanted, a person, a rights-bearing, interest-laden subject.[13]

Simply because someone does not possess the capacity to exercise the attributes of personhood, it does not follow that he does not possess personhood at all. An entity losing its function does not mean that the entity itself no longer exists, only that it cannot function, or perform all of its functions. If through neurological damage I lose the ability to use my leg, that is one thing. It is quite another to insist that that is the same thing as losing my leg altogether. Even if I never had the use of my leg from birth and will never again have the use of it for the rest of my life, that is not the same thing as having it amputated. Just because some newborns cannot exercise many of the functions of personhood, and through deformity will never be able to ex-

---

11. Richard C. Sparks, *To Treat or Not to Treat?: Bioethics and the Handicapped Newborn* (New York: Paulist Press, 1988), 256–57.
12. Ibid., 260.
13. Ibid., 259.

ercise them, it does not follow that they do not possess the essence of personhood. Function is grounded in essence. If the former is absent, the latter may
be defective, but it is still real.

## Personhood and Active Euthanasia for the Terminally Ill

A second area in which the human being-person distinction is maintained
is in cases of terminal illness in which active euthanasia is considered a merciful
and justifiable course of action. The general term *euthanasia* is derived from
classical Greek and literally means "good death." It refers to the process by
which a person eases into death without unnecessary pain and suffering.
Death is considered a natural and normal part of life, and after a certain point
it is not something to be resisted any longer. Euthanasia is often associated
with terms such as "death with dignity," highlighting the indignity of the dying process surrounded by unwanted medical technology. The current debate
concerns the morality of *active euthanasia*, in which a physician, with the consent of the terminally ill patient,[14] administers a lethal injection of drugs,
quickly and quietly ending the patient's life, thereby mercifully ending substantial suffering. This is different from what is called *passive euthanasia*, in
which the patient is allowed to die rather than his or her death being intentionally caused by a physician's intervention. In passive euthanasia, life-sustaining medical treatment is either withheld or, in most cases, withdrawn, allowing death to take its natural course.

The idea of physicians assisting in suicide, or as some term it "medical killing," is at odds with a long tradition of medical practice. But the longtime taboo against active euthanasia has come under increasing scrutiny since the
mid-1970s. In recent years, well-publicized organizations such as The Hemlock Society and The Society for the Right to Die have increased their efforts
to legitimize euthanasia. The Hemlock Society's founder, Derek Humphry,
published a best-selling book in 1991 that was the boldest statement to date
in support of euthanasia and assisted suicide. Entitled *Final Exit: The Practi-
calities of Self-Deliverance and Assisted Suicide for the Dying*, it is a "how-to"
book, describing how one can be released from the torments of a terminal illness, with or without professional medical assistance. Right-to-die initiatives
are appearing on the ballots more frequently. The best known of these have
been The Humane and Dignified Death Initiative in California, which nar-
rowly missed gathering enough signatures to get on the 1988 ballot (though
influential state legislators confidently predict its eventual passage), and Ini-

14. Advocates of euthanasia insist on strict guidelines governing its administration. For example, the patient must be in the last stages of a uncontroverted terminal illness, with death imminent and with unalleviable and severe pain. Though most physicians are hesitant to predict the
longevity of a terminally ill patient, usually euthanasia is considered for patients with less than a
few months to live.

tiative 119 in Washington state, which did get enough signatures to appear on the 1991 ballot, but was defeated. At the time of this writing, similar initiatives are also being considered in Oregon, Colorado, and Florida.

In the late 1980s and early 1990s, Michigan pathologist Dr. Jack Kevorkian made the headlines with his "suicide machine," which allowed a terminally ill patient to release a lethal dosage of drugs into his body, thereby ending his life. Once the patient was connected to the machine, releasing the drug was a simple matter and it was in the hands of the patient, not the physician. Kevorkian was indicted on two occasions for second degree murder, and though the charges were eventually dropped, he has been prohibited by state law from assisting people with active euthanasia.

A similar prohibition exists in many countries in Europe, but in the Netherlands, for example, the law is rarely enforced, making active euthanasia legal for all practical purposes. The degree to which it is practiced is difficult to determine accurately. The Dutch Ministry of Justice maintains that only approximately two hundred deaths per year result from active euthanasia, but pro-euthanasia groups insist that close to twenty thousand people are administered active euthanasia annually, accounting for more than fifteen percent of the Dutch mortality rate. What is clear is that very few of the cases of active euthanasia are ever brought to a prosecutor, and the few that are almost never end up in court.[15]

Two strong traditions in Western societies, the sanctity of life and the "inevitable" progress of medicine, have created a legacy of aggressive medical treatment that has only recently been reexamined. The increasing ability of medicine to prolong life in increasingly poor quality-of-life circumstances has contributed to a growing fear among the elderly to face end-of-life medical decisions. These fears include ending up powerless to make these decisions for themselves, being held "hostage" to life sustaining medical treatment that they do not want, and living out their last days with an extremely poor quality of life. Thus there are growing pressures to legalize active euthanasia and allow consenting physicians to assist a dying patient in ending his life.

The distinction between *active euthanasia* and *passive euthanasia* is critical to this discussion. Active euthanasia refers to the direct and intentional efforts of a physician or other medical professional to aid a dying patient in suicide. It is commonly called "mercy killing." Passive euthanasia refers to withdrawing (terminating treatment that has already been initiated, such as a respirator) or withholding (that is, not initiating treatment that one considers futile, such as cardio-pulmoninary resuscitation [CPR] for a near death, terminally ill cancer patient) medical treatment from a dying patient and allowing the patient to die. In passive euthanasia death is not intentionally caused as in active

15. Carlos Gomez, *Regulating Death: Euthanasia and the Case of the Netherlands* (New York: Free, 1991).

euthanasia; instead the disease or condition affecting the patient is simply allowed to take its natural course. Thus the disease, not the doctor, is responsible for the patient's death. The principal difference between the two is that in active euthanasia the patient is killed, whereas in passive euthanasia the patient is allowed to die.[16] Most bioethicists, even those in the Christian community, hold that passive euthanasia is morally justified, since the patient has the right to refuse any medical treatment he or she so desires. There is no obligation for any patient to be sustained on life-support systems and live out his or her final days surrounded by invasive medical technology. Thus, if it is clear that a patient does not desire to face death in this way, they have the right to refuse that treatment. Increasingly, the term *euthanasia* is used to refer to *active* euthanasia, thus restricting the debate to legalizing physician-assisted suicide.

The case for active euthanasia has been argued most persuasively by University of Alabama at Birmingham philosopher James Rachels.[17] A critical component of his case is the distinction between *biological* and *biographical* life. Biographical life is the sum total of one's goals, dreams, aspirations, accomplishments, and human relationships. It is those things that form the narrative of one's life and the essence of one's personhood. According to Rachels, modern medicine has enabled one to exist biologically while the person's biographical life has ended. That is, corporeal existence continues, but the person has died. Persons in a persistent vegetative state or in intense suffering with death imminent can be said to have lost their biographical life. This is that which separates man from the animals. Though one implication of this distinction is that animals do have some sort of biographical life, only human beings can have a coherent, whole biographical life. A further implication is that certain handicapped newborns, the elderly, and those who have suffered (for example) permanent severe brain damage have lost their biographical life, and only have biological life or corporeal existence. Since it is biographical life that gives human beings their distinctive value, Rachels reasons that when that has been lost, what is essential about personhood has been lost, or more accurately, has died. Thus, he suggests that concerns about killing persons in active

16. This distinction is not accepted by most advocates of active euthanasia. For example, James Rachels, perhaps the most prominent academic advocate of active euthanasia, has suggested that there is no moral difference between a physician killing a patient by a lethal injection and allowing that patient to die by removing life support systems and allowing death to occur naturally. See Rachels, *The End of Life,* 112. For a thoughtful critique of this point, which Rachels calls the "bare difference argument," see J. P. Moreland, "James Rachels and the Active Euthanasia Debate," *Journal of the Evangelical Theological Society* 31 (March 1988): 81–94; idem, review of *The End of Life,* by James Rachels, *The Thomist* 53 (October 1989): 714–22.

17. See Rachels, *The End of Life.* For the original statement of the position, prior to the more expanded book form, see Rachels, "Active and Passive Euthanasia," *New England Journal of Medicine* 292 (9 January 1975): 78–80.

euthanasia are minimized, which, in turn, according to Rachels, deflects much of the sanctity of life criticism of his position.

He uses a well-known case to bioethicists known as "Dax's case" to illustrate this distinction. Dax Cowart was a strong, athletic young man in his early twenties when he and his father were standing close to an underground gas pipeline that exploded, leaving him severely burned over 90 percent of his body and resulting in the loss of his sight. As he was lying in the field following the explosion, he begged a passerby to shoot him and end the misery that he was experiencing and that he knew he would experience as he underwent painful burn therapy. The passerby refused and arranged for him to be taken to a burn unit at a metropolitan hospital. The treatment was exactly as he anticipated; slow, depressing and excruciatingly painful. Repeatedly he asked the doctors to stop the treatments and simply allow him to die. Though he never requested active euthanasia (but he surely would have had he known it was an option, albeit an illegal one), Rachels suggests that he lost much if not all of his capacity for biographical life as a result of his accident. Those priorities that were most important to him were now impossible for him to pursue. Thus, Dax not only should have been allowed to refuse the painful burn treatment, but had he requested it, he should have been allowed to have active euthanasia administered.

Dax's case, however, is probably not the best example for Rachels to use to illustrate this distinction between biological and biographical life. Throughout the course of the treatment, and in his recovery after it was finished, Dax *recovered* his biographical life. He married, went to law school, and set up a legal practice in his hometown, with a focus on protecting the rights of patients wishing to refuse medical treatment. The irony of this case is that Dax not only regained his biographical life, but one of its significant goals revolves around this very distinction between biological and biographical life. For Dax and others to defend the right to die, and active euthanasia in particular, it is important that the distinction between biological and biographical life be maintained. Yet Dax's own experience of recovering his biographical life indicates that this distinction cannot be upheld as clearly as one would like. In other words, a biographical life is not something you either have or don't have. Rather, it can be possessed in degrees and it can be lost and regained. If this is true, as Dax's case suggests, then the loss of biographical life is hardly an appropriate basis for justifying active euthanasia. It further calls into question the validity of the distinction between biological and biographical life.

In response to this distinction, many would argue that biographical life, far from rendering biological life morally irrelevant, rather presupposes it. The notion of *secondary substance*, first put forth by Aristotle and expanded by Thomas Aquinas, is helpful here. The capacity to have biographical life is grounded in a person being of a specific kind, namely, human being. A human being has an essence that is capable of constructing those necessary elements of biographical life. In other words, a thing has certain qualities because it is a thing of a particular kind. That is, it has second order qualities (those necessary to construct a biographical life) because of its first order qualities (that of being a person, created in God's image). For example, my two-year-old son cannot yet speak in coherent sentences, an ability that is a second order quality. But because of his being of a specific kind, or having the essence of humanness, a first order quality, he will develop that quality as a manifestation of membership in the kind, *homo sapiens*. The possibility of a coherent, full biographical life is grounded in biological life, both of which are part of the essence of being human. Thus personhood is not lost when the ability to exercise its capacities is lost. Losing the use of my arm is not the same thing as having it amputated.

A second criticism of this distinction is that it leads to a subjective view of the value of one's biographical life. For Rachels, it seems that biographical life is independent of any normative (i.e., a judgment that some things are more intrinsically valuable than others) standards of validity. That is, one's biographical life is meaningful simply because it is one's own, and no one can make any normative judgment about the value of one's biographical life. But surely some biographical lives are dehumanizing and inconsistent with being human. For example, suppose that a prostitute had as her goal in life to be the best prostitute she could be and specialized in providing sado-masochistic sex for her clients. Or take a person whose life goal was to be the most effective administrator of torture in his country. We would certainly insist that the biographical lives constructed around those aspirations would be inconsistent with membership in the human community, and that they would devalue someone's life rather than give it value. Yet Rachels's insistence on biographical life being that which gives value to life has nothing in it that keeps biographical life from demeaning life as well as contributing positively to it.

A third criticism extends this point. If biographical life is that which gives life its value and, when it is gone, essentially only a body can be said to exist, then what is to prevent us from stripping the "person" of all his rights? If biographical life gives life its value, then that would seem to be the basis for all other rights. But if biographical life is lost, can we bury the "person" and treat him like a corpse, assuming proper respect for the dead is given? Can we take organs with consent of next of kin? Can we experiment on him, again with appropriate proxy consent? If the essentials of one's life and one's rights are tied up with biographical life, and if that is lost, there does not seem to be any consistent way of preventing any of these scenarios, as long as they are done in a way compatible with our respect for the dead. One could even argue that if rights have been lost with biographical life, not even consent would be necessary for active euthanasia. Opponents of active euthanasia point out that this move from voluntary to involuntary euthanasia, which is performed without the patient's consent, and at times without the patient's knowledge (called *crypthanasia*) is already happening in parts of Europe.[18] Thus it is not surprising to them that this biographical-biological life distinction is problematic and could lead to abuses in its administration.

Thus in cases in which active euthanasia would be considered a desirable alternative (though at present, it is against the law in every state), one cannot justify it by suggesting that a person is not being actively killed, even though it would normally be at the patient's request. If this distinction between a person and a human being cannot be upheld, then active euthanasia is indeed killing innocent people. The long standing tradition, both in society in general and in the medical profession in particular against killing and assisted suicide is rooted in the fifth commandment, "Thou shalt not kill" (KJV).

## Personhood and the Patient in a Permanent Vegetative State

A third area in which the distinction between a person and a human being is suggested is again at the end of life, specifically when a patient, normally through a traumatic injury, is in a permanent vegetative state, in which all brain function except for the activity of the brain stem has ceased. It is suggested that these patients have lost the essence of their personhood, thereby justifying removal of the feeding tubes that are keeping them alive.

On June 25, 1990 the U.S. Supreme Court, in a landmark case, set a precedent that allows for medically provided nutrition and hydration to be withdrawn if there is clear and convincing proof that the patient would have so desired.[19] In this case, Nancy Cruzan had been in a permanent vegetative state as a result of a tragic auto accident. Her family and physicians viewed the continuation of artificial feeding not only as intrusive, but against her wishes as well. They claimed that on a handful of occasions Nancy had commented that she would never want to live in a condition that resembled the one in which she now existed. The Court ruled against her family's request to have the feeding discontinued, but in doing so, clearly affirmed the right of patients in a permanent vegetative state to refuse even such life-sustaining treatment as food and water, if there is clear and convincing evidence that the decision to do so reflects the patient's desire. However, questions are still being raised concerning the ethics behind the Court's decision. Some contend that food and water are basic necessities of life and under no circumstances should members of the medical profession be allowed to starve someone to death.[20]

18. Richard Fenigsen, "A Case Against Dutch Euthanasia," *Hastings Center Report Special Supplement* 19 (January/February 1989): 24–26.
19. Cruzan v. Director, Missouri Department of Health, 110 S. Ct. 2481 (1990).
20. See, for instance, Gilbert Meilander, "On Removing Food and Water: Against the Stream," *Hastings Center Report* 14 (December 1984): 11–13.

Supporters of withdrawal insist that it is pointless treatment that only prolongs dying, often for extended periods of time at exorbitant cost to the family and, in most cases, to the public. Others would hold that the reason the treatment is futile is that the patient has ceased to be a person, and only the biological body is being kept alive.[21]

Without commenting on the ethics of the Missouri law, the Cruzan Court held that the incompetent patient may refuse any medical treatment with clear and convincing proof that such was the patient's desire. In addition, they affirmed that medically provided nutrition and hydration was indeed medical treatment, and that there was essentially no place for proxies (people, usually family members, who are entrusted with making medical decisions for patients when they lose the capacity to do so themselves) in treatment decisions of the patient in a permanent vegetative state.

Even though the Cruzan decision did not allow for the withdrawal of treatment, in December, 1990, a subsequent lower court in Missouri did authorize it. This was based on new evidence brought forth from former roommates and work associates who testified to her desire to avoid ever being sustained in a situation in which she was entirely dependent on artificial life support systems. The lower court held that this constituted clear and convincing proof, and the decision was not challenged by the state. In early January, 1991, within two weeks after medically provided nutrition and hydration was withdrawn, Nancy Cruzan died.

The reason that Cruzan was rightly decided at the Supreme Court level has little to do with the ethics or the wisdom of the Missouri law that the Court upheld. Rather, the Court correctly held that no Constitutional rights were violated in the decision to sustain her, and thus the state could legally impose those restrictions. In addition, the provision of clear and convincing proof is not an unreasonable burden given the life and death consequences of the decision. Granted that most people do not talk about life and death issues in such a formal manner, it is neither unreasonable nor burdensome to require advance written directives or other clear evidence of the patient's wishes to terminate treatment. It is a protection, not a denial of a person's rights, for states to insist that clear directions be made when life and death medical decisions are being considered. The claim that the state of Missouri and the Court denied was the right of the family to decide their daughter's treatment based on *its impact on them*. It may be that treating Cruzan against the wishes of her parents is not the wisest course of action, but it does not follow that her rights are being violated if treatment is maintained.

However, the Court did recognize the right to have nutrition and hydration withdrawn. This is a significant victory for the "right to die" groups.

21. See Joanne Lynn and James F. Childress, "Must Patients Always Be Given Food and Water?," *Hastings Center Report* 13 (October 1983): 17–21.

Whether this will further open the door to active euthanasia is debatable, and in my judgment unlikely, since the bioethics community is still rightly very cautious about active euthanasia. But the Court in Cruzan clearly affirmed the liberty of a person to refuse even life-sustaining food and water.

The *Permanent Vegetative State* (PVS hereafter) is defined by the President's Commission as the state in which "all components of mental life are gone, including self-awareness, thought, emotion, feeling and sensation."[22] According to the consensus of the American Neurological Association, the patient cannot feel pain and has no capacity for anything except involuntary activities. All higher brain function is lost, and only the brain stem is still functioning. However, the person in this state is not dead, according to the medically accepted definition of death (the cessation of *all* brain activity). Most people would be uncomfortable with treating the PVS patient like a corpse and subjecting the person to either burial or organ donation. Many ethicists and physicians reject the higher and lower brain death distinction as a valid way to redefine death. Thus the PVS patient still has all the essential elements of personhood. All that is lost is the ability to exercise them. Simply because a person has lost the ability to exercise the key functions of personhood, it does not follow that they have lost the essence of it. In addition, though they cannot experience harm (and, again, the neurological consensus is that they are not able to experience any sensation, including pain), it does not follow that they cannot be harmed, since treating them as a corpse or a premature organ donor would clearly be harming them, since it treats them as a thing and not as a human being with intrinsic value. Had someone amputated Nancy Cruzan's leg prior to her death, she would certainly have been harmed, though unable to experience it as such.

Actually, discussions about the personhood of the PVS patient are irrelevant and unnecessary in making decisions about artificial feeding and hydration. Most people who draw a distinction between biological and biographical life do so in order to justify withdrawing or withholding treatment. Even some evangelicals involved in medical ethics suggest that the PVS patient has lost something of both personhood and the image of God.[23] For example, Dr. Kenneth Schemmer, a Christian surgeon, writing on the Cruzan case

22. President's Commission for the Study of Ethical Problems in Medicine and Biomedical and Behavioral Research, *Deciding to Forego Life-Sustaining Treatment*, (Washington, D.C.: Government Printing Office, March 1983), 174–75.

23. To illustrate the diversity of opinion in the evangelical community, see the debate over the Brophy case in Massachusetts, referred to later in this chapter. Paul Brophy was the first person in the United States to die after a court had authorized removal of artificial feeding. The debate appears in John J. Davis, "Brophy v. New England Sinai Hospital," *Journal of Biblical Ethics in Medicine* 1 (July 1987): 53-56. He argues against the Court's decision. For a counterargument, see Franklin E. Payne, "Counterpoint to Dr. Davis on the Brophy Case," *Journal of Biblical Ethics in Medicine* 1 (July 1987): 57–60.

prior to the decision of the Supreme Court, suggested that Nancy Cruzan's "living corpse be allowed to die." In his judgment, "Nancy actually died on January 11, 1983, of anoxia, as a result of an auto accident that produced cardio-respiratory arrest."[24]

Robert Wennberg of Westmont College has provided the most extensive evangelical exposition of this distinction between personhood and corporeal existence in the PVS patient. He states:

> [T]hose operating within a Christian belief system may be attracted to the conclusion that death is the total and irreversible loss of the capacity to participate in God's creative and redemptive purposes for human life. For it is reasonable for Christians to believe that it is precisely this capacity which endows human life with its special significance. More specifically, this is the capacity to shape an eternal destiny by means of decision-making and soul-making, requiring as it does both spiritual agency and spiritual receptivity—and not mere organic functioning (that is, somatic life). Indeed it is reasonable to suppose that human organic life has no value in its own right but receives its significance from the fact that it can make possible and sustain personal consciousness, and thereby make possible the capacity to participate in God's creative and redemptive purposes. However, when the human biological organism can no longer fulfill that function, its significance has been lost. . . . When an individual becomes permanently unconscious, the *person* has passed out of existence, even if biological life continues. There cannot be a person where there is neither the capacity for having mental states nor even the potentiality for developing that capacity (e.g., as with infants). For persons are beings who have the capacity (potentially or actually) to think, will, affirm moral and spiritual ideals, love and hate, desire, hope, plan and so forth . . . where no such capacities exist *at all* due to permanent loss of consciousness, there we no longer have an individual who commands the special respect due a person, because we no longer have a person.[25]

Though Wennberg does not specifically mention the image of God being bound up with personhood that dies when an individual's higher brain ceases to function, others make that express connection. For example, Robert Rakestraw of Bethel Seminary accepts Wennberg's view of the personhood of the PVS patient, and extends the argument to hold that the PVS person has lost something essential of the image of God. He states:

> [F]rom a Christian perspective, the relation between image of God and person is that being the image of God is the ground for having the rights of a person. . . . I believe that Scripture equates being God's image with being a person . . .

24. Kenneth E. Schemmer, "Nancy Cruzan is Already Dead," *Update* 5 (December 1989): 4–5.

25. Robert N. Wennberg, *Terminal Choices: Euthanasia, Suicide and the Right to Die* (Grand Rapids: Eerdmans, 1989), 159–60.

the Biblical passages (on the image of God) give good reason to believe that the image concept has a great deal to do with our relationships, or capacity for dominion and our reasoning abilities. . . . However we view the imago Dei, unless it is in terms of a physical body alone, it is difficult to see the PVS individual as being or having the image of God . . . It appears then, that neocortical destruction equals the end of personal life because the correctly diagnosed PVS individual is a body of organs and systems, artificially sustained without the personal human spirit that once enabled this body-soul unity to represent God on earth. While the body still has some kind of residual life, the *person* is dead. . . . A body without neocortical functioning cannot image God according to my understanding of the image concept. . . . The Christian, then, has a theological basis for distinguishing between the death of the body, with its residual movements, and the death of a person.[26]

This functional rather than essential view of personhood and the image of God should give rise to caution, as was outlined in the section on defective newborns. In addition, this distinction is unnecessary here. There is no need to open the door to other possible abuses based on this distinction between a living human being and a person. Rakestraw wants to see only two alternatives for the PVS patient. First, the patient is still alive and thus a person with all the attendant rights to life. Thus it is not justifiable to remove artificial feeding because it would be killing a person. Or second, the PVS patient is dead in any meaningful and Christian sense. He states,

If we accept the view that the PVS patient is not dead, the matter would appear to be settled. Since we must not do anything to contribute deliberately to the death of an innocent person, the artificial feeding and hydration must continue. . . . If we can determine that the PVS patient is dead, then we need not hesitate to withdraw food and water. If, on the other hand, the patient is alive, we must not take his or her life.[27]

However, those are not the only two alternatives. A third, and in my judgment the most satisfactory, option is to admit that artificial nutrition and hydration are indeed medical treatments, and as such, the patient, or legitimate proxy decision maker, has the right to refuse them, similar to other forms of life-sustaining treatment.[28] To take this alternative view avoids the problems

26. Robert V. Rakestraw, "The Persistent Vegetative State: Should Fluids Be Withdrawn?" *Journal of the Evangelical Theological Society.* Even though he maintains the distinction between a body and a person, he does insist on proper respect for the body, both in death and dying as well as in life, because of the connection of the body with the image of God.

27. Ibid., 2, 4.

28. In personal conversation with Rakestraw, he admitted his hesitancy to concede that medically provided food and water were forms of medical treatment that could be refused. I insisted that he would have an easier time persuading the evangelical community of that fact than of his more functional view of the image of God.

inherent in separating biological life from personhood and does not open the door to further potential abuses.

The reason that this alternative position is viable is that *medically provided nutrition and hydration can be legitimate medical treatment*, which, similar to other life-sustaining treatments, can be refused by a patient or by a appropriate surrogate decision maker. The Cruzan Court was very helpful in clarifying the precedent set by the 1985 Conroy decision in New Jersey.[29] Some of the reasons for their decision on this parallel the Brophy case in Massachusetts, which further clarified the legal background.[30] In this case, Paul Brophy was in a PVS due to a head injury. He was the first well-publicized person to be allowed to die following removal of feeding tubes. In the decision of the Massachusetts Court of Appeals, the judges cited the highly invasive nature of the treatment to provide food and water artificially. This is particularly the case when the feeding tube is inserted by gastrotomy (a process in which the tube is directly placed into the wall of the stomach)—clearly a surgical procedure. It is typically treated as medical treatment by health insurance companies and by Medicare, and must be done under the supervision of a physician or nurse, normally in a licensed medical facility. Insertion of the tube has risks and possible side effects like other medical treatments; this is especially true of the nasogastric tube and the risk of pneumonia. Though less invasive than a respirator, in principle medically provided nutrition and hydration functions in the same way: through mechanical and medical means it provides a basic function that the body is no longer able to do itself.

The term *medically provided nutrition and hydration* is used intentionally to underscore the technological nature of it. There is a strong parallel to the respirator in that medical technology is performing an essential bodily function that the body, through injury or disease, can no longer perform itself. Certainly air to breathe is as basic a human need as food and water. Yet very few question the morality of removing a respirator, since it is considered legitimate medical treatment. Wennberg makes this parallel in his attempt to show that nutrition and hydration is optional treatment for the PVS patient. He rightly points out, "Why should artificial feeding be any more mandatory

29. In re Conroy, 98 N.J. 321, 486 A.2d 1209, 1223 (1985).

30. Brophy v. New England Sinai Hospital, Inc., 398 Mass. 417, 497 N.E. 2d 626 (1986). In this case, the court ruled that withdrawal of nutrition and hydration did not violate any of the key state interests in 1) the preservation of life, since the state interest was broader than simply *extending mere corporeal existence* (appearing to make the distinction between personhood and biological life), and the interest in preserving life applied only when an affliction is curable; 2) the prevention of suicide, since it is the initial injury that is the ultimate cause of his death (he would not have been in this condition at all unless the injury had occurred and his need to have N/H artificially provided was the direct result of the injury); and 3) maintaining the integrity of the medical profession, since they are not the ultimate cause of Brophy's death, and thus have not violated any code of ethics or the Hippocratic oath.

than a respirator? Indeed, it is difficult to see why the one (artificial feeding) should be required and the other (artificial breathing) not required if neither bring any benefit to the *person*."[31] My point here is simply that the parallel between a respirator and artificial feeding is sufficient morally to allow for its removal, all other things being equal. In cases in which it is moral to remove a respirator, it is also moral to withdraw artificial feeding and hydration. There is no qualitative difference between the two types of treatment. Once this parallel is accepted, and artificial feeding is accepted as medical treatment, *then the personhood of the patient is no longer a necessary or relevant consideration.*

Of course, if the definition of death is altered to include the PVS patient under its heading, then there is no moral tension with removing the artificial feeding tubes. However, most bioethicists are hesitant to so alter the definition. But if medically supplied nutrition and hydration is indeed medical treatment, then it falls under the heading of that which can be refused, and as such is similar to the respirator. If this is so, and if substituted judgment (the notion that the judgment of the proxy decision maker accurately represents the wishes of the patient) is in some way valid, *then questions of personhood do not need to be entertained here.* Hospitals and ethicists don't ask those questions of people who are being sustained on a respirator or who are contemplating refusal of some other form of life-sustaining medical treatment, and there is no need to ask them here.

Opponents of removal of medically provided nutrition and hydration have focused their position around four principal arguments. First, it is maintained that nutrition and hydration are necessary to preserve patient dignity in the dying process. But it should be noted that many PVS patients are not actually in the process of dying, but could live in a PVS on artificial feeding for many years. The longest recorded PVS survivor lived in this condition for thirty-seven years. Elaine Esposito was maintained on artificial feeding between 1941–1978.[32] In addition, once it is removed, it is not difficult to keep the patient looking comfortable (even though they cannot experience comfort or discomfort) by periodically applying ice chips to the face and lips.

A second argument is that nutrition and hydration is ordinary treatment and thus should be provided. This comes out of the distinction between ordinary and extraordinary treatment, the former always being mandatory and the latter being optional. Ordinary treatment is that which is expected to bring a benefit to the patient that is proportionately greater than the burden imposed. Extraordinary treatment is treatment in which the burden may outweigh the benefit to the patient. Rather than a predetermined distinction, many are more comfortable with the distinction between obligatory and op-

31. Wennberg, *Terminal Choices,* 164–65.

32. David Lamb, *Death, Brain Death and Ethics* (Albany: State University of New York Press, 1986), 6.

tional treatment. What is important is the weight of benefit over burden in each particular case as opposed to a predetermined distinction. There are cases in which the denial of extraordinary treatment would clearly be unjustifiable and times when ordinary treatment could be withheld. For instance, in the case of a patient in the last stages of a terminal illness, antibiotics to ward off pneumonia (traditionally, the dying person's friend) would not be mandatory—since they would only be prolonging an imminent death—yet they would fall under the heading of ordinary treatment. Though there is a presumption in favor of continuing treatment (that is, the moral burden of proof in favor of discontinuing treatment must be established), even for nutrition and hydration, whether such treatment is obligatory or optional depends on the facts of the case in question. The distinction between ordinary and extraordinary treatment cannot be used as a predetermined formula for mandating the course of treatment.

A third objection is that this is starving a patient to death, something that is inhumane and not worthy of a community that cares for the dying. Though there are clearly cases in which nutrition and hydration should be provided, withdrawing them, or refusing to initiate them, does not constitute starving someone to death any more than the removal of a respirator constitutes suffocating someone to death. Even though the PVS person is not terminally ill, it is the injury suffered that is responsible for the patient being in the present condition. Were it not for the injury (or sometimes a disease; in most cases, a traumatic head injury), the patient would be able to take nutrients orally. The injury caused the condition, and had food and water not been initially provided by medical technology or otherwise had not been available, the patient would have died in a relatively short time period and the death would been seen as a result of the injury. Thus parallel to the removal of other types of medical treatment, the injury is the ultimate cause of the patient's death.

The fourth, and most common argument against withdrawal is that food and water are symbolic of basic human care for the dying, and we don't dare neglect it for what it will say about our care for people at the edges of life. It is parallel to the "cup of water" administered to the dying by a loved one or family member. This symbolism is built on the assumed parallel between medically provided and non-medically provided nutrition and hydration. Proponents of this argument stress the parallel between medical and non-medical means of feeding and insist that this establishes a presumption in favor of feeding the PVS patient. In general, we would hold to the presumption in favor of life sustaining treatment.

However, one may ask if medically provided nutrition and hydration is any more symbolic than any other kind of treatment, such as a respirator. In addition, the way in which it is provided medically has little resemblance to the "cup of water" administered to the dying, and it is rarely administered by a family member or other loved one. Loved ones of the patient are sometimes involved in the process of caring for the patient, but not in the actual feeding. In most cases it occurs in sterile hospitals, done by hospital personnel who have no connection to the patient. Others would suggest that it is symbolic, but of something different. It is symbolic of someone being held hostage to medical technology, likely against his or her wishes. It may even be symbolic of something further, namely, exile from the human community. Life in a PVS can be seen as the modern equivalent of a punishment that was considered worse than death, exile, in which the person is cut off from loved ones and dies alone.[33] Thus one can argue that continuing nutrition and hydration is symbolic of a patient being held hostage to medical technology and state intervention against his or her wishes (or to put it another way, symbolic of the fact that his or her wishes are irrelevant, with caregivers ironically and symbolically ignoring them), or as one writer has suggested, symbolic of exile from the human community (exile in a condition that most of society considers worse than death). Nor is it clear that providing artificial feeding necessarily upholds the sanctity of life. Rather, it appears that the sanctity of life is being equated with merely postponing death.

## Conclusion

Questions of human nature and personhood are becoming much more than simply abstract philosophical or theological issues. The debate over these issues is coming out of the academe and moving into the intensive care units of hospitals around the world. These questions have a tremendous bearing on a growing number of real life ethical decisions that have life and death implications associated with them. Never before has there been such a need for clear and biblically informed thinking about what it means to be a person made in God's image.

## Suggested Readings

Beauchamp, Tom L., and LeRoy Walters. *Contemporary Issues in Bioethics.* Belmont, Ca.: Wadsworth, 1989. [I]

Hauerwas, Stanley. *Suffering Presence: Theological Reflections on Medicine, the Mentally Handicapped and the Church.* Notre Dame, Ind.: University of Notre Dame Press, 1986. [B]

Lammers, Stephen E., and Allen Verhey, eds. *On Moral Medicine: Theological Perspectives on Medical Ethics.* Grand Rapids.: Eerdmans, 1987. [I]

33. For further development of this parallel, see Lawrence J. Schneiderman, "Exile and PVS," *Hastings Center Report* 20 (May/June 1990): 5.

Lynn, Joanne, ed. *By No Extraordinary Means*. Bloomington, Ind.: Indiana University Press, 1986. [A]

Moreland, J. P. and Norman L. Geisler. *The Life and Death Debate: Moral Issues of Our Time*. New York: Praeger, 1990. [I]

President's Commission for the Study of Ethical Problems in Medicine and Biomedical and Behavioral Research. *Deciding to Forego Life-Sustaining Treatment*. Washington, D.C.: Government Printing Office, 1983. [B]

Rachels, James. *The End of Life*. New York: Oxford University Press, 1986. [A]

Ramsey, Paul. *The Patient As Person*. New Haven: Yale University Press, 1984. [B]

Wennberg, Robert N. *Terminal Choices: Euthanasia, Suicide and the Right to Die*. Grand Rapids: Eerdmans, 1989. [A]

# A Response to Scott B. Rae

## Klaus Issler

Technological progress offers us something "new" and something "old." Such advances in medical technology make available *new* medical procedures and devices for improved diagnoses and treatment. The attendant complexity in decision making regarding the use of these improvements directs our attention to the *old*: the necessity of rigorous philosophical inquiry, as exemplified in Professor Rae's chapter. As we are confronted by the failing health of an aged parent, by a brother or sister in an automobile accident, or by our new infant born with multiple deformities, we are forced to make immediate life-and-death decisions—decisions we are, oftentimes, ill-prepared to make.

We have become accustomed to discarding our possessions when they are no longer useful or needed. Inevitably, such a consumer-oriented perspective is being directed toward *people*. Is an individual just another high-tech piece of machinery, worthy of value only when he or she functions within a range of acceptable levels? What is the essence of personhood? This chapter directs us toward ways of thinking which are consistent with an evangelical view of persons created in the image of God.

To make some headway in a discussion of matters related to euthanasia, Rae introduces a number of conceptual distinctions: some that are problematic for evangelicals (e.g., "human being" and "person"; "biographical" and "biological" life) and some that are essential (e.g., "active" and "passive" euthanasia; "medically provided" and "non-medically provided" nutrition; "obligatory" and "optional" treatment).

After perusing the chapter, readers may regard such distinctions as obtuse and esoteric, and conclude that discussions of this kind have no value outside of the ivory tower. This judgment may hold until we face a crisis involving a family member or a member of our church. But then it is too late to prepare ourselves to understand what biblically-consistent options we may take. The counsel we receive from the attending medical officers may or may not square with an evangelical view of personhood. Since we may not do our best thinking in such times of emotional strain, it behooves us, as Christian leaders, to educate ourselves and to train our fellow believers in matters of medical ethics and principles to guide our decision-making.

In this chapter, Rae has highlighted for us the deontological or rule-based ethical tradition. In many cases, it is possible to choose the right course of action according to a set of moral principles (e.g., "we ought to keep a promise"). Yet a rule-based ethic does not exhaust our understanding of the moral life. Not only must we *do* the right kind of act, but we must also *be* the right kind of person. Such a virtue-based ethic focuses on the *character* of the agent who accomplishes the moral act.

Virtue ethics affirms that it is important not only to act correctly, but also to exhibit the necessary habits, dispositions, motives, and attitudes of goodness. Our motivations for doing good and whether or not we are tempted to do wrong are important factors to consider. Such a character-based ethics offers essential guidance where a principle-based ethics leaves off. The patterns of moral character must be learned in the crucible of life. A central means of moral education in this particular tradition is gleaned through watching good moral models and then following their example.

Thus, our moral education as Christians should include two significant thrusts as we grow to full maturity in Christ. We must emphasize ethical instruction in which we are able to employ relevant moral principles to resolve the difficult situations of life. Rae's chapter provides a helpful example within this important direction. In addition, we must cultivate godly virtues of character, providing a boundary of habits and dispositions to guide our actions when moral reasoning is not enough. We are best prepared to make the right decisions when we regularly internalize God's principles into our character. For it is the mature "who by constant use [of the Word] have trained themselves to distinguish good from evil" (Heb. 5:14).

# A Response to Scott B. Rae

## *J. P. Moreland*

I am in hearty agreement with the vast majority of what Professor Rae has said. In my view, the main theme he has surfaced involves the ethical importance of the notions of the image of God, being human, and personhood. Thus, my response will develop and comment on these notions to offer further support and clarity to Rae's treatment of them.

In my view, being is prior to and the ground of functioning, doing, and relating. A thing can function or relate in a certain way because of what it is. A brick can function as a doorstop or be to the left of my desk because of what it is (a material object). The number two does not have the capacity to function or relate in these ways because of what it is (an abstract object). Similarly, personhood, humanness, and the image of God specify primarily what certain kinds of things are (namely, human beings) and secondarily what functions or relationships certain individuals can exemplify because of the capacities inherent in personhood, humanness, and the image of God.

Now, part of a thing's being is its capacities (dispositions, abilities, potentialities). A bowling ball has the capacity to reflect light, I have the capacity to speak English. Individual human beings are kinds of things, that is, they fall under the natural kind "being human," and being human constitutes the essence or nature of each and every human. If I lose my humanness, I cease to exist.

Further, as a human, I have a heirarchy of capacities that culminate in ultimate capacities determined by the kind of thing I am. There are first-order capacities, second-order capacities to have these first-order capacities, third-order capacities to have the second-order capacities, and so on, until ultimate capacities are reached. I have the first-order capacity to speak English, I have the second-order capacity to develop the first-order capacity to speak English (or Russian), and so on.

My ultimate capacities are mine, not as a result of anything I do to develop anything, but just in virtue of being a member of my natural kind, being human. A thing's natural kind is a deep unity of a thing's ultimate capacities. These set limits to the kinds of changes and developmental processes a thing can undergo and still exist. A thing cannot change in its ultimate dispositions. A thing's "inner nature" is just a unity of its ultimate dispositions. These dispositions determine a lawlike path through which a substance can move over time as it develops (or fails to develop) its lower order capacities that typically unfold the higher order ones. An acorn has the ultimate capacity to draw nourishment from the soil, but this can be actualized and unfolded only by developing the capacity to have a root system, then developing other capacities *of* the root system, and so on, until nourishment can be derived from the soil.

Now, just because something cannot exercise or develop its lower order capacities (a defective newborn cannot develop linguistic skills) through some defect, it does not follow that the thing's ultimate capacities are gone. I may not have the capacity to develop the capacity to speak English, but I may have the capacity to develop the capacity to develop the capacity to speak English.

In my view, the image of God specifies our highest order capacities that constitute being human. The absence of first or second order functional abilities to exercise these capacities does not mean that the highest order capacities are not still present, as Wennberg seems to suppose when he claims that the capacities to think, will, and so forth do not exist at all when a person is in a persistent vegetative state. Such persons, he claims, are *permanently* unconscious. However, they are not permanently unconscious, since God can make them conscious again in the intermediate state following death, even if we admit that they are *irreversibly* unconscious from a medical point of view.

Now, when God revives such persons in the intermediate state, he does not create them all over again (he would have to do so if they ceased being a person in the PVS and became one again in the intermediate state); rather, he merely actualizes certain higher order capacities which are still present (their presence maintains personal identity and continuity for these persons). Thus, a human is still a person in God's image with a full set of highest order capacities even if a defect causes that person to fail to be able to develop lower order capacities.

Further, it is not "the capacity to participate in God's creative and redemptive purposes for human life" that endows human life with special significance, as Wennberg supposes. Rather, it is being an example of the kind of thing—being human—that gives me value. Moreover, as a human, I have the higher order capacity to participate in God's purposes, even if through loss or defect, I cannot develop the lower order capacities that flow from the higher order capacity. In fact, the very notion of a defect (a failure to have something I ought to have) presupposes the defective entity is still a member of its natural kind, and as such, it *ought* to have the lower order abilities to develop the ultimate capacities it still possesses in virtue of its kindedness. Ultimate capacities are developed through the cultivation of lower order capacities that realize the ultimate ones, and defects do not signal the non-existence of ultimate capacities, but merely the failure for those capacities to be realizable in the appropriate ways.

Sometimes properties relate to each other as a genus does to a species. Here are some genus/species relationships: being a color/being red; being a shape/being square; being a person/being a human. The species is a *way* by which the genus exists. Being red, square, or human are ways that being colored, shaped, or being a person exist in individual things.

There can be colored things that are not red things, but there cannot be red things that are not colored things. Similarly, there can be persons that are not humans (Martians, angels), but there are no humans that are not persons. In fact, there is no such thing as a colored thing or person plain and simply. There are only kinds of colored things (e.g., red things) and kinds of persons (e.g., divine, human, angelic). Thus, in my view, there are no such things as human non-persons (e.g., defective newborns, PVS patients).

As Rae suggests, if we are going to justify the claims that 1) all human beings have equal rights and value and 2) human beings as a class have more intrinsic value than do animals, and if our justification is going to be grounded in the way things really are, then we must do two things. We must find some property (or properties) that all humans as such distinctively have in common, and this property (or properties) must be relevant to the question of value; that is, it must be a value-making property (as my daughter suggested, the property of having a belly button doesn't count). The image of God serves as a metaphysical ground for such a task. Once it is abandoned, it becomes hard to justify the two claims above, especially if various functional criteria are utilized (e.g., rationality, awareness of one's self through time, ability to use language). Why? Because these are degreed properties that something can have more or less of (e.g., psychologists may have more of them than, say, plumbers), and certain animals (e.g., higher primates) may have more of them than some humans (e.g., defective newborns). Speciesism notwithstanding, both of the claims above are reasonable, and the non-Christian labors to justify them in a way unnecessary for the believer. Thus, the doctrine of the image of God is crucial for ethical deliberation regarding the value and rights of human beings.

# 9

# Conscience

## *Moral Sensitivity and Moral Reasoning*

### *Klaus Issler*

In the midst of cooking that favorite meal, a shrill sound interrupts your creative art. "There goes that dumb smoke alarm again," you shout to your roommate. Though you are a little irritated about the disturbance, you are very happy that the alarm works. An operative smoke alarm could mean the difference between life and death. These fire detectors have become standard equipment in most homes and office buildings. In a similar fashion, our wise Creator equipped us all with a comparably-designed standard feature: a conscience—a fully operational moral detector or prompter.

In the first chapter, Robert Saucy indicated that we are moral beings, created with a faculty for moral self-awareness.[1] Although we may not know how conscience functioned prior to the fall, this critical faculty has been operative from Genesis 3 onward.[2] Scripture records the promptings of conscience in such notable figures as Moses (Exod. 2:11–12), King David[3] (1 Sam. 24:5),

1. For analysis purposes, conscience is viewed as a distinct conceptual entity, although it is a function of the whole person.
2. How conscience operated before the fall, or how it may operate in the eternal state is a matter of speculation. Currently, we can only fully study the *fallen* and the *regenerate* conscience.
3. In Psalm 32, David penned an explicit description of the pangs of conscience.

and the apostle Paul (Acts 23:1). And newspapers frequently report unusual cases of restitution, based on a guilty conscience, such as this one:

> Nearly 25 years after two brass bells were stolen from his ice-cream truck, Joe Queen got them back for Christmas. "Do you remember?" a note read. "I did." The note said the bells were taken in 1967, 1968, or 1969. "Sorry. Merry Christmas." "Somebody took those bells and evidently their conscience bothered them ever since," Queen said.[4]

Maturing in Christian character involves growth in two essential aspects:[5]

*Conscience* (e.g., Ps. 119:11; Acts 24:16)

a. Educating, evaluating, and responding to a sensitive conscience—the seat of our convictions of morality (e.g., Rom. 14:22–23; James 1:22–25),

b. Improving our moral reasoning and decision making—conscience being the locus of arbitration regarding moral decisions (e.g., Heb. 5:14),

*Lifestyle Habits* Developing and maintaining our self-control and participation in moral actions (through personal habits and spiritual disciplines) (e.g., 1 Cor. 9:24–27).

The purpose of this chapter is to describe certain aspects of the functioning of conscience (item 1) as outlined by biblical data and as informed by social science theory.[6] Although our experience of a functioning conscience is commonplace, discussions of conscience per se have fallen on hard times in the social sciences. Few psychology or human development textbooks list that specific term in their indexes aside from a review of Freud's concept of the

---

4. *The Orange County Register,* 30 Dec. 1991.

5. In summarizing social science studies on moral development, James Rest ("Morality," in *Manual of Child Psychology,* 4th ed., ed. Paul H. Mussen, 4 vols. [New York: John Wiley and Sons, 1983], 3:557–629) suggests that four major components are involved in making a moral action: (1) *moral sensitivity* (being aware of and correctly interpreting a situation as involving a moral issue); (2) *moral reasoning* (making a decision as to the ideal course of action); (3) *moral motives and values* (considering other extenuating factors that will affect the final course of action to be taken); and (4) *moral character or courage* (executing the plan of action, despite any countervailing forces). Aspects of Rest's framework have been incorporated in my outline and an eleven-step outline recently presented by Arthur Holmes, *Shaping Character: Moral Education in the Christian College* (Grand Rapids: Eerdmans, 1991).

6. Two resources offer introductory guidance for item 2: Lifestyle habits. Dallas Willard (*The Spirit of the Disciplines* [San Francisco: Harper Collins, 1988]) reviews the necessity of practicing spiritual disciplines. Though not from a Christian perspective, David L. Watson and Roland G. Tharp (*Self-Directed Behavior: Self-Modification for Personal Adjustment,* 5th ed. [Pacific Grove, Calif.: Brooks/Cole, 1989]) provide a helpful guide on developing new habits.

Superego. Yet, studies and theories are available that touch on matters that we would relate to a biblical concept of conscience. Although such information may help us understand how we grow and learn, as evangelical believers, we must affirm that genuine morality (i.e., Spirit-led righteousness) issues from and is an evidence of a growing relationship with God.

Following a review of biblical terms for conscience, a three-component model of conscience will be briefly outlined. This framework will then be used as we investigate two particular aspects of the functioning of conscience: moral sensitivity and moral reasoning. The applicational thrust of the chapter is to provide insight and guidelines for those believers who have a more or less healthy conscience.[7]

## Conscience and Scripture

There is no specific term for "conscience" in the Hebrew language. The pangs of conscience are expressed as one of the many functions of the "heart" (*heart* is most often used in Scripture for the seat or center of personality). Compare the following translations:

Genesis 20:6:

NASB: "Yes, I know that in the *integrity of your heart* you have done this. . . ."

NIV: "Yes, I know you did this with a *clear conscience*. . . ."

2 Samuel 24:10:

NASB: "Now David's *heart troubled* him after he had numbered the people."

NIV: "David was *conscience-stricken* after he had counted the fighting men. . . ."

Following his sin with Bathsheba, David composed Psalm 51 in which he requests: "Create in me a *pure heart*, O God" (v. 10). This Hebraic metaphor is occasionally used in the New Testament: "When the people heard this, they were *cut to the heart* and said to Peter and the other apostles, 'Brothers, what shall we do?'" (Acts 2:37). The NASB translators provide the marginal rendering, "smitten in conscience," for what the NIV renders as *cut to the heart*.

7. For a study of conscience from a therapist's perspective, consult the insightful book-length treatment of conscience and psychological guilt, S. Bruce Narramore, *No Condemnation: Rethinking Guilt Motivation in Counseling, Preaching, and Parenting* (Grand Rapids: Zondervan, 1984). Narramore's book offers particular guidance for those believers suffering from an overly scrupulous or "weak" conscience. On one point Narramore and I differ in our respective views of conscience. I take a "higher" view—that conscience is a gift of God, whereas Narramore holds a "lower" view—that it is not necessarily a gift of God.

The Greek term for conscience is *suneidēsis*. It is used about thirty times in the New Testament, mostly within the Pauline corpus. Singular references portray the non-regenerate conscience as "guilty" (Heb. 10:22), "corrupted" (Titus 1:15), and capable of being "seared" (1 Tim. 4:2). With primary reference to the believer, conscience is described as being "cleansed" (e.g., Heb. 9:14) and capable of being "good" (e.g., Heb. 13:18), "clear" (e.g., 1 Tim. 3:9), and "weak" (e.g., 1 Cor. 8:7). Narramore offers an explanation of the latter three terms: "A clear, or good, conscience is related to consistency in living. . . . A strong conscience (and its opposite, the weak conscience) results from a mature and properly educated faith or lack of it."[8] In 1 Corinthians 8 and 10:25–11:1 Paul treats matters of Christian liberty in which questions of conscience arise. A similar discussion takes place in Romans 14, though the word *conscience* is not specifically used.

In the classic passage in Romans 2:14–15, Paul describes the basic function of conscience: it either accuses us or defends our actions. We commonly think of conscience as just a "post-act monitor"—when the pangs of guilt or sorrow are aroused following something we did. But in addition to being a *judge* of *past* thoughts, feelings, and actions, our conscience also serves as a *guide* for *future* decisions.

> To think of conscience in this way as the judge of past action is to be on the verge of thinking of it also as the guide of future action. And though this latter aspect is not developed in the New Testament as part of the meaning of [the term] conscience, the duty to live by norms revealed by God is clearly affirmed in the teaching of Jesus and of his apostles.[9]

## Components of Conscience

Before moving to an investigation of moral sensitivity and moral reasoning, we need to explain a few key concepts that will be relevant to the discussion. Though conscience involves a variety of complex processes, for ease of analysis, we may identify three essential components: the capacity, the call, and the convictions of conscience.

8. Ibid., 212. For the believer, a "clear" conscience is a subjective judgment of our degree of obedience toward God. Yet, Acts 23:1 raises a question as to how objective that assessment may be, since Paul appears to include his pre-conversion life in this statement to the Sanhedrin: "My brothers, I have fulfilled my duty to God in all good conscience to this day."

9. Peter Toon, *Your Conscience As Your Guide* (Wilton, Conn.: Morehouse-Barlow, 1983), 39. As a guide for future action, conscience also prompts deeds of courage. The Carnegie Hero Fund Commission recently cited fifteen people for trying to save the lives of others while risking their own. Four of those honored heroes died in their rescue attempt ("Group Honors 15 Heroes," *The Orange County Register,* 27 Dec. 1991).

## The Capacity of Conscience

"We intuit the moral dimension in human life because we still have the sense for genuine humanity that God created us with."[10] Since we have been created in the image of God as moral beings, we have a unique, innate capacity to discern what right and wrong means. That is, regardless of the particular convictions we happen to acquire, whether we are Christian or not, whether we are American or not, we all experience a sense of "ought" or "should." The particular moral norms we hold dear are learned from birth onward. But the capability for moral sensitivity is part of God's special design for humankind. It is one characteristic that distinctly separates us from the rest of God's creation.

## The Call of Conscience

Like the smoke alarm mentioned at the beginning of the chapter, conscience has been designed with an "alarm" mechanism—it beckons for our attention. The call of conscience may take on many forms. Following a good deed, we may feel the peace and affirmation of conscience (2 Thess. 2:16–17). When we notice someone in distress or in dire circumstances, our heart goes out to him or her (empathy sends forth a call for action) (Rom. 9:1–3).[11] If we actually hurt a friend or when we disobey God, we experience a troubled conscience, a sorrow that can lead to repentance and restoration (2 Cor. 7:8–13a).[12] The call of conscience acts as an internal reminder of our convictions and as a moral prod to consider a plan of action.[13]

For believers, conscience is the vehicle through which the Holy Spirit *may* subjectively prompt us to action (Rom. 8:14, 16).[14] If we are filled by the Spirit (Eph. 5:18) and keep in step with him (Gal. 5:25), we can respond positively. Or, we may decide to quench (1 Thess. 5:19) or grieve the Spirit (Eph. 4:30).[15]

10. Lewis B. Smedes, *Choices: Making Right Decisions in a Complex World* (San Francisco: Harper and Row, 1986), 20.

11. Charles M. Shelton (*Morality of the Heart: A Psychology for the Christian Moral Life* [New York: Crossroad, 1990]) gives empathy a prominent place in his view of Christian morality. His discussion is largely based on Hoffman's psychological studies of empathic arousal (e.g., M. Hoffman, "Empathy, Its Limitations, and Its Roles in a Comprehensive Moral Theory," in *Morality, Moral Behavior, and Moral Development,* ed. W. M. Kurtines and J. L. Gewertz (New York: Wiley, 1984), 283–302.

12. Narramore (*No Condemnation,* chap. 11) makes a helpful distinction between destructive psychological guilt, (which Christians need not and should not experience) and constructive or godly sorrow (which leads to repentance) (2 Cor. 7:9–10).

13. Believers will vary in their need for such conscience "reminders." It may be helpful to view conscience as a divine "safety net"—a final moral checkpoint—to encourage us to do what is right, rather than as a Skinnerian behavior modification mechanism. Responding to the call of conscience is not the *primary* reason or motive for us to be obedient to God. But conscience is always ready to prod us when we may need that extra nudge.

14. Not all promptings of conscience are divine as discussed later in the chapter.

15. When mature believers sin, they may also experientially share in the grief of the Holy Spirit, the one who indwells them.

## The Convictions of Conscience

The particular *convictions* within our conscience largely determine on what basis the *capacity* and the *call* of conscience will operate. But these convictions are not set and fully formed at birth. "The biblical notion of conscience does not imply that we are given an innate moral code common to all human beings, as popular usage sometimes suggests. It is rather a conscious sensitivity . . . that needs to be informed, sharpened, and directed."[16] Like a personal computer, our conscience must be programmed with appropriate input for it to be useful. Since our convictions are learned throughout life, largely in an *unconscious* manner (as will be explained), we will acquire both *good* and *sinful* values.[17] Thus, the urgency arises for growing believers to regularly evaluate and educate their conscience toward righteousness. To that task we now turn.

## Educating a Sensitive Conscience

Should we always *listen* to our conscience? Yes! Should we always *follow* our conscience? No! The conscience is very fallible. But if we wish to maintain a highly sensitive conscience, we must always be willing to listen to and evaluate the message our conscience offers. To repeatedly ignore the promptings of conscience will desensitize the conscience's promptings regarding a given conviction. As blind persons regularly use sandpaper to keep their fingertips

16. Holmes, *Shaping Character,* 27. Whether Romans 2:15 indicates that some basic moral content is innately common to all consciences or whether these values were learned after birth is difficult to discern. Regardless, all are held morally accountable before God (Rom. 1–2).

17. Anthropologists have made distinctions between guilt- and shame-cultures regarding the function of conscience and the motivation to conform to cultural norms. "Cultures which give rise to norm-internalization are termed 'guilt-cultures,' for cultural conformity is motivated by guilt. Those which do not produce norm-internalization are termed 'shame-cultures,' for the members of society conform to cultural norms only when their fellows are present to shame them" (Melford E. Spiro, "Social Systems, Personality, and Functional Analysis," in *Culture and Human Nature: Theoretical Papers of Melford E. Spiro,* ed. Benjamin Kilbourne and L. L. Langness [Chicago: University of Chicago Press, 1987], 138–39). Yet Spiro questions the validity of this guilt-shame dichotomy since "[t]he existence of agents of shame implies that at least some members of the society have internalized at least some norms" (ibid., 136). He suggests an alternative internal distinction between guilt-oriented and shame-oriented Superegos. "A person with a guilt-oriented superego suffers guilt when he transgresses, even if no one perceives his transgressions, because the [internalized] agent of punishment (the introjected figure) is always with him. However, a person with a shame-oriented superego does not suffer shame when he transgresses unless others witness his transgression, for no agent of punishment (the external others) is present. Instead of experiencing *actual* punishment (shame), he continues to anticipate punishment; he suffers from anxiety" (ibid., 139). Although guilt- and shame-oriented superegos function differently after a transgression occurs, "both types inform the individual that his anticipated behavior is wrong, and both motivate him to refrain from transgressing a norm, *whether others are present or not*" (ibid., 138–39, emphasis added). Since in both cases something is internalized, the concept of "convictions" of consciences as used in the chapter can incorporate both guilt- and shame-oriented superegos. Appreciation is expressed to colleague Sherwood Lingenfelter for making me aware of these issues.

sensitive for reading braille, so those who wish to pursue righteousness must be ever alert to the promptings of conscience. Through inattention and neglect calluses easily form on one's conscience rendering it useless toward a given conviction. To change the metaphor, like a glass-enclosed anniversary clock, the conscience is a very delicate mechanism—it must be treated with tender loving care. How do we do this? We first need to understand how the call and the convictions of conscience are linked together.

### Linking Call and Convictions

The process of linking the call and the convictions of the conscience is basically automatic, unconscious, and operative throughout life. Just like the regulation of our breathing, it *requires* no cognitive supervision, yet the linkage *can* be modified by deliberate effort. As an expression of God's wisdom, this particular arrangement allows young children, without significant cognitive capabilities, to acquire important foundational convictions.[18] Then, as cognitive functioning matures in the teen and adult years, these internalized moral norms developed in childhood can be affirmed, modified, or discouraged by conscious choice. Yet, even in the adult years, we continue to acquire convictions of conscience, in an unconscious manner.

This special process of convictions development is reflected in the common

18. One of the most significant gifts parents can provide their children is a sensitive conscience developed through consistent parenting practices. Conscientious parents should pursue this task with diligent effort but without being unduly anxious about their own imperfections, since "love covers a multitude of sins" (1 Pet. 4:7). In addition, God may provide a period of grace during the early years of life in which fallible parents can instill convictions of conscience in their children, without children being judged for their parents' imperfections (e.g., Deut. 24:16; Ezek. 18:20). Deuteronomy 1:39 and Isaiah 7:15–16 suggest that during their early years, children are not held accountable for moral actions. After reaching such an age of moral accountability (a point in time which varies with each child, somewhere between ages 5 to 13), children are morally responsible for their actions and are capable of making sound moral decisions, regardless of how well or how poorly their consciences had been educated.

Two standard evangelical theology textbooks comment on the "age of accountability" concept:

"We all were involved in Adam's sin, and thus receive both the corrupted nature that was his after the fall, and the guilt and condemnation that attach to his sin. With this matter of guilt, however, just as with the imputation of Christ's righteousness, there must be some conscious and voluntary decision on our part. Until this is the case, there is only a conditional imputation of guilt. Thus, there is no condemnation *until one reaches the age of responsibility*. If a child dies before he or she is capable of making genuine moral decisions, there is only innocence, and the child will experience the same type of future existence with the Lord as will those who have reached the age of moral responsibility and had their sins forgiven as a result of accepting the offer of salvation based upon Christ's atoning death" (Millard Erickson, *Christian Theology* [Grand Rapids: Baker, 1985], 639).

"All who have come to an age of responsibility for decisions between right and wrong are accountable for their behavior" (Gordon R. Lewis and Bruce A. Demarest, *Our Primary Need, Christ's Atoning Provisions,* vol. 2 of *Integrative Theology* [Grand Rapids: Zondervan, 1990], 222). For a detailed study of this issue, see Thomas Cragoe, "An Examination of the Issue of Infant Salvation" (Th.D. diss., Dallas Theological Seminary, 1987).

expression: "Values are more 'caught' than 'taught.'" How we learn or "catch" convictions of conscience can be best explained by behavioral and social learning theories.[19] The actual process is much more complex than can be clarified here, but the following remarks will help the reader get some idea of how this primarily unconscious procedure occurs.

*Behavioral learning theory.* The two major aspects of behavioral learning theory are interrelated: (1) operant conditioning and (2) classical conditioning. Imagine that you receive a speeding ticket with a fine of $75. In most cases, the fine will discourage you from exceeding the speed limit in the future. *Operant conditioning* suggests that, based on the consequences or the kind of feedback we receive, we will either repeat or discontinue specific thoughts, feelings, or actions (cf. 1 Thess. 4:1; 2 Thess. 3:6, 14–15). We tend to appreciate affirmation and we try to avoid discipline.

Now let's imagine that the next day on the road you notice a police car. At that instant, you may feel the pangs of conscience and you may look at your speedometer or slow down a little. It is evident that an unconscious linkage has been made between a symbol or an object (e.g., the police car) and what that object represents (e.g., a fine for speeding). This principle undergirds *classical conditioning.* The Lord's Supper represents another example of classical conditioning. The bread and cup (symbols) remind us of our Lord's suffering and atonement and of his future return (Matt. 26:26–28).

*Social learning theory.* How we learn by watching the example of others is explained by social learning theory. Through such vicarious learning we discover what to do and what not to do. Imagine that I was riding in your car when you received the speeding ticket. Though I did not have to pay the fine, I too will probably be more careful about how fast I drive (cf. 2 Thess. 3:6–10).

Our experiences of the joys and reproofs of life continuously influence our thoughts, feelings, and actions (operant conditioning). Yet, convictions can be *unconsciously* altered by the next experience (e.g., a police officer later helps you or me fix a flat tire). We can also *consciously* evaluate the particular rewards and punishments we receive, analyze our resident linkages, and attempt to modify them. To repeat, the conditioning process is automatic, but the results are *not* permanent or inaccessible to rational evaluation.

We develop certain sets of expectations (though largely unconscious) about the matters of our lives (classical conditioning). We acquire "approach" tendencies toward what brings us success, peace, and enjoyment. To pursue these values, we will surmount almost any barrier. For example, a strong conviction about sharing the Good News would dispose us to talk freely about our faith when an opportunity arises. But we also acquire "avoidance" ten-

19. See Ronald Habermas and Klaus Issler, *Teaching for Reconciliation: Foundations and Practice of Christian Educational Ministry* (Grand Rapids: Baker, 1992), chap. 8, for more explanations of these principles of learning.

dencies toward those things that bring us pain, embarrassment, and discomfort. When we don't genuinely value an activity, we usually create some excuse to legitimize our lack of participation. For example, in relation to sharing the Good News, we could offer a variety of reasons for our inactivity: we don't have the gift of evangelism, the other person is probably not interested, we don't feel as qualified as the pastor to explain the Good News, we've tried it in the past and it has proved unsuccessful.

Habitual thought, feeling, and behavior patterns deepen these tendencies or dispositions—they become characteristic of our lives. Thus, whenever conscience prompts us (whether it be with affirmation or sorrow), we are given a glimpse into our actual or *functional* set of core values.[20] Since our conscience always operates based on resident convictions, the acquisition of biblical values must be a lifelong process. It represents an essential element in character formation.

### Developing Convictions of Conscience

Based on our understanding of how this process operates, we can take a conscious, proactive stance to use it for our good. But first, the principles of *learning* elaborated must be translated into principles of *teaching*.[21] A four-part educational strategy emerges. We need (1) emphasis (classical conditioning theory), (2) examples (social learning theory), (3) exercise (behavioral learning theory), and (4) evaluation (behavioral learning theory, particularly operant conditioning). To illustrate how these four principles can work for us, let us imagine we want to become more compassionate to our fellow human beings.

*Emphasis.* Through a variety of means, God can direct our attention to the concept of compassion (e.g., a sermon or a Bible study, an event we hear about or observe or one we experience ourselves) and what particular aspects of compassion he wishes to highlight.

*Examples.* What does "compassion" look like? We need to clarify the various facets of compassion. Our present awareness of the concept of compassion must be taken to a deeper level of understanding. Stanford professor Albert Bandura, the major proponent of social learning theory, outlines three kinds of examples or models: (a) verbal modeling (spoken or written examples), (b) direct modeling (live encounters), and (c) symbolic modeling (examples through mass media, including newspapers, television, and movies).

20. Such a *functional* set of core values or convictions (internalized dispositions) must be distinguished from our *professed* values, that is, those values we may "claim" to hold, but norms that do not actually characterize our lives.

21. This translation is necessary since a theory of learning is a "descriptive" subject (i.e., how *do* we learn), while a theory of teaching is a "prescriptive" one (i.e., how *should* we teach). For a discussion of learning and teaching from a Christian perspective, see Habermas and Issler, *Teaching for Reconciliation*.

Verbal and direct modeling have been the only forms of observational learning for most of human history. In its fullest expression mass media is a twentieth century phenomenon. Bandura notes the power of symbolic modeling for the effective dissemination of ideas and values over large geographical regions:

> Whereas previously modeling influences were largely confined to the behavior exhibited in one's immediate community, nowadays diverse styles of conduct are brought to people within the comfort of their homes through the vehicle of television. Both children and adults acquire attitudes, thought patterns, emotional bents, and new styles of conduct through symbolic modeling. In view of the efficacy of, and extensive public exposure to, televised modeling, the mass media play an influential role in shaping human thought and action.[22]

For each of the three categories of modeling, we could seek a variety of examples of compassion, with differing degrees of exposure. In the category of verbal modeling, we could study relevant passages of Scripture, take a seminar or course related to compassion, read biographies of Christian servant-leaders who demonstrated compassion. As for direct modeling, we might visit a soup line at the city mission, live with a missionary in a Third World country and observe his ministry. Under the heading of *symbolic modeling*, we could view television programs or movies that exemplify compassionate values whether they involve Christians (e.g., World Vision television specials) or not (e.g., *Ghandi*). It is critical to use many and varied examples to help develop a comprehensive concept of compassion.

*Exercise.* Next, we need to begin experimenting with and practicing compassionate actions. Whatever we genuinely value will eventually evidence itself in outward acts. And habits of compassion develop through individual acts of compassion. So, for example, we may help distribute sandwiches and soup at the city mission. We could help build or repair a church facility in Appalachia or Mexico. We could serve on a short-term mission team to a Third World country. If we wish to be characterized by compassionate values, then regular participation in compassionate acts offers proof of our convictions, since "faith without deeds is dead" (James 2:26). Our actions will help clarify how serious and committed we are about becoming more compassionate.[23]

22. Albert Bandura, *Social Foundations of Thought and Action: A Social Cognitive Theory* (Englewood Cliffs, N. J.: Prentice-Hall, 1986), 70. Regarding the mass media, it is well known that most editors, journalists, producers, and directors do not view life from a Christian perspective. The pervasiveness of a secular world view throughout most television programs, commercial advertising, and movies, coupled with such a subtle, yet powerful, learning medium, presents a grave danger to all believers who "hunger and thirst after righteousness."

23. God superintends our lives so that unplanned experiences help us grow to become more compassionate. Such trials of life and the suffering he allows can prompt growth (James 1:2–4) and prepares us for ministry to others (2 Cor. 1:3–7).

*Evaluation.* Finally, we must receive specific feedback from mature believers about our thoughts, feelings, and actions, in general, and those of compassion, in particular. This is the most critical phase of convictions development. Without some manifestations of affirmation and guidance we have no way of telling if we are on the right track in becoming more compassionate. We may invite a mature brother or sister in Christ to be our mentor. On a regular basis, we could share our life and ministry experiences in order to gain our mentor's evaluation and guidance. The mentor could observe us as we engage in compassionate ministry and offer "on-the-job" feedback.

Without some measure of accountability, our good intentions can easily become distracted and forgotten as time goes on. For example, in a conversation among friends, we happen to tell a joke that disparages a person because of intellectual or athletic disabilities or based on race or gender. A good friend in the group must say to us, "The joke may be funny, but it's not a very compassionate way of speaking." Because it is difficult to receive constructive criticism, often we hesitate to offer evaluative comments, even among close friends. Thus, we must *invite* our friends to "invade our privacy" a little by giving us necessary feedback (e.g., Rom. 15:14; James 5:19–20).

In summary, an application of these basic teaching guidelines (emphasis, example, exercise, and evaluation) is necessary to acquire principles which we would *like* to characterize our lives into *internalized* convictions of conscience. In general in our teaching ministry, we do well in emphasis and in giving examples, but we do poorly in getting our students to exercise or in offering personal evaluation. The process is not accomplished in a day, but over a period of time with concerted effort.[24] Since the task is so complex,

24. Once a value becomes a functional conviction of conscience, it needs to be consciously affirmed and acted upon (when conscience sounds off), since convictions of conscience are not *permanently* registered. If we do not regularly maintain our convictions of conscience, they will erode away over time and be useless against the onslaughts of Satan, this world system, and the sin that indwells our members.

Of course, the impermanence of our convictions of conscience is also a help to us. In cases where a functional value is problematic and needs modification we must repeatedly ignore the call of conscience. Over a period of time, the linkage between that particular conviction and the call of conscience will weaken and eventually disappear.

To illustrate, let us assume that in our upbringing, we developed a conviction that watching *any* movie was sinful and, during that time, our parents had never allowed us to watch a film. Later, as a young adult, we recognize that some movies can be very helpful in our Christian walk, such as the film *Jesus,* and the Academy Award-winning *Chariots of Fire.* Let us imagine that we watch one of these movies, and it happens to be the first movie we have ever viewed. Even though we regard the movie as appropriate, the pangs of conscience will still sound. By repeatedly ignoring this particular call of conscience and by upholding our convictions through avoidance of other kinds of movies, we will eventually desensitize our conscience in this particular area.

educating a mature conscience must be the responsibility of a loving and holy Christian *community*—it cannot be done alone. "Flee the evil desires of youth, and pursue righteousness, faith, love and peace, *along with those who call on the Lord out of a pure heart*" (2 Tim. 2:22, emphasis added). The community can affirm and guide the exercise of values and the development of convictions.[25]

We are now in a better position to understand more fully what Psalm 119:11 teaches us: "I have hidden your word in my heart that I might not sin against you." Because we talk of memorizing Scripture "by heart," we have mistakenly believed that this passage refers exclusively to Scripture memory. We assume that, in and of itself, such mental recall will prevent us from sinning. If memorization alone guaranteed holiness, then even Satan would practice righteousness—an abhorrent thought. He knows the Bible very well; he easily quoted passages to Jesus in the wilderness (cf. Matt. 4:1–11). Rather, Psalm 119:11 speaks of "the heart" as the conscience, and of "hiding your word" as inculcating moral values, not just items of verbatim recall. By "treasuring" God's principles in our conscience (as in the process described in this chapter), our sensitive conscience will call us when we begin to violate these principles. Thus, the Spirit through our conscience prompts us not to sin—if we choose to be obedient. The promise of Psalm 119:11 is for all believers based on our resident convictions of conscience, be they shallow or deep.

Maintaining a sensitive conscience requires regular attention to the call of conscience. But its message must *always* be evaluated in light of biblical truth. Educating one's conscience requires diligent and faithful effort through focused emphasis, specific examples, regular exercise, and mature evaluation of progress. Now we turn to another important aspect of educating our conscience.

## Improving Our Moral Decision Making

When conscience calls us in a situation where a moral issue is at stake, what is our response?[26] Once conscience calls, we must evaluate the message, consider the important facts, and render a final decision. Due to the limitations of space, we will not provide guidelines for making good moral choices; such

25. The critical need for regularly encouraging the saints toward steps of positive growth and regularly practicing church discipline/reconciliation for any type of sin becomes obvious (e.g., 1 Thess. 5:14).

26. If the call of conscience does not sound or is not heard in the midst of a situation, one of three possibilities exists: (1) a previous, mature decision has been made about the matter, and either (a) this is not an issue needing our attention, or (b) sufficient habits have been established so that we respond automatically to the situation; (2) conscience has not been educated about the matter (a point of concern and need for growth); or (3) conscience is no longer sensitive to the matter due to repeated disregard of previous promptings.

material is available elsewhere.[27] Our purpose here will be to describe certain psychological processes undergirding this evaluation and decision making process. Specifically, we will look at *how we perceive and frame our understanding* of moral issues. Such information can help us understand what present limitations constrain us in making sound moral decisions. And it can help us identify where there is room for growth—an important aspect of educating our conscience. The writer of the letter to the Hebrews challenges us that if we wish to be characterized as "mature," we must train ourselves "to distinguish good from evil" through constant use (5:14). In this section we focus on three particular factors: (1) perceiving issues as moral or not, (2) articulating both the content and rationale of our decisions, and (3) aligning our decisions as viewed through three lenses of concern.

## Perceiving Moral Issues[28]

On occasion, parents and teens battle over such issues as hairstyle, dress, and orderliness of the bedroom. How can teens and parents navigate through such common conflicts? In making decisions about life situations, we tend to categorize situations within three distinct domains: moral, social, or personal.[29] We resolve issues using guidelines appropriate to each domain. In the moral domain, we view principles and practices as constituting universal and unalterable obligations. An affirmative reply is given to the question: "Is it wrong for everyone?" Principles for the social domain are more relative and contextual in nature, thus alterable to some extent. Here we include such matters as cultural norms and matters of etiquette. Finally, the personal domain incorporates matters of individuality, what pertains to "one's own business." These describe expressions of self and personal taste. Questions related to this domain would include: "Is this only a personal issue?" "Does this have any impact on others?" "Would this matter to anyone else?"

How are these three categories useful? They may help us explain why in conflict situations, we talk past each other—when no real communication is taking place. For example, John, a teenager, feels that the orderliness of his bedroom is a *personal* matter. His parents may consider it a *social* issue or,

27. For readable treatments of *command*-oriented and *consequences*-oriented ethical traditions, the two most common systems, see J. P. Moreland and Norman L. Geisler, *The Life and Death Debate: Moral Issues of Our Time* (New York: Praeger, 1990), chap. 8, and Smedes, *Choices*. See Louis P. Pojman, *Ethics: Discovering Right and Wrong* (Belmont, Calif.: Wadsworth, 1990) for a helpful introduction to ethics as well as guidelines about a third ethical tradition (*character*-oriented ethics).

28. I am indebted to David Rahn, "Faith Domain Distinctions in the Conceptualization of Morality and Social Convention for Evangelical Christians" (Ph.D. diss., Purdue University, 1991), for much of the summary provided here. This study explored moral and "faith-moral" distinctions among Christian college students.

29. Research into the "distinct domains" model of social reasoning was pioneered by Elliot Turiel. For a recent introduction, see Elliot Turiel, "Domain-Specific Social Judgments and Domain Ambiguities," *Merrill-Palmer Quarterly* 35 (1989): 89–114.

even more seriously, a *moral* issue. From the start, coming to some understanding of the situation between John and his parents is *not* possible, since the issue is perceived from such diverse perspectives.

Thus we can see that how we perceive an issue affects our decision making. If we can clarify within which domain we view an issue, we can then genuinely dialogue about the matter, rather than become embroiled in a debate comparing "apples" and "oranges." Another implication would suggest that growth may be necessary. On the one hand, we may have an overly sensitive conscience when the matter is more of a social or a personal matter. On the other hand, we may *not* place an issue in the moral domain when it should be there. For example, in a study cited by Rahn, some women perceived abortion to be an individual matter (*personal* domain) rather than a *moral* issue.[30] We turn now to a second factor which affects our moral decision making.

### Content and Rationale

In discussions of morality in the church, we have tended to focus exclusively on right answers with little concern for the reasoning behind those answers. Yet Scripture affirms that *why* we do (rationale) *what* we do (content) is just as significant (e.g., Matt. 6:1–18). Kohlberg's research into the psychology of moral judgments suggests that, as we mature physically from childhood to adulthood, the reasons for our actions must also mature.[31] The dif-

---

30. Rahn, "Faith Domain Distinctions." The women's perception of abortion as an individual matter, not a moral issue, signals the presence of an insensitive conscience. By "an individual matter" one usually means an amoral decision without a right or wrong evaluation being relevant to it. An individual matter is a private choice made in an amoral area. However, it should be clear that relegating a decision to the sphere of being an amoral, individual matter can only be done subsequent to a judgment that the issue in question is either not objectively moral, or, if it is, there is no way to justify one view of the matter versus another view. Such judgments clearly involve the conscience. A clear mark of an insensitive conscience is precisely the act of classifying a moral issue as a private matter. Such acts of classification usually follow from and contribute to a searing of conscience.

31. It is generally acknowledged that Lawrence Kohlberg (1927–1987) pioneered the study of moral reasoning during the second half of this century. Some of the major limitations or criticisms of Kohlberg's moral reasoning theory from a Christian perspective include (1) its naturalistic-atheistic basis (morality can stand on its own apart from religion); (2) its anthropocentric view of moral autonomy (the highest stage of moral reasoning involves freedom from all outside influences, including divine authority, so that Christians and others holding to divine authority typically receive lower moral stage scores); (3) its narrow view of the essence of morality which focuses on justice and fairness, thus eliminating Christianity's important twin foundations of truth (including justice) *and* love; and (4) its overemphasis on the liberal agenda of individual rights and individualistic decision making, thus devaluing individual *responsibility* and ignoring the *community* as an important resource in decision making. Despite these limitations, certain features of Kohlberg's theory offer helpful insights about the operation of moral thinking. For a recent summary of Kohlberg's theory, see Lisa Kuhmerker, *The Kohlberg Legacy for the Helping Professions* (Birmingham, Ala.: R. E. P. Books, 1991). For a readable discussion geared for parents, see Thomas Lickona, *Raising Good Children: Helping Your Children Through the Stages of Moral Development* (New York: Bantam, 1983) and Ted Ward, *Values Begin At Home*, 2d. ed. (Wheaton: Victor, 1989).

ference between these two concepts of "content" and "rationale" can be illustrated through the following interview responses.

Interviewer:     Ruth, should people tell lies to each other?
Ruth (age 6):    No. [*content*: lying is wrong]
Interviewer:     Why is it wrong to tell a lie?
Ruth:            Because if I get caught telling a lie, my parents will punish me. [*rationale*]

Interviewer:     Daniel, should people tell lies to each other?
Daniel (age 26): No. [the same *content* as Ruth's response]
Interviewer:     Why is it wrong to tell a lie?
Daniel:          Because if I get caught telling a lie, my parents will punish me. [also the same *rationale*]

Daniel's response to the first question is appropriate. But his second response seems out of place for a twenty-six year old. As we grow, although our beliefs and values (content; e.g., "Do not lie") may not change much, our reasons why these beliefs and values are true *do need to change* (rationale). When teens and adults continue to use *child-appropriate* reasons they significantly hinder their moral growth. Then, what are appropriate reasons in moral decision making at each stage of development?

### Aligning Spheres of Concerns

Young children tend to consider exclusively their own needs and concerns.[32] Then, in late childhood and the early teen years, in addition to concern for themselves, adolescents begin to attend to the approval of their peers. Finally, in adulthood, an additional third lens of concern emerges: being able to consider and live by universal moral principles. Thus, with each new stage of growth, we increase the number of factors we consider in evaluating and responding to the call of conscience. But only with the complex cognitive capabilities of adulthood are we able to keep in mind *all three lenses of concerns* in moral decision making.[33] The mature believer should have an appropriate

32. The following discussion is also based on Kohlberg's theory of stages of moral reasoning (Lawrence Kohlberg, Charles Levine, and Alexandra Hewer, *Moral Stages: A Current Formulation and A Response to Critics* [Basel: Karger, 1983]). Rather than focusing on six stages or three levels of hierarchical reasoning, I will focus on three "lenses" of concern identified in the three levels. This adaptation, though related to Kohlberg's theory, issues from a scriptural basis.

33. Kohlberg's theory suggests, and we would agree, that becoming an adult does not guarantee that one would regularly incorporate universal moral principles in decision making. Reaching adulthood only suggests that we are now *capable* of such thinking, not that we actually *use* it. Thus, we see the need to challenge teens and adults to more comprehensive patterns of thinking.

concern for self, others, and moral principles—all three lenses being viewed within a divine perspective.

Teens and adults encounter problems when they focus exclusively on the concerns of "self" and "others" without regard for the third lens: moral principles. For example, how might the Golden Rule be understood when consideration is restricted to a few lenses of concern? Examples of these restricted perspectives followed by scriptural cases that illustrate each view are listed below. Remember, for children and younger teens, it is normal[34] to focus exclusively on self and others due to their limited cognitive capabilities. But these restrictions do not apply for mature teens and adults (see fig. 1).

## Figure 1
## Lenses of Moral Growth

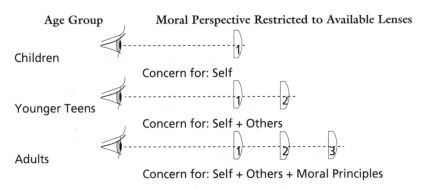

| Age Group | Moral Perspective Restricted to Available Lenses |

Children

Concern for: Self

Younger Teens

Concern for: Self + Others

Adults

Concern for: Self + Others + Moral Principles

*Note:* With each new life phase, a new lens capability emerges.

*Sources:* Adapted from Kohlberg (1981); Lickona (1983); Ward (1989).

*Exclusive Focus on Me:*

"I will do what I like to do since everyone else would do the same thing if they were in my shoes."

"Let's make a deal: I will do this for you if you do this for me."

John 12:3–8: Judas claimed that the money used to purchase expensive perfume should have been given to the poor. He wasn't concerned about the poor but about the disciples' treasury since he regularly stole money from it.

34. "Normal" is understood as a descriptive term. An exclusive focus on "self" is normal for young children, and older children and young teens tend to focus exclusively on "self and other" concerns. The challenge for children's and youth workers is to customize God's truth so it can be understood with the student's respective lens capability.

Mark 7:9–13: Jesus castigated the religious leaders for the deceptive practice of "dedicating" their possessions to God ("Corban") so they could set up a life estate for themselves while avoiding the obligation to provide for the needs of their aged parents (dedicated property could not be used for secular purposes) (cf. also 1 Tim. 5:8).

*Exclusive Focus on Self and Others:*
"If everybody in the group does it, then I will do it too."
"I try to put myself in your shoes and do what would be best for you—whether the action itself is right or wrong."
Matthew 6:2: Jesus claimed that the religious leaders gave to the poor, not to please God, but to show off and to build up their reputation among the people.
Acts 4:36–5:11: Ananias and Sapphira, apparently in order to copy the example of Barnabas and to gain the acclaim of the early church, pretended to give the full proceeds of a sale, when they had actually kept back a part. (Note Peter's response which aligns all three lenses.)

The examples indicate that, although actions can be perceived by others as being good, what may be an appropriate rationale for a child may be totally inappropriate for a teen or adult. Another implication: the number of lenses of concerns we *regularly* consider in our decision making affects our *interpretation* of Bible passages and *understanding* of moral messages. For example, a pastor may preach a sermon on the Golden Rule, but members of the congregation will comprehend the message within their own thinking patterns, as illustrated above.

Our goal as teachers, then, is to help teen and adult believers consider and align all *three* spheres of concerns with God's truth as they evaluate and respond to the call of conscience.[35] Ideally, harmony is possible among the

35. In 1974, Kohlberg and his associates began to study growth in both moral reasoning *and* moral behavior in what they labeled "the just community." Working with a few groups of high school students (in an on-campus alternative setting in which both students and staff participated by choice), they challenged students to deal with their own "real life" moral situations. Staff and students would agree on corporate solutions and actions regarding matters of school governance (related to both academic and student conduct issues). The central feature of the program involved a "town hall"-like meeting in which policy was debated and enacted and punishment was meted out to those who violated these policies. Based on this kind of research (especially studies completed within the last decade of his life), Kohlberg concluded that the most effective way for individuals to become people of justice and morality is to experience this within a democratically-oriented "just community" (F. Clark Power, Ann Higgins, and Lawrence Kohlberg, *Lawrence Kohlberg's Approach to Moral Education* [New York: Columbia University Press, 1989]). Since the church aspires to be a community of holiness, this particular line of research offers potential implications for church leaders to consider.

three lenses because God's truth is not ultimately opposed to our concerns for ourselves, for others, or for moral principles. Even in difficult situations, we can experience the harmony of God's truth among the three lenses. Compare the example of Daniel's three companions (Dan. 3) and the apostles Peter and John (Acts 4:1–31). So, just as the optometrist aligns various lenses to help us see clearly, we must align *all three lenses of concern* to gain a clear perspective of God's truth. Some biblical examples regarding decisions about money are provided to illustrate this more holistic perspective.

> Believers who benefit from those teaching God's Word should financially support these teachers (Gal. 6:6; 1 Tim. 5:17–18).
>
> "Do not be deceived: God cannot be mocked. A man reaps what he sows." "Whoever sows sparingly will also reap sparingly, and whoever sows generously will also reap generously" (Gal. 6:7 and 2 Cor. 9:6).
>
> God's grace was manifest in the sacrificial giving of the (mostly Gentile) Macedonian believers (Philippi, Thessalonica, and Berea) that, despite their poverty, they made a generous contribution for the poor in Jerusalem (2 Cor. 8:1–5; cf. Rom. 15:26; Acts 24:17).
>
> Based on Christ's example of gracious selfless giving, Paul urges the (mostly Gentile) Corinthian believers to complete the generous commitment they had previously made to collect additional money for the poor in Jerusalem. In the future, these Jewish saints may be able to help the Corinthians in their need (2 Cor. 8:6–15; 9:5; cf. Rom. 15:26; Acts 24:17).
>
> God loves cheerful givers (2 Cor. 9:7).

## Conclusion

The challenge of educating our conscience is always before us. In this chapter we have surveyed certain psychological aspects involved in improving our moral sensitivity and moral reasoning. We can maintain a high level of sensitivity by always listening to the call of conscience. Still, we must evaluate the particular message and respond appropriately. We acquire our convictions in a rather happenstance manner; this involuntary process is always operational. By employing some basic educational concepts (emphasis, examples, exercise, and evaluation), we can proactively work with this automatic process to internalize convictions that we would like to characterize our lives.

In our response to the call of conscience, as we deliberate what actions we may take, how we understand and perceive the issue at hand will significantly affect our decision making. We may perceive a matter as not being moral, when, in reality according to God's principles, it is. We may perform the right moral action, yet do so with immature or wrong motives and reasons. A holistic strategy for believers is to consider all three lenses of concern in our decision making: ourselves, others, and moral principles.

The goal of educating our conscience is aptly expressed in Psalm 119:11: "I have hidden your word in my heart that I might not sin against you." Like the smoke alarm, God's built-in moral detector and prompter can alert us to potential dangers and urge us toward courageous action.

## Suggested Readings

### Conscience

Holmes, Arthur. *Shaping Character: Moral Education in the Christian College*. Grand Rapids: Eerdmans, 1991. [B]

Toon, Peter. *Your Conscience As Your Guide*. Wilton, Conn.: Morehouse-Barlow, 1983. [B]

### Moral Sensitivity

Narramore, S. Bruce. *No Condemnation: Rethinking Guilt Motivation in Counseling, Preaching and Parenting*. Grand Rapids: Zondervan, 1984. [I]

Shelton, Charles M. *Morality of the Heart: A Psychology for the Christian Moral Life*. New York: Crossroad, 1990. [I]

### Moral Decision Making

Kuhmerker, Lisa. *The Kohlberg Legacy for the Helping Professions*. Birmingham, Ala.: R.E.P. Books, 1991. [I]

Lickona, Thomas. *Raising Good Children: Helping Your Child Through the Stages of Moral Development*. New York: Bantam, 1983. [B]

Power, F. Clark, Ann Higgins, and Lawrence Kohlberg. *Lawrence Kohlberg's Approach to Moral Education*. New York: Columbia University Press, 1989. [A]

Smedes, Lewis B. *Choices: Making Right Decisions in a Complex World*. San Francisco: Harper and Row, 1986. [B]

Ward, Ted. *Values Begin At Home*. 2d ed. Wheaten: Victor, 1989. [B]

# A Response to Klaus Issler

## Sherwood G. Lingenfelter

The principal thrust of Dr. Issler's paper is excellent. Christians must indeed educate a sensitive conscience through a careful study of the Word of God, continuing regular practice in which we try to apply through modeling the relevant principles of Scripture in our lives, and consistent evaluation and feedback from the Christian community and from Scripture in relationship to moral sensitivity and moral living. Too often Christians allow their consciences to be shaped by the world around them. When this happens the results are counter to God's Word and disastrous in the Christian life. Issler has outlined for us a practical plan that any believer may employ to improve our moral sensitivity and our moral decision making.

Early in his chapter Issler notes that we should always listen to our consciences but we should not always follow them. This point is worthy of further emphasis. Our consciences are always framed within the context of our social world. We learn the standards of right and wrong through feedback in our relationships with our parents and our peers. Paul argues eloquently in Romans 1 that people who reject the knowledge of God are given over to a depraved mind. In the social sciences we talk about this as the contextual problem of right and wrong. For example, the Sawi men in New Guinea, described by Don Richardson in his book *Peace Child,* saw Judas as the hero in the crucifixion of Christ. They reached this conclusion on the basis of their social context in which treachery and deception were esteemed as highest values. Their moral reasoning was obviously inconsistent with the Word of God, an illustration of what Paul calls the "depraved mind."

To understand the contextual problem of conscience is crucial. Students come to Christian and secular campuses these days with very different conscience issues than they had two decades ago. The issues of premarital sex, alcohol, cheating, and managing finances are handled very differently by the students of the nineties. Are these differences due to changes in God's Word or changes in social context? Obviously the issue is social context. Issler's chapter provides excellent direction and help for Christians who want to heal what may be "seared" consciences through the overexposure to and pressure of secular society.

Issler's work provides for the young person a "how to do it" guide for those who want to genuinely grow in their moral reasoning and sensitivity to Scripture. The process he provides is a very reasoned, intentional program toward developing one's conscience. To affect this result, the person must practice diligently as they would practice their basketball or golf skills. Without intentional practice one cannot develop athletic skills; skill in moral reasoning is as difficult to acquire if not more so.

The person who attempts to apply his methodology should be aware that there are often non-rational and at worst irrational pressures upon us to shape our consciences in non-biblical ways. Students who are regular movie goers are not merely "symbolic modeling"—they are participating in a social event, they are talking about the issues, and they are affirming the "neat", "provocative," and "yuk" which all reinforce values and attitudes. Our consciences are constantly shaped by our interactions which are not planned or directional. Issler's work highlights then the need for intentional self-assessment and a biblical refocusing of our conscience development.

# A Response to Klaus Issler

## Scott B. Rae

Issler's work on the function of conscience provides much helpful material in the critical area of moral decision making. My response to this chapter involves matters of emphasis and practice, as opposed to fundamental disagreement in areas of content.

He has rightly maintained the need for ongoing reeducation of a fallen conscience. This is a helpful corrective for many believers who, in practice, though not in theory, consider the conscience the virtually infallible voice of God to guide and direct their moral actions and decision making. It is anything but that. The conscience is just as fallen, and thus prone to mislead the believer, as is any other part of his or her constitution. Take the sociopathic killer, for example, who has committed heinous crimes, yet feels little if any regret over crimes committed. Or on the other end of the spectrum, take the believer with the particularly sensitive conscience, who feels guilt, falsely so, for many actions that are morally neutral, or for actions that may even be morally proper. The capacity of the conscience to mislead the believer should not be underestimated, and thus there is the need that Issler emphasizes for evaluation of the message that the conscience brings to the believer according to biblical standards. One needs a theory of the good, philosophically speaking, to accompany any concept of the conscience functioning as the mirror of morality. The conscience, in biblical perspective, functions to bring the awareness of sin to the believer.

Frequently associated with the functioning of conscience is the feeling of guilt. It is common to assume that the feeling of guilt accompanies the awareness of sin that the conscience delivers. However, it is not clear from Scripture

284

that this is the way the conscience is designed to function, though in practice it can be very effective in producing change by inducing guilt in the believer's mind. The Old Testament background to the notion of guilt indicates that the term is used to describe a legal verdict that says whether someone has lived up to the standard of the law. This forensic idea of guilt is the foundation for the New Testament concept of justification. To be justified is to be acquitted from the penalty of sin, for the believer, accomplished at the cross. Thus in Scripture, guilt is primarily a fact, not a feeling.

The feeling of guilt, on the other hand, is a feeling of self-condemnation based on one's awareness of sin. The conscience rightly produces an awareness of sin, but it is debatable whether the conscience is designed by God to produce the feeling of guilt, though, again, in practice it surely functions in this way, and very effectively. But its effectiveness is not necessarily related to its being consistent with Scripture. The feeling of guilt is a conclusion about the individual and his or her worth, based on the sin committed and the conscience's bringing it to conscious realization. The feeling of guilt says, "I'm bad, because of my sin," and it involves a tearing down of one's self-esteem. But that is an incorrect conclusion in light of the believer's new position in Christ. Since the legal *fact* of guilt was settled for the believer at the moment that saving faith was exercised, and since the feeling of guilt is essentially one of self-condemnation, and since Romans 8:1 is clear that there is no longer any condemnation for the believer, then it would appear that the feeling of guilt is not being used by God to produce change. Thus the proper role of conscience is to bring sensitivity to one's sin, not to produce the self-destructive feeling of guilt.

When the feeling of guilt is associated with the proper functioning of conscience, it distorts the proper motive for obedience in the spiritual life. The feeling of guilt is essentially a self-centered motive for obedience and can even function as a means of self-atonement for one's sin. Rather the proper motive for the moral life is a relational one, that is, out of a desire to please someone whom I love. The reason that I don't hit my close friend Dr. Issler in the face the next time I see him is not because of conscience, though it would properly point out to me that that would be wrong. It would not even be out of a desire to avoid the feeling of guilt that I would very likely feel. The ultimate reason why I don't hit Issler is because I don't want to hurt someone for whom I care about very much. It is because of my relationship with him that I am constrained from doing something that would hurt him. It seems that this is what Paul means in 2 Corinthians 5:14 (NKJV) when he declares that, "the love of Christ constrains [or 'compels' in some translations] us." That is, my love for Christ is what provides the ultimate motive for my moral actions and decisions. This context for the moral life is one of the principal things that is unique about Christian ethics. It is an ethic that is relationally motivated out of a person's love for Jesus Christ.

This motive for moral behavior is what Paul calls "godly sorrow" (2 Cor. 7:8-13). He contrasts godly and worldly sorrow (or guilt) and says that godly sorrow is the intended response to one's awareness of sin. Though it is not clear from that text, a person feeling godly sorrow essentially feels sadness over having hurt someone he or she loves. It does not produce a negative conclusion about one's worth or value as a person, as does the feeling of guilt. Thus the conscience acts to produce an awareness of sin and the feeling of godly sorrow, as opposed to the feeling of guilt.

Though the conscience is a smoke alarm designed to detect sin in the believer's life, that does not mean that its message is correct every time it goes off. There is clearly a need to evaluate the information that the conscience brings to light, and sometimes that information should be rejected. Indeed, one should always reject the information given out by the conscience when the feeling of guilt is part of the message that it delivers.

# Conclusion

## David M. Ciocchi

In our secular society religion has become a culturally marginal thing, practiced by millions more like a casual hobby than like an all-encompassing world view. This approach to religion is so well known that references to it can pop up in all sorts of places. I will give two examples. Digby Anderson, food columnist for the London *Spectator,* criticizes "Sods" (Special Occasion Diners), the people who normally eat fast, prepared foods but occasionally spend all day doing some fancy cooking. As Anderson puts it, these Sods "are turning what was a habit, an integrated part of daily life, into an occasional hobby to be indulged in when they feel like it."[1] He then adds that "[i]t is the way so many modern persons treat religion."[2] In a review of Robert Conquest's work, Charles H. Fairbanks, Jr. claims that in the history of the West, the greatest obstacle to utopian-minded totalitarianism "was religion, which argued that the good social order is not attainable on this earth."[3] Fairbanks says that the West no longer has this obstacle to totalitarianism because "in our secular society religion occupies the place of a hobby among other hobbies."[4] To say that religion is practiced as a mere hobby is a provocative way of saying what can be said more politely, namely, that many religious persons have only a *nominal* faith.

The nominal Christian does to the faith of Jesus Christ what Anderson's "Sods" do to cooking. They take what should be integral to daily life and

---

1. Digby Anderson, "Sods and Squawkers," *National Review,* 27 April 1992, 55.
2. Ibid.
3. Charles H. Fairbanks, Jr., "The Bard of Terror," *National Review,* 17 Feb. 1992, 48.
4. Ibid.

make it an occasional hobby to be indulged in when they feel like it. The Christian church does not need nominal believers, and Jesus himself does not want them: "I know your deeds, that you are neither cold nor hot; I would that you were cold or hot. So because you are lukewarm, and neither hot nor cold, I will spit you out of My mouth" (Rev. 3:15-16 NASB). The nominal Christian, however, may not contribute as much to the cultural marginalization of the Christian faith as does his more earnest fellow believer, the *fideist* Christian.

The fideist Christian may be a thoroughly earnest believer who is anything but a casual hobbyist about his faith, but all the same he implicitly accepts the secular culture's definition of religion as private opinion. As private opinion, Christianity is seen as both irrelevant to public debate and incapable of rational justification. If some people want to follow the Christian way, this is fine, provided that they don't "impose" their personal beliefs on others, or have the temerity to air their religious values in the public square. The fideist may even be ill at ease with this church-as-cultural-ghetto approach to his faith, but he has no intellectual defense against it. He has, as I said, an implicit belief that the secularist is basically correct about the private, personal, and nonrational nature of (any) religious faith, including Christianity.

The fideist may want to engage unbelief *morally* and *spiritually*, but he will not engage it *intellectually*. The result of this is that the intellectual high ground is left largely under the control of philosophical naturalists who have thereby managed to secure strong positions in many of our culture's leading institutions, including the universities, the news media, and the entertainment industry. These naturalists—people who believe that nature (or "the universe") is the only reality—perpetuate the idea that religion is and ought to be culturally marginal. As long as they remain unopposed intellectually by literally millions of Christians of the fideist sort, the culturally dominant naturalists will continue to dictate most people's ideas about the intellectual status of the Christian faith. And as long as that status is "religious hobby," the Christian message will seem to many to lack any relevance to their lives.

The nominal believer probably will not care very much that his faith is culturally marginal, but, as I have suggested, the fideist believer may well be truly uncomfortable about this, sensing that something is very wrong and that perhaps he should try to do something about it. But there isn't much that he *can* do about it. A fideist understanding of faith implies that any attempt to build a rational justification for Christian belief must be a mistake. An upshot of this is that any serious intellectual engagement with unbelief is impossible for the fideist. No matter how "hot" his faith is in terms of love for Jesus, it is likely to remain culturally impotent. The Christian church needs not nominal believers nor earnest fideists, but *rationally assertive Christians*.

The rationally assertive Christian should have the fideist's hot faith without the fideist's implicit intellectual submission to the culturally dominant naturalists. This will mean that the rationally assertive believer can and will *engage unbelief intellectually*, mounting a spirited rational defense of Christian belief and an equally spirited assault on all the cultural and intellectual pretensions of unbelief. In the language of the New Testament, he will be "destroying speculations and every lofty thing raised up against the knowledge of God, and . . . taking every thought captive to the obedience of Christ" (2 Cor. 10:5).

The rationally assertive Christian will hold certain basic philosophical beliefs. He will believe that there is such a thing as truth, that all truth is of God, and that at least some of this truth is knowable by human beings. He will consider himself under obligation to argue for his beliefs rather than just to assert them, understanding that the Christian faith is not a "private opinion" but a public truth claim. A rational person does not simply accept truth claims, but rather investigates them to the degree that it is possible to do so. The rationally assertive Christian is prepared to assist others in their investigation of the claims of Christ. This Christian flatly rejects the tacit relativism of the "religion as private opinion" way of thinking. Truth stands in opposition to falsity, and there is a truth about God, and this is a truth that can be rationally defended. It is on these basic beliefs that the rationally assertive Christian builds his program of intellectual engagement with unbelief.

If the rationally assertive Christian really shares the hot faith of the fideist (and he ought to), then he will supplement his intellectual program with serious moral and spiritual engagement with unbelief. All the rational arguments in the world are unlikely to commend the Christian faith if they are advanced by cold, loveless people who seem intent only on winning debates and making themselves look good and others look foolish. The rationally assertive Christian's *life* should win over the hearts of unbelievers, and his *arguments* should win over their minds. Whether anyone is actually won to Christ or not, of course, depends finally on the work of the Holy Spirit. But what we are looking at here is not the power of God as such, but the proper role of the Christian as a representative of Christ in our secular society. That role requires the believer to engage unbelief on all fronts, moral, spiritual, and intellectual, letting the results of this work be whatever God chooses them to be.

As described, the rationally assertive Christian appears to be an apologist only, a defender of the faith who keeps in mind the apostolic injunction that we are to be ready to "make a defense," an *apologia*, for the hope that is in us (1 Pet. 3:15). But moral, spiritual, and intellectual engagement with unbelief requires the Christian not only to *defend* the faith, but also to *explain* it, to set it in the context of everything human beings know or think they know. In other words, the rationally assertive Christian must articulate an all-encompassing world view. This will involve a great deal more than studying the Bible and reading apologetics books, and anything approaching a proper job will take the cooperation of *many* rationally assertive believers.

The nine contributors to this book have made a modest attempt to think and write as rationally assertive Christians. We have both *explained* and *defended* our faith, trying to learn all we could from whatever sources of knowledge were available to us. Our aim was to demonstrate what it means to articulate and defend a Christian world view by directing our attention to just one topic: the nature of man. We took a variety of approaches to this topic, partly because we represent several academic disciplines. One approach was to argue that research in a given discipline is coming to conclusions that are in substantial agreement with the traditional teachings of the Christian church. Nancy Duvall gave us a sample of this with her study of developments in psychoanalytic theory. Another approach took what is of value in a discipline but supplements this with something from Christian belief that the practitioners of the discipline have overlooked. Sherwood Lingenfelter took this approach when he argued that anthropologists have taught us much of value about what it is to be human, but they have overlooked the spiritual dimension of man. A third approach was to take on a popular view of the nature of man that is inconsistent with Christian belief, arguing against it and arguing for an alternative that fits Christian teaching. J. P. Moreland did this by arguing against the popular physicalist accounts of man and arguing for a substance dualist account. Through these and other approaches we have tried to model the intellectual work of the rationally assertive Christian.

In this book we have at least indirectly called on our fellow believers in Christ to abandon fideism and to embrace the challenge of an intellectually engaged, and engaging, faith. This will mean rejecting the dominant culture's marginalization of religion, and taking on the entrenched cultural and intellectual elites of our society. If that sounds intimidating, it is. Or at least it is if we forget God, and that is something a rationally assertive believer with a hot faith will not do.

# Contributors

**David M. Ciocchi** holds the B.A. degree from Biola College and M.A. degrees from Talbot Theological Seminary and the University of California at Santa Barbara; his Ph.D. degree is from Fuller Theological Seminary. He is associate professor of philosophy in the School of Arts & Sciences at Biola University, and is the author of "Understanding Our Ability to Endure Temptation: A Theological Watershed," *Journal of the Evangelical Theological Society* (forthcoming). His primary research interest is in theological applications of free will and related philosophical concepts.

**Nancy S. Duvall** is an associate professor at Rosemead School of Psychology, Biola University. She has a M.A.T. from Duke University, and a Ph.D. from the University of North Carolina at Chapel Hill. Her teaching and interests focus on the psychodynamic perspective in psychotherapy, perspectives on the self, the integration of psychology and Christianity, and missions and mental health. Professionally, she has been actively involved in the Christian Association for Psychological Studies.

**Keith J. Edwards** is academic dean of Rosemead School of Psychology, Biola University, where he also serves as professor of psychology. Edwards holds two Ph.D. degrees, one from New Mexico State in Educational Administration/Research and one from the University of Southern California in Clinical & Social Psychology. Edwards is a licensed psychologist; he has served as a psychological consultant for dozens of organizations, and he has delivered professional papers and presentations all over the country. Edwards is the co-editor of the *Journal of Psychology and Theology,* and he has written over ten articles or book chapters in scholarly publications.

**Klaus Issler** is an associate professor of Christian education, primarily teaching in the Doctor of Education program, at Talbot School of Theology, Biola University. He holds the Th.M. degree from Dallas Theological Seminary and M.A. degree from the University of California, Riverside; his Ph.D. degree in Education was received from Michigan State University. Issler is co-author, with Ronald Habermas, of *Teaching for Reconciliation: Foundations and Practice of Christian Educational Ministry*; articles published in *Best of Theology*, vol. 1, *Journal of Moral Education*, and *Christian Education Journal*. Klaus Issler has served on the pastoral staffs of churches in Ohio, Michigan, and California; he has been a seminar leader for Walk Thru the Bible, 1981-89.

**Sherwood G. Lingenfelter** is provost and senior vice president at Biola University where he also serves as professor of Intercultural Studies at Biola's School of Intercultural Studies. Prior to coming to Biola University, Dr. Lingenfelter taught for 15 years at the State University of New York. He holds the Ph.D. from the University of Pittsburg; he has served as consultant, workshop leader, and lecturer with various missions organizations around the world, and he has written a number of articles in scholarly journals. Lingenfelter has authored or co-authored seven books, most recent of which is *Transforming Culture* (Baker, 1992).

**J. P. Moreland** is professor of philosophy at Talbot School of Theology, Biola University and serves as the director of Talbot's M.A. program in philosophy, apologetics, and ethics. He has a Th.M. in theology from Dallas Theological Seminary, a M.A. in philosophy from the University of California at Riverside, and a Ph.D. in philosophy from the University of Southern California. He has authored or co-authored seven books including *Scaling the Secular City* (Baker), *Christianity and the Nature of Science* (Baker), *The Life and Death Debate* with Norman Geisler (Praeger), *Does God Exist?* with Kai Nielsen (Prometheus), and *Immortality: The Other Side of Death* with Gary Habermas (Thomas Nelson). In addition, he has published numerous articles in such journals as *Philosophy and Phenomenological Research, The American Philosophical Quarterly, Grazer Philosophische Studien,* and *Journal of the Evangelical Theological Society.*

**Scott B. Rae** is currently associate professor of Biblical Studies-Christian Ethics at Talbot School of Theology, Biola University in La Mirada, CA. He earned a B.A.S. in Economics from Southern Methodist University and a Th.M. from Dallas Theological Seminary. He holds the Ph.D. in Social Ethics from the University of Southern California. He has taught and pastored in Southern California for the past twelve years. Scott Rae is the author of "Ethical Issues in Fetal Tissue Transplants," in the August, 1991 issue of *The Linacre Quarterly*, "Spare Parts from the Unborn," in the fall 1991 issue of *Christian Research Journal*, study notes on Ecclesiastes, Song of Solomon, and

Titus in the *Life Recovery Bible* (Tyndale; forthcoming), and *Christian Ethics in the Workplace* (Thomas Nelson, forthcoming). He is also writing a major introductory text in ethics for Zondervan. Rae serves as ethics consultant for Holy Cross Medical Center, Mission Hills, CA, and is associated with the Center for Health Care Ethics, St. Joseph Health System, Orange, CA. He is a member of the Society of Christian Ethics, American Academy of Religion, and the Evangelical Theological Society.

**Walt Russell** is associate professor of New Testament at Talbot School of Theology, Biola University. He has his undergraduate degree from the University of Missouri and a Th.M from Dallas Theological Seminary. He has also earned a M.A. in Theology from St. Mary's Seminary and University (Baltimore, MD) and a Ph.D. in Hermeneutics and Biblical Studies from Westminster Theological Seminary in Philadelphia. His varied ministry experience includes four years on the staff of Campus Crusade for Christ, nine years in the pastorate (including co-planting two churches), and seven years of university teaching. He has published numerous articles in scholarly journals relating to the ministry of the Holy Spirit, the renewal of the church, and the cause of world evangelization. He is presently working on a book for Baker that expands the content of his chapter in the present volume.

**Robert L. Saucy** is Distinguished Professor of Systematic Theology and chairperson of the Christian Thought department at Talbot School of Theology, Biola University. Saucy earned his Th.D. in theology from Dallas Theological Seminary in 1961 and has taught at Talbot since 1961. Saucy is a frequent contributor of articles to journals, dictionaries, and popular publications, and his book *The Church in God's Program* (Moody, 1972) has sold over fifty thousand copies. Currently, Saucy is finishing a major contemporary treatise on dispensational theology soon to be released by Zondervan.

# Index